AMERICAN PLURALISM

AMERICAN PLURALISM

A Study of Minority Groups and Social Theory

William M. Newman
The University of Connecticut

Harper & Row, Publishers
New York, Evanston, San Francisco, London

FOR MOM AND DAD

AMERICAN PLURALISM
A Study of Minority Groups and Social Theory
Copyright © 1973 by William M. Newman

Standard Book Number: 06-044801-6
Library of Congress Catalog Card Number: 72-9059

Contents

PREFACE

This book is intended to be a short text that addresses some basic issues and topics in the sociology of majority-minority relationships. More importantly, this volume is an attempt to evaluate and reformulate the conceptual and theoretical tools of the field. It is argued in Part I that majority-minority relationships must be understood as a case study in social stratification and as an opportunity for the study of total societies. A comparative perspective is employed in order to depict the distinctive features of the United States as a pluralistic society. In addition, various typological approaches to the study of minority groups are examined.

Part II turns to the social processes of intergroup relationships in the United States. Chapter 3 traces the historical emergence of the ideas of assimilation, amalgamation, and cultural pluralism, as well as the application and development of these theories in American sociology. As is the case at several points throughout the text, the sociology of knowledge provides the analytical framework. Chapter 4 places the study of majority-minority relationships in the context of social theory and, especially, social conflict theory. In essence, this chapter is an exercise in general theory construction. A model is developed for the analysis of intergroup conflicts, and the various theoretical propositions presented are applied to the more specific area of minority group studies.

Part III explores three related aspects of the consequences of intergroup conflicts. Chapter 5 reviews some major trends of theory and research about prejudice and discrimination. It is argued that these phenomena are best understood as weapons employed by groups in social conflict. The analytical model developed in Chapter 4 is applied in Chapter 5 to demonstrate that there are important variations in patterns of prejudice and discrimination, depending upon the relative social positions of the conflicting groups. Chapter 6 constitutes a case study in the sociology of science. The central issue addressed is the historical as well as the contemporary role of the sciences in creating and sustaining racism as an ideology. Finally, in a brief epilogue, the social meanings of minority group membership are examined from the perspective of role theory. Each chapter contains an annotated bibliography, which hopefully will provide a point of departure for those students wishing to explore the literature in greater depth.

This volume connects the study of majority-minority relationships with the larger tasks of social theory. It also provides a number of new concepts that may be employed not only in the study of American society but in the comparative study of societies as well. Far from being a final statement, this book is an attempt at a new departure.

This work has benefited from the diverse contributions of many of my teachers, colleagues, friends, and students. I am indeed fortunate to have had the intellectual guidance and personal encouragement of several teachers both within and outside the discipline of academic sociology. I am deeply grateful to Ernest Becker, Paul Meadows, James B. Wiggins, D. B. Robertson, Deborah I. Offenbacher, and Peter L. Berger. Each of them has given generously to me and to my intellectual perspective.

My colleague Harold J. Abramson provided invaluable criticism and encouragement during the early stages of the writing. I am similarly indebted to C. Edward Noll for our continuing dialogue on the contents of this book and to Albert K. Cohen for his review of some selected chapters. Both Lewis M. Killian and Jerold Heiss made extensive suggestions for the revision of an earlier draft of the entire manuscript. I am especially grateful to Jerry for showing me the way in which my ideas and theories could be refined and extended.

My students at The University of Connecticut have been a source of continuing stimulation and criticism. I am particularly grateful to Leslie M. Reed for providing me with an undergraduate's view and assessment of the contents of the book. Some words of thanks are also due Frances Hayward for both an impeccable typing job and her expert editorial assistance, and to Luther Wilson, Duncan Hazard, and Ann Fox at Harper & Row.

Somewhere around midpoint in the writing of this book, my wife remarked that being married to a man who was writing a book was probably second only to being married to a man who had a mistress. Without Sue's love, understanding, and patience I would never have gotten this "mistress" out of our house and into print. Sue has managed the difficult roles of wife, editor, and new mother with remarkable grace.

WILLIAM M. NEWMAN

PART I
BASIC CONCEPTS
AND FRAMEWORKS

CHAPTER I
The Study of Majority-Minority Relationships

A Sociological Perspective

The purpose of this book is to offer an analysis of majority-minority group relationships in the United States. One of the dangers of this task is reflected in a cartoon published in the magazine *Saturday Review*. Three cavemen are shown standing before a mammoth slingshot. An enormous boulder rests in the sling ready to be flung upon some unsuspecting enemy. The first caveman says to the other two, "I'd do it for you but I'm only a technical advisor." Contemporary social scientists have indeed been plagued with the realization that, like it or not, they too have become technical advisors. Given this situation it seems imperative that any new interpretation of majority-minority relationships in the United States must be set in the context of a rigorous evaluation of the concepts and theories to be employed.

College courses on the subject of minority groups are a relatively recent addition to the academic scene. Similarly, the reunion between the sociological enterprise and the study of social problems is a recent trend. One of America's foremost sociologists, Everett C. Hughes, has remarked that during his undergraduate career in the 1920s courses on minority groups were almost unknown. Today there are few colleges or universities that do not offer these kinds of courses (Rose 1968: Foreword).

The relative absence of minority group courses during the 1920s is in large part explained by the fact that sociologists of this period were greatly concerned with establishing sociology as a science. The dividing line between social science and social work was sharply drawn (Hinkle and Hinkle 1954). On the other hand, the apparent popularity of minority group courses among both teachers and students in recent years may be attributed to at least three factors.

Both students and teachers are aware that this area of study focuses upon the most urgent social and moral problems of contemporary American society. These problems are continually portrayed in the mass media, have been the subject of numerous newly created state and federal governmental agencies and programs, and have produced a virtual explosion of paperback literature. A second factor has been the growing awareness among sociologists that science is an institution in society and that the products of social science will inevitably be expropriated by society for the solution of social problems and the creation of new social policies. While an earlier generation of sociologists viewed the relationship between sociology and social problems as a dilemma to be avoided, today's practitioners have accepted this relationship as a problematic but unavoidable fact. While this new definition of the situation has created a growing interest and involvement by sociologists in social problems, it has also produced a wide range of ethical questions about the "proper" role of the scientist in social policy formation. The growing literature on the sociologist's role in society (Reynolds and Reynolds 1970, Friedrichs 1970) is itself testimony to the fact that the study of social problems, majority-minority relationships, and deviancy all enjoy a new and important place in the discipline. Finally, sociologists have recognized that majority-minority relationships involve not only social problems but also fundamental social processes and structures, which are an important domain for social-scientific investigation.

From these observations it should be apparent that social problems and sociological problems are not necessarily the same. Social problems are situations in which dislocations, pain, and suffering exist for society at large or for groups and individuals in society. The resurgence of anti-Semitism in the 1960s (Glock and Stark 1966), the existence of poverty in an affluent society (Keyserling 1964), and deteriorating race relations and civil disorders (Kerner et al. 1968) are all social problems. They demand our attention not only because they are signs of a moral crisis but also because pain and suffering in society eventually affect all of us in some way.

Sociological problems are of a different genre than those just described. It is a frequent complaint that sociologists spend most of their time proving things most people already know. In a sense, this complaint is a fair one. Most scientists are involved in studying the things that most other people take for granted. It is for this reason that science is a unique and specialized institution in society.

The philosopher Eugene Rosenstock-Huessy states this point very poetically: ''May we not suppose that all new discoveries in science were made by the stubborn patience of men who insisted on looking at everyday things with astonishment in spite of the general indifference?'' (1938:6).

The taken-for-granted facts of everyday life are the basic problems of science. It is a fact that ice when heated will melt and become water. For the chemist this fact is an important scientific problem. He wants to know how this happens and why it happens. It is also a fact that prejudice and discrimination, differentiation, and stratification occur in societies. For the sociologist these facts are important scientific problems. He wants to know how they happen and why they happen. As members of society, sociologists may wish to alleviate social problems, but they are also aware, as scientists, of the need to ask important prior questions. Sociological problems are those that concern the structures, processes, and conditions under which events occur in society.

While the study of minority groups involves a uniquely close relationship between social and sociological problems, this is not always the case. The French sociologist Emile Durkheim (1858–1917) asked an important sociological question in his book *The Division of Labor in Society* (1893). Durkheim wanted to know how society is possible. Few men would view this as a problem. As Rosenstock-Huessy suggests, few men react with ''astonishment'' to the existence of society. That society exists is taken for granted in everyday life. The point, then, is that while these two kinds of problems are essentially different, they may also be closely related.

It is a central presumption of this book that one cannot fully understand social problems without first viewing them in a sociological context. If one wishes to alleviate certain social conditions, one must first understand the structures and processes through which these conditions arise and are likely to arise again in the future. This, basically, is the relationship between so-called pure and applied science. It is also the human meaning of the social sciences.

The potential contribution of social science to human understanding was perhaps most concisely explained by the great German sociologist Max Weber (1864–1920). In his essay "Science as a Vocation," Weber argues that as an objective endeavor science cannot formulate moral guidelines and social policies for society. Rather, the unique contribution of science is to provide "methods of thinking" and "tools of training." By revealing the probable consequences of social institutions and individual actions, science may allow us "to gain clarity" in the perception of social problems (Weber 1919/1946:150–151).

More recently, Peter L. Berger has suggested that a truly humanistic social science must exhibit a healthy skepticism, a sense of humor, and a self-critical attitude toward its own products (1963). Regrettably, it is the self-critical aspect of humanistic social science that has been greatly lacking in the sociology of minority groups. While there is now more literature available on the subject of minority groups than any student could read in a dozen academic semesters, few books include a concern for the concepts and theories employed in the field. With rare exceptions (Gordon 1964, Schermerhorn 1970, Blalock 1967, Shibutani and Kwan 1965), one encounters tentative definitions and extended descriptions of the life-style characteristics of the different groups in American society. Various anthologies contain case studies or discussions of social problems with little or no concern for conceptual and theoretical issues.

A former president of the American Sociological Association, Herbert Blumer, has suggested that the lack of clarity of concepts represents one of the major shortcomings of contemporary social theory. In his essay "What's Wrong with Social Theory?" (1954), Blumer maintains that sociologists have failed to emphasize the formulation and reformulation of what he calls "sensitizing concepts." With regard to the study of minority groups, the absence of sensitizing concepts is both a scientific and moral failure. On the scientific side, the continual reshaping of concepts is an essential element for both sound theory construction and meaningful research. On the other hand, if sociologists have become technical advisors for the solution of social problems, the quality of their concepts will have a direct bearing on social policies.

The central focus of this book is the subject of majority-minority relationships in the United States. An essential aspect of our treatment of this subject is the evaluation and reformulation of the concepts and theories of the field. The area of minority group studies represents an instance in which social problems and sociological problems are closely related. While the thrust of this book is sociological and theoretical, the realm of social problems provides the materials with which concepts may be illustrated and theories may be tested.

Minority Groups, Concepts, and Social Theory

Since the task before us involves the development and scrutiny of concepts, it is appropriate to briefly consider the nature of concepts in science. All concepts are abstractions from experience. Language is essentially an arbitrary, though necessary, set of abstractions. There is no inherent or "natural" relationship between a word and the object, social or physical, to which it refers. Trees might by chance have been called "chairs" and vice versa. This arbitrary system of naming things works because, through usage, agreements are sustained about the meanings of these labels. Without this system of symbols, these standard meanings, society and communication in society would be all but impossible. As will be seen later, majority-minority conflict in society may be understood in part as a function of the lack of common meanings.

The situation in science is no different from that in society itself. Scientists are able to study social life and compare the results of different studies by virtue of consensual agreements about the definitions of the objects they study. No scientific concept will ever encompass all aspects of any given object of study. Similarly, no single definition will ever serve all scientific purposes and situations.

Again Max Weber has provided some valuable instruction. In his writings on the methodology of the social sciences, Weber argues that sociological concepts are at best *ideal types*. In Blumer's terminology this means that sociological concepts sensitize us to the most significant or important aspects of the phenomenon under study. Ideal types are useful abstractions to which different actual events and cases may be compared for purposes of classification and analysis. An ideal type, then, is a conceptual device that allows the investigator to isolate an important dimension or aspect of a class of phenomena. It allows one to distinguish significant similarities and differences between actual events. There may be varying degrees of ''goodness of fit'' between the ideal-type model and the actual events that occur in the real world. Thus, Weber argued that it was only through the continual process of formulating ideal-type concepts, studying actual events, and then reformulating the concepts that useful scientific concepts and theories could be created (Weber 1904/1949:90–91). This study employs Weber's method of the ideal type. Whether the topic under study is types of societies, types of minority groups, or types of majority-minority relationships, the purpose of the analysis is to understand important differences and similarities in the social world and to understand the social consequences of these differences and similarities. Just as this study is an attempt to reformulate the concepts in the field, it is also an invitation for further research and subsequent reformulation of the ideal types employed and the theories that they help to produce.

Concepts are the basic building blocks of theories. The relationship is a reciprocal one. Just as concepts make theories possible, so concepts are only meaningful in a theoretical framework. The same may be said of the study of any aspect of society and the study of society itself. While the sociology of minority, religious, political, or criminal groups are all intrinsically interesting, these areas of study are most revealing when placed in the broader context of the ''main drift'' (Mills 1960) of society *writ large*. If one is to understand the nature of group relationships in a society, one must also consider the nature of that society. For society is the context in which those interactions occur. Conversely, the structures and processes of group relationships reveal much about society. The study of minority groups, then, must be viewed in relationship to social theory. The joining of social theory and the sociology of majority-minority relationships is a central aspect of this book.

The Central Questions

Thus far, the purpose of this book, as well as some of the major assumptions that guide it, has been discussed. Sociological analysis is viewed as a critical tool for understanding social problems. Max Weber's method of ideal-typical analysis shall be employed. No concept will ever capture the entirety of the phenomenon it describes. Rather, the formulation and reformulation of ideal types provide an understanding of the essential similarities and differences between social phenomena and events. Majority-minority relationships cannot be understood as isolated phenomena but must be placed in the context of the study of total societies. The study of majority-minority relationships requires not only an understanding of group interactions but also of pluralistic societies. Within the framework of these assumptions, this book addresses several related sets of sociological questions.

Part I provides the basic framework for analysis and attempts to locate some key definitions and typologies within that framework. After examining some previous definitions of the term "minority group," it is argued that majority and minority must be understood and defined in terms of social stratification. The process of ranking between groups, as well as the distribution of social resources between groups, is the starting point for an examination of majority-minority relationships. The pattern of majority and minority as opposed to that of elite and mass can only be understood in a larger comparative framework. Through a discussion of different types of societies it is shown that American society represents an extreme example of the pluralistic type of society. Finally, different typologies of minority groups are examined. The utility of different typologies depends upon the specific sociological question being asked. Part I attempts to raise some central issues for future research and to provide a framework for the analysis of social pluralism in the United States.

Part II assesses previous theories about the processes of group relationships in pluralistic societies. Chapter 3 focuses upon assimilation, amalgamation, and cultural pluralism as alternative interpretations of American society. These three notions are examined both in terms of their significance as social doctrines and as sociological theories. After assessing the major lines of theory and research stemming from these three views of American pluralism, an alternative theory is presented. The major argument is that social conflict theory provides a viable theoretical alternative that avoids the shortcomings of previous theories. Part II of the book provides a model for the analysis of intergroup conflicts and concludes with a related set of theoretical propositions about social conflicts.

Finally, Part III addresses three aspects of the consequences of social pluralism. First, the major trends of theory and research concerning prejudice and discrimination are examined. The theory of social conflict offered in Part II provides a context for integrating these various studies. A second area examined is the concept of race. The central task of Chapter 6 is to understand the unique and controversial role of the concept of race in modern science and modern society. The history and use of the concept is examined from the standpoint of the sociology of knowledge. Finally, in a brief epilogue the problem of social pluralism is examined in terms of its meaning for the individual. This book, then, is organized around three sets of issues. First, what is a viable framework of analysis and what are the concepts that emerge from that framework? Second, what are the basic processes and structures of pluralistic society, and what theoretical approach provides an understanding of those structures and processes? Third, what are the social consequences of these structures and processes for groups and individuals?

This book is intended to provide a new departure for the study of intergroup relations. It is hoped that it will at once provide a conceptual and theoretical framework for assessing the many existing case studies in the field as well as a starting point for new kinds of research. While the explicit focus of this work is American society, the utility of the theoretical and conceptual framework proposed can only be determined through comparative research. In this sense, the book is far from the last word on the subject but rather a call for continued evaluation and reformulation of the tools of the field by both teachers and students alike.

FOR FURTHER READING

BERGER, PETER L.
  1963 *Invitation to Sociology*. Garden City, N.Y.: Doubleday. A widely
         read, short introduction to the nature of sociological thinking in a
         humanistic framework.
BLALOCK, JR., HUBERT M.
  1967 *Toward a Theory of Minority-Group Relations*. New York: Wiley.
         (Paperback ed., 1970. New York: Capricorn Books.) A theoretical
         work focused upon the problems of discrimination and prejudice.
BLUMER, HERBERT
  1954 "What's wrong with social theory?," in *American Sociological
         Review*, Volume 19, pp. 3–10. A presidential address delivered to
         the American Sociological Association that stresses the problem of
         concept formation in contemporary sociology.
DURKHEIM, EMILE
  1893 *The Division of Labor in Society*. Translated by George Simpson,
         1933. New York: Macmillan. This was the first of several classic
         studies by one of sociology's European founders.
FRIEDRICHS, ROBERT
  1970 *A Sociology of Sociology*. New York: Macmillan. A monograph on
         the changing nature and social roles of sociology in the United States.
GLOCK, CHARLES, AND RODNEY STARK
  1966 *Christian Beliefs and Anti-Semitism*. New York: Harper & Row. An
         empirical study of the nature and extent of anti-Semitism in the United
         States and its relationship to Christianity.
GORDON, MILTON
  1964 *Assimilation in American Life*. New York: Oxford University Press.
         An analytical study of the roles of race, religion, and ethnicity in
         the United States.
HINKLE, ROSCOE, AND GISELA HINKLE
  1954 *The Development of Modern Sociology*. New York: Random House.
         A brief and concise history of the subject.
KERNER, OTTO, ET AL.
  1968 *Report of the National Advisory Commission on Civil Disorders*. New
         York: Bantam. An important report by a presidential commission
         on the relationship between racial discrimination and civil disorders
         in the United States.
KEYSERLING, LEON H.
  1964 *Progress or Poverty*. Washington, D.C.: Conference on Economic

Planning. The Keyserling Report was the first of several major studies done in the 1960s on poverty in the United States.

MILLS, C. WRIGHT (ED.)

1960   *Images of Man*. New York: Braziller. A collection of essays by sociology's classic authors, all of whom, according to Mills, attempt to depict the ''main drift'' of modern societies.

REYNOLDS, LARRY, AND JANICE RAYNOLDS (EDS.)

1970   *The Sociology of Sociology*. New York: McKay. An anthology of essays on the social role of sociology written from a sociology-of-knowledge perspective.

ROSE, PETER I.

1968   *The Subject Is Race*. New York: Oxford University Press. A study of the teaching of race in American colleges and universities.

ROSENSTOCK-HUESSY, EUGENE

1938   *Out of Revolution*. Norwich, Vermont: Argo Books. A *magnum opus* on the history of Western man.

SCHERMERHORN, RICHARD

1970   *Comparative Ethnic Relations: A Framework for Theory and Research*. New York: Random House. An important theoretical examination of intergroup relations.

SHIBUTANI, TAMATSO, AND KIAN KWAN

1965   *Ethnic Stratification*. New York: Macmillan. A comparative text on minority groups.

WEBER, MAX

1904   '' 'Objectivity' in social science and social policy,'' in *The Methodology of the Social Sciences*. Translated and edited by Edward Shils and Henry Finch, 1949. New York: Free Press. This essay contains Weber's explanation of his concept of ideal types.

1919   ''Science as a vocation,'' in *From Max Weber*. Translated and edited by Hans Gerth and C. Wright Mills, 1946. New York: Oxford University Press. This essay contains Weber's views on the social contribution of science.

CHAPTER 2
Minority Groups and American Society

The Problem of Definition

If one had asked a sociologist twenty years ago what he meant by a minority group, he most likely would have responded that Poles, Jews, and the Irish are all minority groups in American Society. The same question asked today might well bring the response that blacks and Spanish-speaking people are minorities in the United States. And herein lies the problem of definitions. Some definitions sensitize us to the common features of different phenomena that arise at different times and in different places. Others restrict our vision to events in a specific society or even to a certain time period in that society. While all scientific concepts are abstractions from experience, various types of conceptual abstractions may be formulated. Those that have the greatest utility will provide the greatest latitude for studying different events and situations and then formulating generalized statements about them. With these criteria in mind, the kinds of definitions of the term "minority group" that sociologists have employed in the past may be examined.

Sociologists have used at least three different kinds of definitions of the term "minority group." The oldest type of definition may be called a descriptive or trait definition. The group characteristics or traits that are employed in the society to determine minority status become the elements of the sociological definition. An example of this type of definition is found in Donald Young's pioneering textbook *American Minority Peoples* (1932). Young arrived at his definition in the following way: "There is, unfortunately, no word in the English language which can, with philological propriety, be applied to all those groups which are distinguished by biological features, alike national traits or a combination of both" (Young 1932:viii).

For Young, minority groups are those that American society distinguishes according to their race (biological features) or their ethnicity (national origins). Trait definitions are at best a first step in social science. These kinds of definitions restrict our perspective to particular cases and may often lead to embarrassing scientific conclusions.

An interesting illustration of the shortcomings of definitions based upon one societal experience is found in the sociology of religion. During the middle of the nineteenth century, the British anthropologists Henry Lewis Morgan and John Lubbock began applying evolutionary theory to the study of so-called primitive cultures. Yet both men, having the Judeo-Christian tradition as their definitional framework, failed to give any useful account of primitive religions. In his book *The Origin of Civilization* (1870), Lubbock maintained that primitive rituals and practices could not be viewed as truly religious. Morgan labeled primitive religions as "unintelligible" and "grotesque." The culture-boundedness of their approach created an unfruitful detour in the comparative study of religions (Harris 1968). Anything that did not conform to the definition of religion in their own society could not be viewed as religious and, therefore, could not be understood.

The same may be said for the study of minority groups. While race, national origins, and a factor that Young does not consider, religion, are the most prominent group differences in the United States, they are not the only criteria for minority status in this or other societies. For instance, the combination of geographic and economic factors in Appalachia has resulted in minority status for the people of this region. In highly industrialized societies, age has increasingly become a factor in creating minority status. In many emerging African states, old tribal alliances have led to the formation of minority groups. Given the wide range of criteria for minority status, it seems clear that trait or descriptive definitions provide few avenues for comparative study or theory building.

A second way of defining social phenomena is to focus upon the functions or consequences of social institutions for either the society at large or for groups in society. This type of definition in the area of minority group studies was first formulated by Louis Wirth:

> We may define a minority as a group of people who, because of their physical or cultural characteristics, are singled out from others in the society in which they live for differential and unequal treatment and who therefore regard themselves as objects of collective discrimination (Wirth 1945, in Linton 1945:347).

Wirth's definition contains at least three important elements. First, he has expanded Young's definition by suggesting that minority status may be determined not just by race or national origins but by any physical or cultural trait. Second, Wirth has introduced the aspect of group consciousness. In order to live in a society, people must be conscious of their place in the social structure and of the roles that society expects them to play. Each individual carries a map of the social world in his head, and for society to exist there must be some degree of reciprocity between different peoples' definition of society. Members of minority groups are aware of the way in which they are defined and treated by the larger society. Whether or not members of minority groups view their place in the social structure as justified or legitimate is yet another question. Both the "Uncle Tom" and the Black Power advocate are aware of the place of blacks in American society. The difference between the two is that the Black Power advocate has overtly challenged the legitmacy of the situation.

The third and most important aspect of Wirth's definition of minority groups is his emphasis upon the consequential aspect of minority status. Minority groups are those groups that are subject to discrimination, differential, and unequal treatment in society. Armed with this definition, the sociologist might not look for specific group traits in a given society, but might compare all those groups in different societies that suffer the same social consequences. The practice of defining phenomena in terms of their social functions or consequences has stimulated a wide debate in the social sciences (Cohen 1968, Tumin 1953). While the issues in this controversy need not be reviewed here, several aspects of Wirth's definition of minority groups must be considered.

The German sociologist Georg Simmel (1858–1918) maintained that all social life is permeated by superordination and subordination (1908). It is always the case that one group or party to a social relationship dominates while the other, willingly or unwillingly, submits. In a similar manner, Simmel's friend Max Weber showed that all social life involves the implementation of power (Weber 1922). Power is the ability of an individual or group to determine, to some degree, his own as well as others' actions, regardless of the others' wishes. For anything to occur in society, power and domination must be involved. In this framework it is apparent that equality is rarely the case in society. Even in an ideal socialist society or a commune, it is usually the case that power, in the form of legitimate authority, is delegated to different individuals so that the basic tasks required for living may be accomplished. The alternative is complete anarchy.

The philosopher Alfred Schutz has provided some further insights into the use of the term "equality" for the purpose of sociological definition. Schutz argues that different groups are very likely to disagree on what is equal. Members of the majority group, minority group, and even the social scientist may all disagree about what constitutes equality. Schutz further contends that equality is a relational term. Echoing the philosopher Aristotle, Schutz asks, "equality of what?" One might mean equality before the law, equality of opportunity, or equal distribution of goods and services in society (Schutz 1957/1964:240).

While the term "equality" is a particularly difficult one to employ sociologically, it should be noted that the relational aspect of the term cannot be avoided simply by focusing upon some alternative aspect of majority-minority relationships. Most social phenomena are studied and measured in terms of relative quantities. Thus, the frequently employed terms "social class" and "social power" are also relational concepts. The focus upon inequality stems from the predominant concern of the field with the problems of prejudice and discrimination. As Richard Schermerhorn observes, this "victimological" approach tends to depict all minority groups as oppressed victims of the system (1970:8).

It provides little understanding of the diversity of both minority groups and majority-minority relationships.

For instance, by concentrating upon blacks and Spanish-speaking groups, contemporary sociologists may overlook important social processes that involve Jews and Italians, groups that are also minority groups but are not objects of extreme prejudice and discrimination today. The focus upon prejudice and discrimination may severely restrict the framework of analysis. It is perhaps not merely a coincidence that the sociological concern with prejudice and discrimination has not resulted in a concise theoretical framework for understanding majority-minority relationships. Moreover, as will be seen in Chapter 5, the research on prejudice and discrimination has produced one of the most confusing and controversial theoretical areas in the social sciences. The argument here is that prejudice and discrimination are merely one aspect of majority-minority relationships and can only be understood in a larger context. As long as prejudice and discrimination remain the central focus, the kinds of group differences and similarities that inform the larger theoretical picture remain obscured. Accordingly, in this study the task of articulating a theoretical perspective for the analysis of majority-minority relationships has taken the center stage. Once this task has been addressed (Chapter 4), it will then be possible to review the research on prejudice and discrimination in that context (Chapter 5). It is for these several reasons that a definition of minority groups focused primarily upon prejudice and discrimination must be rejected.

Finally, a third type of definition that is formulated at yet a higher level of abstraction may be examined. As will be seen, this third approach is preferable because it is amenable to comparative analysis, allows us to see majority and minority in relationship to one another, and carries with it the roots of a theoretical perspective located in the study of social stratification both across and within societies. As Peter L. Berger and Thomas Luckmann have suggested, the impetus to all sociological inquiry is that societies, institutions, and groups are observed to differ from one another along similar dimensions (1966). The essence of scientific analysis, sociological or otherwise, is the specification of variation, the appearance, absence, or relative strength of different phenomena or important dimensions of phenomena.

Richard Schermerhorn has defined minority groups, not according to specific group traits or by the consequences of those traits (prejudice and discrimination), but on the basis of the variation of three important aspects of social groups: size, power, and a third aspect that he calls "ethnicity." He first defines the term "ethnicity" to mean:

> . . . a collectivity within a larger society having real or putative common ancestry, memories of a shared historical past, and a cultural focus upon one or more symbolic elements defined as the epitome of their peoplehood. Examples of such symbolic elements are: kinship patterns, physical contiguity (as in localism or sectionalism), religious affiliation, language or dialect forms, tribal affiliation, nationality, phenotypical features, or any combination of these. A necessary accompaniment of these is some consciousness of kind among the members of the group (Schermerhorn 1970:12).

Having defined ethnicity, Schermerhorn offers the following schema in which ethnic groups may differ according to the two variables, size and social power (Table 1).

Schermerhorn defines minority groups as those ethnic groups that form less than one-half the population of their society and are subordinate with regard to the distribution of power in that society. While this definition involves the specification of two variables, size and power,

TABLE 1. Dominant and Subordinate Ethnic Groups[a]

	Dominant groups		
	Size	Power	
Group A	+	+	Majority group
Group B	−	+	Elite
	Subordinate groups		
Group C	+	−	Mass subjects
Group D	−	−	Minority group

[a]AD and BC = typical intergroup configurations.
Source: R. A. Schermerhorn, *Comparative Ethnic Relations: A Framework for Theory and Research* (New York: Random House, 1970), p. 13. Copyright © 1970 by Random House, Inc. Used with permission of the author and publisher.

the definition hinges upon the term "ethnic group." The latter is defined by Schermerhorn to mean groups that possess any trait, cultural or physical, that serves as a symbol of the group's distinctiveness.

Two modifications of Schermerhorn's approach may be offered. First, it should be noted that the term "ethnic group" has been employed in several different ways in sociology. The earliest definition of ethnicity as national origin arose during a period when most students of minority groups were interested in the migration of European nationals into the United States. This interest was not simply within the scientific community but, rather, part of the American consciousness. The unprecedented immigration to the United States of Italians, Germans, Poles, and other national groups reached peak levels between 1900 and 1925. The National Origins Quota Act of 1924 and subsequent immigration legislation must be viewed as the context in which sociologists discovered the sociology of ethnic groups.[1]

As was seen earlier, Louis Wirth's definition of minority groups marked an important conceptual turning point. His distinction between physical and cultural minorities has been employed widely ever since. In practice, the term "ethnicity" has been used to describe both national origins and religion. Jews of all national origins, Irish Catholics, Italian Catholics, and German Protestants are all viewed as ethnic groups. It is interesting to note that there is still much disagreement among sociologists as to whether national origin or religion is the more significant variable in the experience of these groups. Will Herberg in his well-known work *Protestant-Catholic-Jew* (1955) and Gerhard Lenski in his study *The Religious Factor* (1961) argue that religion is an important factor in American life. In his classic *Race and Nationality in American Life* (1957), Oscar Handlin stresses the role of national origins. In practice, the term "ethnicity," taken to mean cultural traits, has served as a convenient label for describing those groups that have experienced the complex interaction of the variables national origin and religion.[2]

[1]See the discussion on pp. 53–67.
[2]Harold J. Abramson has made a convincing argument for studying ethnic differences within religious groups. His particular focus is upon ethnic diversity within Catholicism (1971a, 1971b).

Returning to Schermerhorn's use of the term, "ethnicity" is stretched even further to mean any physical or cultural group trait. In this framework, national origin, race, and religion would all be viewed as ethnic factors. Etymologically, the English word "ethnic" stems from the Greek word *ethnikos,* which means nations. It appears in the Bible as *ta ethne*, which means peoples of the nations. The first modification of Schermerhorn's definition of minority groups shall be to return to the older, literal meaning of the term "ethnicity." Ethnicity will be used in this book to mean national origins.

Second, what Schermerhorn seems to be suggesting in his use of the term "ethnicity" is that minority groups are groups that differ or vary in some manner from the social norms or archetypes of their societies. The difference between "we" and "they" is that "they" are different.[3] In other words, the terms "majority" and "minority" are status designations. They refer to the relative social status (honor, privilege, and prestige) of a group in the social structure. The fact that a group either exemplifies or varies from the most highly valued social norms or archetypes in a society becomes a measure of its social status. As the late Judith Kramer suggests (1970), a minority group is a "status community," which because of some real or alleged group characteristic(s) is assigned a low degree of social status. As shown in Table 2, minority groups may be defined and clearly distinguished from other types of social collectivities on the basis of three social variables: size, power, and social norms or status. *Minority groups may be defined as groups that vary from the social norms or archetypes in some manner, are subordinate with regard to the distribution of social power, and rarely constitute more than one-half of the population of the society in which they are found.* In other words, an ethnic group is merely one type of minority group. While minority groups rarely constitute more than one-half of the total population, they may vary greatly in size within this general upper limit. In the United States, Jews, blacks, and Catholics (roughly 3 percent, 12 percent, and 35 percent of the population, respectively) are all minority groups of differ-

---

[3]The phrase "we and they" is, of course, taken from the title of a poem by Rudyard Kipling, in which the poet depicts the tendency of people to value the cultural norms of their in-group (we) and to disvalue those of the out-group (they).

TABLE 2. Dominant and Subordinate Groups: A Three Variable Typology[a]

Type of group	Groups' norms and archetypes compared to those of society (a measure of status)	Relative group size	Relative group power
Elite	Exemplify archetypes, create and/or enforce norms	Small	Much
Majority	Exemplify archetypes, create and/or enforce norms	Neither extremely large nor small	Much
Minority	Differ from archetypes and/or norms	Rarely more than one-half the total population	Little
Mass	Differ from archetypes and/or norms	Large	Little
Deviant	Explicitly reject and violate legal norms	Small	Little (never legitimate)

[a]Elite-mass and majority-minority are alternative patterns. Deviancy may accompany both patterns.

ent sizes.[4] In contrast to minority groups, majority groups may be defined as those groups that create or enforce the social norms or exemplify the social archetypes (trait characteristics of groups that are the most highly desired or rewarded), are superordinate with regard to the distribution of power, and are neither extremely large nor extremely small. It is important to note that sociological minorities or majorities are not the same as political minorities or majorities. For instance, in the United States the sociological majority, white Anglo-Saxon Protes-

[4]Any estimate of the size of American religious groups must be rough "guesstimates," as the last census data collected in the United States on religious groups was in 1957.

tants, is neither a political majority (meaning more than one-half) nor a political plurality (meaning simply the largest group). The minority group, Catholics, possesses a voting plurality but is still less than one-half of the population. This, of course, does not rule out the possibility that in some societies a single group will be both the sociological and political majority. But the two phenomena are conceptually and empirically distinct.

While the size limits for majorities and minorities offered here are by no means exact, they are meaningful when viewed in relation to the other two variables (social norms and social power). The definitions proposed in Table 2 also assume that minority groups are typically encountered in multiple numbers. In other words, it is extremely unlikely that a society will contain only one minority group. Whether the same can be said for majority groups is an open question, although clearly most social scientists have tended to use the term "majority group" as though there is only one majority group in a given society.[5] Turning to the remaining three definitions in Table 2, an elite is a superordinate group that creates, enforces, and exemplifies social norms and archetypes but is typically small in size. A mass population is extremely large, subordinate, and varies from the norms or archetypes. Finally, a deviant group is small, subordinate, and explicitly rejects the legal norms of a society.

The definition of minority groups that has been proposed here also implies that there is a wide range of ways in which groups may vary from the social norms or archetypes and that it is only under certain conditions that minority groups become the objects of extreme prejudice and discrimination. Blacks, Quakers, Jews, Asians, vegetarians, and the handicapped might all be viewed as minority groups. Similarly, the relationship between deviant and minority status in society and the processes through which groups may move from one position to the other are important areas for further investigation. These questions are addressed in Chapter 5.

There are three important themes, central to this book, that underlie the definitions proposed here. First, as both Schermerhorn (1970) and

---

[5]Some theorists have suggested that pluralistic societies may be understood in terms of *codominance,* meaning several dominant groups.

Shibutani and Kwan (1965) have argued, majority-minority relationships must be viewed in terms of social stratification, or ranking. The concepts of majority, minority, elite, mass, and deviant are meaningful only in the larger context of the distinction between dominant and subordinate groups. Schermerhorn stresses this theme by employing variance in social power as one of several criteria for defining the different types of groups. The definitions proposed here extend Schermerhorn's theme by adding variance from social norms as a criterion for distinguishing groups. In essence, variance from social norms is a measure of social status (honor, privilege, and prestige). Thus, the two social resources, power and status, provide basic descriptive information about the social positions or ranks of different groups. The third social resource, class (wealth), is often the first important reward over which groups fight. As will be seen later, the pattern of majority-minority interaction, especially social conflict, depends upon how much of which resources the different groups possess.

A second aspect of the definitions offered here is that they allow comparative analysis of groups both within societies as well as across societies. Unlike definitions that are based upon specific traits, these definitions identify groups in terms of their location in the social structure, regardless of the kinds of traits that place them there. In this way the definitions become portable for the purpose of research. Wherever there are societies and stratification systems within those societies, groups can be understood on the basis of their locations in those social structures. Finally, the definitions proposed here view groups in relation to each other. As Schermerhorn suggests (1970), the task is to understand groups in relation to each other, as opposed to approaching minority groups as an occasion for victimological analysis.

For the moment, the most important relationship between the different groups described in Table 2 is that they do not all usually appear in the same kinds of societies. While deviant groups appear in almost all societies, as Schermerhorn has shown (1970), one tends to find either one or the other of the two ideal types of paired relationships: elite-mass or majority-minority. As was suggested earlier, the study of group relationships must be placed in the broader context of the study of society. The utility of these proposed definitions, as well as the range of groups encompassed by them, cannot fully be appreciated without first examining the social context in which the different kinds of group configurations appear. The structure of American society as a pluralistic society must be examined. Since the very beginning of the sociological enterprise, successive generations of social theorists have argued that there are important differences between types of societies and that these differences have an immense impact upon the kinds of social relationships found within them. The next section of this chapter addresses two central questions. First, what are the important differences between types of societies? Second, how do these differences relate to the structure of group relationships, particularly the two patterns of elite-mass and majority-minority? Answers to these two questions may provide a general model for future comparative research as well as a useful context for examining the problem of majority-minority relationships in the United States.

Differentiation, Stratification, and Types of Societies

In attempting to characterize different types of societies, sociologists have traditionally emphasized two distinct, but related, phenomena: differentiation and stratification. These two concepts may be explained by comparing extreme cases. *The term "differentiation" refers to the degree of separation between institutions in a society as well as to the degree of internal diversity within those institutions.* The degree of differentiation in a society may vary from simple to complex. Simple societies are those that exhibit a small number of social institutions and in which each of the major institutions has a number of social functions. In a society composed of a single tribe or clan, one may find a rudimentary division of labor, but membership in the tribe is at once a social, religious, and political membership. Complex societies contain a large number of separate and distinct social institutions. Each institution is also internally differentiated. In the United States, religious, political, and economic institutions are distinct from one another, and there is a wide variety of options for activity in any of these institutional spheres.

Stratification means ranking. Some positions or roles in society are more highly valued or desired than others. Some social groups hold a larger stock of social resources (class, status, power) than others. Just as differentiation is measured on a scale from simple to complex, stratification systems vary from closed to open. Closed ranking systems are based upon ascription. One's rank or position in society is ascribed at birth, and there are subsequently few, if any, ways of changing that rank. The caste system in India and the estate system in Europe during the Middle Ages are both closed systems.

In contrast, open stratification systems evidence a high degree of social mobility. One's position in adult life is not ascribed but achieved. Of course, all societies involve ascription, but the important question is whether or not groups and individuals are allowed to achieve new positions through social mobility. Max Weber showed that the stratification of industrial societies into social classes resulted in part from an achievement ethos. This is the theme of Weber's controversial essay *The Protestant Ethic and the Spirit of Capitalism* (1904–1905). It has already been suggested that the two patterns, elite-mass and majority-minority, are characteristic of different types of societies. It may now be specified that the elite-mass configuration is typical of simple societies with closed stratification systems. Majority-minority relationships are typical of complex, differentiated societies with relatively open stratification systems. These two ideal types are shown in Table 3.   The two ideal-type linkages between stratification, differentiation, and group configurations suggested here are similar to those discussed by Pierre van den Berghe in his study *Race and Racism* (1967). Van den Berghe argues that race relationships tend toward two typical patterns that he calls "paternalism" and "competition." These two terms refer to the

TABLE 3. Comparative Societies: Two Ideal Types

Type of society	Type of social stratification	Type of social differentiation	Type of group configuration
I	Ascribed and closed	Simple	Elite-mass
II	Achieved and open	Complex	Majority-minority

ideological aspects of closed and open stratification systems. While paternalism characterizes the dominant group attitude in a closed stratification system, the ideology of competition is more likely to be found in an open stratification system. As van den Berghe suggests, the strategy of studying the relationships between social structures and group relationships should be applied not just to the study of race, as he has done, but to the study of dominant-subordinate relationships generally (1967:25–34). Van den Berghe, of course, is primarily concerned with the relationship between structural aspects of societies and those phenomena he views as being social-psychological, such as prejudice, discrimination, paternalism, and the ethos of competition (1967:31–33). An alternative approach is provided by Schermerhorn, who argues that historical variables such as voluntary group migration, colonization, and annexation should be viewed as the independent variables that create different structural features of societies and group relationships within them (1970:14–16). The questions of how historical sequences emerge and how structural features of societies influence social-psychological relationships between groups are, of course, important. But it must be remembered that, regardless of the social-psychological aspects of group interactions, these interactions are themselves a structural phenomenon. Moreover, the structural relationships, mass-elite and majority-minority, are dependent upon other structural characteristics of societies. As van den Berghe suggests, ". . . it is reasonable to accept that basic aspects of the social structure exert a considerable degree of determinism on the prevailing type of race relations" (1967:26).

The important question, then, for comparative study is, What specific "aspects of the social structure" determine the type of relationships, not just between races but between dominant and subordinate groups generally? Van den Berghe's study of race relations in Mexico, Brazil, South Africa, and the United States provides a few clues for a more general analysis. Van den Berghe discusses eleven ways in which the four societies he studied are either different or similar. Of these eleven, at least three of them point to structural arrangements that affect not only race relationships but group relationships generally. They are the economic structure of society, the degree of group pluralism, and the political structures of society. The following discussion attempts to map the relationships between several structural features of societies. As was previously noted, the central question is, What combination of structural features produces the ideal-type patterns elite-mass and majority-minority? While this question is addressed in terms of two polar ideal types, it is presumed that a wide range of mixed patterns falls between the two types discussed. Moreover, the model presented here points to the importance of comparative social research into the various mixed types that fall between these two poles. For the moment, comparative examination of societies in terms of two ideal types will provide some perspective on where American society falls within the range of possible occurrences.

It has already been suggested that the degree of overall social differentiation in a society may be viewed as an important variable affecting the nature of group relationships. Yet the three variables discussed by van den Berghe are essentially measures of the degree of internal differentiation within the economic, political, and social-institutional structures of societies.

Turning first to the degree of economic differentiation in societies, sociologists and economists have traditionally employed the categories of preindustrial and industrial economies. The elementary forms of preindustrial societies, gathering, hunting, fishing, horticultural, and agricultural societies (Lenski 1966), all offer a relatively limited number of ways in which groups and individuals may participate and compete economically in society. Conversely, highly industrialized societies exhibit a wide diversity of economic roles and positions for groups and individuals. As the French social critic Jacques Ellul has argued, the essence of "technological society" is the uncontrolled proliferation of new industries, products, and social roles. Whether this is a curse, as Ellul has argued (1954), or a blessing, the fact remains that the United States exhibits almost unlimited economic diversity. The more undifferentiated an economy, the easier it is for an elite to dominate and control that economy. On the other hand, as an economy expands, it becomes more difficult for one group to maintain dominance while, at the same time, more avenues are created for subordinate populations to compete and advance. A first proposition, then, is that high economic differentiation seems more disposed to majority-minority competition than to the paternalistic rule of an elite. It must be noted that the traditional distinction between preindustrial and industrial societies does not adequately convey the argument here. For instance, it is conceivable that an industrialized society could easily be controlled by an elite if the economy contained only a few major industries. There are, in fact, numerous situations of this type in the Middle East, South and Central America, and Africa. Thus, the concepts preindustrial and industrial are not descriptively accurate terms for studying the degree of economic differentiation in societies and might better be replaced by the terms "high diversity" and "low diversity."

The second variable discussed by van den Berghe is the "attitudes and policies of the dominant groups." In structural terms this means the political and legal institutions of a society.[6] The differentiation within the political institutions of a society may be measured on a continuum from high participation to low participation. While this notion is perhaps already conveyed in the distinction between elites and majorities, the opportunity to attain political power in the United States represents, again, an extreme case in terms of ideal types. The federal system of government involves three levels of political office: national, state, and local.[7] In addition, the political system at all of these levels is differentiated between executive, legislative, and judicial power structures. Finally, the national legislature and all but one state legislature (Nebraska) are bicameral (i.e., contain two legislative bodies: a house of representatives and a senate). This is not to say that in the United States all groups share equally in the political system or that the system is administered fairly for all groups. But the high degree of differentiation, both between and within the different levels of the American political system, provides a wide range of opportunities for participation by different social groups. In spite of the shortcomings of the system, the degree of differentiation in it is not conducive to the control of an elite throughout.

Finally, the third variable suggested by van den Berghe is the degree of group pluralism in society. Societies range from those that are monistic

[6]Van den Berghe's preference for treating legal and governmental institutions as different spheres is rejected here in favor of viewing political institutions as the general category (1967:33).
[7]The existence of county governments provides an even more differentiated set of political structures.

(composed of one group) or dyadic (composed of two groups) to those that are pluralistic (composed of many groups). While at a first glance group differentiation may be measured in terms of the number of groups in a society, it is also necessary to examine the relative sizes of groups. There are undoubtedly situations in which relatively small subgroups blend into the mass or become minorities within the mass. On the other hand, societies that are customarily described as pluralistic are composed of numerous groups that, either by virtue of coalitions between minorities or on the basis of their own critical size, are able to resist being lumped into an undifferentiated mass. While a monistic society represents an extreme case in terms of numbers, American society represents the other end of this polarity in terms of both numbers of groups and relative sizes of groups. There has not yet been enough comparative study to specify the exact limits of what is meant by group pluralism. For instance, even in the United States, Jews represent only 3 percent of the population. Can this be viewed as a significant numerical limit? This is difficult to answer, for it must be remembered that American Jews dwell in a society containing a large number of even larger minority groups and that some of these larger minorities acting in coalition (such as Irish Catholics and Italian Catholics) may constitute a voting plurality. In other words, it remains an open question as to whether there are significant upper limits, in terms of numbers of groups in a society and relative sizes of those groups, beyond which it becomes unlikely that an elite-mass pattern of group relationships can be sustained. While the measures employed, then, must be very rough until more comparative study has been undertaken, it is still clear that American society is highly differentiated in terms of group pluralism, whether the number or the size of groups is considered.[8]

To summarize, American society reveals a correlation of high overall social differentiation; high internal economic, political, and social differentiation; a relatively open, achievement-oriented stratification system; and a structural pattern of majority-minority, as opposed to elite-mass, relationships. In simple terms, American society is structurally complex and contains a large number of sizable groups that compete

[8]In addition to the number of groups and their sizes, the relative proximity or geographical distribution of the groups is a third aspect of group pluralism. This problem is discussed on pp. 54–56.

for the various economic and political resources in the society. Majority-minority relationships seem to be the probable pattern, as opposed to elites and masses, when all these forms of differentiation are present.

Which of these six variables—degree of overall social differentiation, internal economic diversity, political differentiation, degree of group pluralism, the stratification system, and the form of group relationships —may be viewed as causes and which may be viewed as effects? The possible alternatives among these six aspects of society offer some complex, though important, avenues for comparative study.

Some tentative guesses may be offered. The history of western Europe suggests that some combination of political and economic diversification, within an existing framework of large-scale social differentiation, caused a new stratification system and a new type of group configuration. The differentiation of religion, economics, and politics has been called secularization. Similarly, as Marx observed, the rise of economic diversity, capitalism, caused a change from an estate system of stratification to a more differentiated class system. With expanding economics came expanding trade and travel. The result was pluralistic group structures. Most, but not all, western European countries no longer have nobles and peasants but, rather, majorities and minorities.

Yet alternative scenarios are available. In spite of a diverse political system and a relatively high degree of economic diversity, conflicts in Northern Ireland during the early 1970s suggest a pattern of elites and masses, Protestants and Catholics. Would a greater degree of group pluralism have altered this pattern? The future history of this situation, as well as those of several South American and African countries, may provide some important answers to these questions. At best, as is shown in Table 4, these variables may be divided into three categories: determinant, intervening, and dependent variables. Clearly, the group configuration and the stratification system in a society are somehow determined by the other four elements.[9]

For the moment, the important point is that American society represents one of the most diverse and complex of all possible outcomes.

[9]Daniel Lerner's study *The Passing of Traditional Society* (1958) provides a useful approach for the kind of comparative research required to employ the model in Table 4. Leo Kuper and M. G. Smith's anthology *Pluralism in Africa* (1969) also provides some important avenues for further research.

TABLE 4. Two Types of Societies: Six Comparative Dimensions

Dimensions	Type I	Type II
Independent variables:		
1. Overall differentiation	Simple	Complex
2. Economic differentiation	Low diversity	High diversity
3. Political differentiation	Low participation	High participation
Intervening variable:		
4. Group differentiation[a]	Nonpluralistic (monadic, dyadic, etc.)	Pluralistic
Dependent variables:		
5. Social stratification	Ascribed and closed	Achieved and open
6. Group configuration	Elite-mass	Majority-minority

[a]To be measured in terms of number of groups, relative sizes of groups, and geographical distribution of groups.

Whether this society is the best of all possible societies is yet another question. The purpose here has been to characterize American society in a comparative framework. The study of majority-minority relationships in the United States must be viewed in relation to the nature of American society as an extremely differentiated society in which achievement, mobility, and competition are the dominant trends.

Finally, it may be noted that while sociologists often speak of majority-minority relationships, the study of minority groups also involves the study of minority-minority relationships. The distribution of power in societies is always relative. No single group is either totally powerful or absolutely powerless. Rather, the position of any given group is relative to that of all other groups, and the relationship between any two groups will involve dominance and subordination. Thus, when viewed in the context of the overall distribution of power, a particular group may appear to be a minority group. Yet from the perspective of a group that is ranked below it, this minority group may appear to be a power-holding group. As is depicted in Figure 1, it is appropriate to view group A as the majority and to view groups B through E as minority groups. Yet from the perspective of group C, minority group B appears to be a majority or power-holding group.

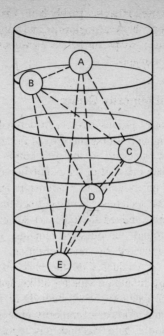

FIGURE 1. Distributions of power in majority-minority and minority-minority relationships.

There are many examples of minority-minority conflicts. The fight in New York City during the late 1960s over local community control of schools by blacks generated a great deal of black anti-Semitism. While Jews were not the most powerful group in determining this policy issue, there were large numbers of Jews in teaching and administrative positions in the city's schools. From the standpoint of blacks, Jews were a powerful group. Similarly, while Irish Catholics and Italian Catholics are not majority groups in the United States, they do appear as dominant groups from the perspective of blacks and Spanish-speaking peoples attempting to gain positions in Irish- and Italian-dominated trade unions. For this reason, the term ''intergroup relationships'' is probably more accurate than ''majority-minority relationships.'' The two terms will be used interchangeably here. Group conflicts and coalitions occur not simply between majorities and minorities or between dominant and subordinate groups, but between groups that possess varying degrees of social dominance.

Typologies of Minority Groups

Thus far, minority groups have been defined as those groups that vary from the social norms or archetypes of the society in some manner, are subordinate with regard to the distribution of power, and rarely constitute more than one-half of the population of the society in which they are found. Majority-minority relationships appear to be a distinctive feature of pluralistic societies. Having defined the concept of a minority group and having examined the types of societies in which they are most frequently found, the question remains, What specific types of groups are encompassed by this definition? Typologies of social phenomena may be evaluated on the basis of at least two criteria. First, any typology should provide for all known events or phenomena within the general category being studied. In other words, it should be possible to locate all types of minority groups within the categories of the classification system. Second, any typology may be evaluated according to the criterion of utility. Does the classification system organize the data in a way that helps solve the scientific problem at hand? Does it sensitize the investigator to an important or significant set of distinctions between the different types? There are relatively few typologies in the social sciences that are universally applicable to all investigations about a particular class of phenomena. Rather, any typology involves distinctions relevant to the particular question being asked. Typologies are collections of ideal types formulated in terms of a specific question or problem. There are several different perspectives from which minority groups may be typologized and studied.

Sociologists have generally tended to classify minority groups according to specific social traits. Many books in the field contain the words "ethnic" and "racial" in their titles (Handlin 1957, Simpson and Yinger 1953, Berry 1951, Segal 1966). Such descriptive labels as "ethnic," "racial," and "religious" fail to encompass the entire range of groups that may be defined as minorities. Moreover, these three categories of minority groups differ greatly. While race is a physical trait, religion and ethnicity involve group differences in beliefs and life-styles. Groups that differ from the social norms or archetypes rarely differ in terms of only one dimension of social life. For instance, the Mormons in the 1830s may represent a cognitive minority because they evidenced distinctively different religious beliefs.[10] But they also may be viewed as a behavioral minority because their patterns of social conduct, most notably the practice of polygamy, were a severe departure from the social norms of the surrounding culture (O'Dea 1957). While these various ways of differing from the social norms may overlap, it is still possible to distinguish those one or two dimensions of social life in any situation that are the most important differences for the social interaction between groups. The essential question being asked by this first typology is, What general types of social aspects of groups seem to determine minority status in societies? The typology includes three distinct types: *physical minorities, cognitive minorities,* and *behavioral minorities.* While these three types may not always be mutually exclusive, as ideal types they may assist in identifying some important underlying elements in majority-minority relationships. Overall, two points should be kept in mind. First, the range of specific groups encompassed by the definition of the term "minority groups" and the typology suggested here is much broader than the traditionally studied racial, ethnic, and religious groups. Second, group traits, which on the surface may appear important, after further analysis may prove to be only coincidental to the essential factors of division between groups. The major categories in this typology are shown in Table 5.

Physical minorities are those that differ from the social norms or archetypes according to their appearance. The handicapped are an important example of this type of minority group. As Robert Scott has shown in his excellent study of the blind, there are no natural or inherent social roles that are played by blind people. Rather, one must be socialized into this minority group just like any other (Scott 1969). The most important social limitations of blindness are not those that result from the inability to see; the limitations imposed by the prejudices

[10]The term "cognitive minorities" was coined by Peter L. Berger (1967:152). Burkhard Holzner's term "epistemic communities" (1968) conveys a similar distinction.

TABLE 5. Three Types of Minority Groups: Physical, Cognitive and Behavioral

Type of minority group	Variance from social archetypes and/or norms in terms of	Some examples in the United States
Physical	Appearance	Blacks, the handicapped, the aged, Asians
Cognitive	Beliefs	Jews, Irish Catholics, various religious sects, social communes
Behavioral	Conduct	Homosexuals

and reactions of the wider society are the most damaging. The handicapped are viewed as undesirable in all spheres of American society. Physical minorities are usually relegated to obscure positions in society. In this way, most individuals with visible handicaps become invisible to, and in, society. They become both dependent upon, and marginal to, society.

While most societies evidence some form of social stratification according to age, in highly industrialized societies old age has become another physical factor in determining minority status. To a large extent, as the nuclear family has replaced the extended family as the basic social unit, the aged have been set adrift from the important social ties of the family. While medical science has lengthened the average life span of individuals, business and industry have tended to view the aged as bad business risks. Consequently, the aged are deprived of the social and economic benefits of both job and family. They have few avenues for establishing and sustaining meaningful social relationships and roles, and they are continually drained economically by the increased medical expenses typical of the later years. Like the handicapped, the aged are a marginal physical minority in society.

Race, of course, is a persistent example in most, though not all, societies of minority status that is assigned on the basis of physical characteristics.[11] Yet even where race is present as a differentiating

[11]The term "race" is used here to mean skin color differences between groups. Issues surrounding the concept of race in the social sciences are discussed in Chapter 6.

factor between groups, it is not always the essential variable. The treatment of the American Indians provides a striking illustration of this point. By relegating Indians to reservations and denying them participation in society, the host society was placing a stronger emphasis on cognitive rather than physical difference. The unique social enclave of the Indian reservation resulted from the implicit view of the dominant group that Indians were uncivilizable and, more specifically, un-Christianizable. This is the major difference between the position of Indians and blacks in American society. In spite of the severe discrimination against blacks and the history of bizarre race mythologies about blacks in the United States, they were granted minimal entrance into society and were baptized into the "flock of the saved." On the other hand, Indians were viewed as savages and were allowed to keep their indigenous religions. While race was surely a related factor, the real conflict was one of cultures and cognition.

It must also be stressed that situations involving more than one important social difference between groups may change over time. As American prejudices and beliefs about the "noble savage" recede and American Indians attempt to enter the society in larger numbers, racial (physical) differences may become the paramount aspect of relationships between Indians and white society. The processes through which social definitions of groups change and majority-minority relationships move from one type of focus to the next are an important area for further study. In this context the distinction between cognitive, physical, and behavioral minorities may provide a point of departure for separating social facts from social fictions.

The important point is that once the larger society has focused upon one type of variance from the social norms, others are typically alleged. While Jews exhibit cognitive variance in Christian-dominated societies, it is often erroneously claimed that the Jews are a race (physical difference). While homosexuals evidence behavioral variance from the norm, it is frequently argued that they are cognitively different as well (mentally ill or sick). While the initial influx of Irish Catholics into the United States in the early nineteenth century was marked by protests concerning their cognitive variance (a papal conspiracy), by the late nineteenth century all foreign ethnic groups were being called races (physical variance).[12] While blacks vary physically from the norm in white-dominated societies, it is erroneously argued that this physical variance is evidence of cognitive variance as well (intelligence). As will be shown later, the precarious evidence gathered from various types of IQ tests does not validate or justify the claim that blacks and whites differ in terms of innate intelligence. Moreover, students of the subject have long known that observable differences such as skin color are extremely poor and unreliable criteria for classifying human groups biologically.[13] The task for social science is first to distinguish the apparent differences between human groups and then to analyze and understand the inaccurate and sometimes absurd social meanings that are attached to these differences. Human groups do differ from one another in terms of a large number of physical, behavioral, and cognitive (meaning beliefs, not intelligence) traits. What requires social-scientific understanding is the social significance assigned to these differences and the ways in which the existence of one kind of difference leads to the allegation of others.

Groups that differ from the social norms in terms of political, religious, and social doctrines may all be viewed as cognitive minorities. While sociologists have traditionally studied the experiences of various ethnic Catholics and Jews in America's Protestant-dominated society, there are a wide variety of smaller religious groups that may appropriately be viewed as cognitive minorities. At different points in American history one might include among such groups the Society of Brothers, the Amana Community, Seventh Day Adventists, Christian Scientists, Theosophists, Buddhists, Quakers, Muslims, and Black Muslims—to mention but a few of the wide variety of smaller religious groups in the United States. In the realm of political groups, the history of the Communist party in the United States is an interesting case study in the movement of a group from minority to deviant status (Howe and Coser 1957). The Communist party was not originally a secret organization in this country. Once the host society began to view this new political philosophy as a threat, the party was driven underground through the Palmer Raids in the 1920s and subsequent anti-Communist

[12]These events are discussed in Chapter 3.
[13]Chapter 6 contains a detailed examination of these issues.

legislation. In addition, many of the "hippie communes" formed in the late 1960s and early 1970s may be viewed as cognitive minorities that differ from the norms of the society in terms of social philosophy.

The distinction between behavioral and cognitive minorities is perhaps a difficult one to illustrate in many instances. After all, patterns of social conduct are ways of acting out ideas, while ideas are essentially reflections about human action. Yet in this dialectic between thought and action there are situations in which differences in conduct are much more important for group relationships than cognitive differences. Homosexuals are disvalued in society, not because of what they think, but because of what they do. This minority group also represents an interesting reversal of the deviant-minority transition just discussed. Unlike the Communist party, which began as a minority group and is now legally defined as a deviant group, homosexuals have been in the process of moving from a deviant position to a minority position in society. There is even an Episcopal congregation of homosexuals in one West Coast community. The movement of groups between these two statuses, deviant and minority, should provide another important area for future research. Not only is this area important for understanding group relationships, but it could also provide additional information about the overall process of social change and changing social values.

The distinction between physical, behavioral, and cognitive minorities stems from the question, What general types of group differences are employed by dominant populations to assign minority status in society? It is equally useful to ask, How do different types of minority groups define and approach the societies that surround them? There are several typologies that classify minority groups from this perspective. The best-known typology of this kind is Louis Wirth's distinction between *pluralist, assimilationist, secessionist,* and *militant* minorities (Wirth 1945). Wirth contends that emerging minority groups generally attempt to obtain social tolerance of their group differences. Wirth calls groups that follow this route pluralist minorities. Groups that go beyond the attainment of tolerance for their differences and attempt to be absorbed into the dominant group are called assimilationist minorities. Wirth contends that groups that are prevented from assimilating will become secessionist and either attempt to establish their own separate geographical domain or withdraw to another state or geographical area where their group traits are normative or tolerated as closer to the norm.

Finally, he argues that the conflict between dominant and secessionist groups can produce a militant group that, rather than withdrawing, attempts to dominate socially through more extreme methods of social conflict.

Wirth's typology has both its shortcomings and its advantages. One of the advantages is that it examines majority-minority relationships, not as a set of interactions between static types of groups, but as a process in which situational variables play an important role in shaping minority groups and their approaches to society. The degree to which a minority group may become militant in many situations depends upon the level of dominant group prejudice and discrimination and minority group frustrations stemming from these policies of the dominant group. On the other hand, it is not accurate to presume that all groups will assimilate into the society even if they are allowed to do so. Rather, as will be examined at greater length in Chapters 3 and 4, there has been a greater tendency in pluralistic societies for minority groups to seek toleration of their differences. Moreover, there are some groups that overtly differ from the social norms and make no attempt to assimilate. For instance, religious groups like the Quakers or the Society of Brothers see little hope for the values of modern American society and simply attempt to maintain a sort of society-within-society withdrawn from the larger culture. Groups that advocate Afro-American culture and Black Power have surely resulted from the failure of the host society to grant acceptance to the black community. But there is little reason to expect that they would now assimilate even if they were invited to do so. Rather, advocates of Afro-American culture are likely to continue to reject the cultural norms and values of the host society. Wirth's typology, then, is useful if one is interested in the process of assimilation between minority groups and their host societies. Wirth viewed assimilative, secessionist, and militant groups as successive minority group responses to majority group prejudice and discrimination. This, of course, is consistent with Wirth's use of prejudice and discrimination as criteria for defining minority groups.[14] This approach provides little understanding of pluralist minority groups, the one type that Wirth does not integrate into his interactive model of how minority groups move from one position to the next. Thus,

[14]See the discussion on pp. 15–17.

while Wirth's typology has both advantages and disadvantages, it is ultimately informed by his definition, which views minority groups as victims of the majority.

Irvin L. Child in his study *Italian or American?* distinguishes between minority group members who *rebel* and disassociate from the minority community, those who *withdraw* and build a strong in-group identification with the minority community, and those who are simply *apathetic* about the problem of assimilation (1943:69–75). While Child's typology has not been widely employed in recent years, J. Milton Yinger (1970) and Bryan Wilson (1963) have utilized a similar typology for religious sectarian groups, which might fruitfully be applied to the study of minorities. Their distinction between groups that avoid and *withdraw,* those that attack, proselytize, and *aggress,* and those that attempt to *ignore* society provides some insights into the question of why certain minority groups become the object of extreme prejudice and discrimination. While this topic will be treated more fully in Chapters 4 and 5, some preliminary observations may be offered here.

During the first few centuries of the Christian Church, the Donatist and Arian parties represented revisions of, rather than complete departures from, the Church's doctrines (Walker 1918/1959). Moreover, both groups attempted to aggress or proselytize their beliefs. Both groups were viewed as heresies and were eventually eliminated. This suggests that it is not necessarily those groups that differ greatly from the social norms that become the object of prejudice and discrimination. As Coser (1956) has observed, threats from within the system are often viewed as more serious problems than threats from outside the system. The Arian and Donatist groups were close enough to the dominant belief system to be viewed as dangerous and, most importantly, took an aggressive stance toward the Church. In contrast, Buddhist groups may enjoy a situation of peaceful coexistence in a Christian-dominated society as long as they do not attempt to convert everyone to their view of things.

Finally, J. Milton Yinger has suggested an important distinction between *subcultural* groups and *contracultural* groups (1960).[15] All groups that vary from the norms of society in some distinctive way

---

[15]The term "subcultural" does not mean that one culture is less desirable or less valuable than the next. It simply means that one culture is different from, but found alongside of the other. Thus Italian culture is a subculture within American society.

may be viewed as subcultural. But some subcultural groups are also contracultural, for they explicitly reject the norms of society. Such groups are likely to be viewed as deviant and become the object of prejudice and discrimination even though they do not necessarily violate the laws. During the late 1960s in the United States, hippies who symbolized their disagreement with society's norms by wearing their hair long found it very difficult obtaining jobs in the "straight" world. Prospective employers resented their defiance and viewed them as "deviants."

Which of these several typological distinctions proves most useful depends upon what aspect of majority-minority relationships are being studied. Future research that goes beyond the realm of the frequently studied racial, religious, and ethnic groups may produce even more enlightening ways of classifying minority groups.

In summary, the first part of this study has addressed several basic questions. The term "minority group" has been defined in a way that places the study of majority-minority relationships within the context of the study of social stratification and the study of total societies. All minority groups, regardless of their goals or objectives in society, are distinguishable within certain size limits by the fact that they are subordinate with regard to the distribution of power and evidence some form of variance from the social norms. Moreover, it has been argued that the pattern majority-minority, as opposed to the pattern elite-mass, is a distinct feature of pluralistic societies, societies possessing a high degree of overall differentiation, economic and political differentiation, and an open stratification system. Within this framework, several alternative ways of typologizing and analyzing minority groups have been examined. The next part of this study examines various theoretical perspectives for understanding what the social processes in a pluralistic society are all about. The purpose of the next two chapters is to examine some old theories and to present a new one.

FOR FURTHER READING

ABRAMSON, HAROLD J.
    1971a "Ethnic diversity within Catholicism: A comparative analysis of contemporary and historical religion," in *Journal of Social History*, Volume 4 (Summer), pp. 360–388. Abramson approaches religion

and ethnicity as interrelated variables and stresses the importance of ethnic differences within religious groups.

1971b "Inter-ethnic marriage among Catholic Americans and changes in religious behavior," in *Sociological Analysis,* Volume 32 (Spring), pp. 31–44. See annotation for Abramson 1971a.

BERGER, PETER L.

1967   *The Sacred Canopy.* Garden City, N.Y.: Doubleday. A theoretical analysis of religion in the United States in which the term "cognitive minorities" is introduced.

BERGER, PETER L., AND THOMAS LUCKMANN

1966   *The Social Construction of Reality.* Paperback ed., 1967. Garden City, N.Y.: Doubleday. A theoretical essay on the sociology of knowledge.

BERRY, BREWTON

1951   *Race and Ethnic Relations.* Rev. ed., 1968. Boston: Houghton Mifflin. This is a widely used text on minority groups.

BLALOCK, JR., HUBERT M.

1967   *Toward a Theory of Minority-Group Relations.* New York: Wiley. (Paperback ed., 1970. New York: Capricorn Books.) A theoretical study of prejudice and discrimination.

CHILD, IRVIN L.

1943   *Italian or American?* New Haven: Yale University Press. Child's typology of minority groups is similar to those later developed by Yinger (1970) and Wilson (1963) to study religious sects.

COHEN, PERCY S.

1968   *Modern Social Theory.* New York: Basic Books. The author discusses the major types and problems of social theory, including an extended critique of sociological functionalism.

COSER, LEWIS

1956   *The Functions of Social Conflict.* Paperback ed., 1964. New York: Free Press. Coser's theoretical study of social conflict is based upon the writings of Georg Simmel.

ELLUL, JACQUES

1954   *The Technological Society.* Translated by John Wilkinson, 1964. New York: Knopf. This is an important essay on the dilemma of technological societies written by a leading French social philosopher.

HANDLIN, OSCAR

1957   *Race and Nationality in American Life.* Boston: Little, Brown. (Paperback ed., 1957. Garden City, N. Y.: Doubleday.) This fine collection of essays has attained the status of a classic.

HARRIS, MARVIN
  1968   *The Rise of Anthropological Theory: A History of Theories of Culture.*
         New York: T. Y. Crowell. This volume contains some important
         insights into the different avenues of theoretical analysis of religion
         and other social institutions.

HERBERG, WILL
  1955   *Protestant-Catholic-Jew.* Garden City, N.Y.: Doubleday. This well-
         known essay is an historical treatment of the same theme stressed
         in Lenski's survey research (1961), that religion is an important vari-
         able in the minority group experience in the United States.

HOLZNER, BURKHARD
  1968   *Reality Construction in Society.* Cambridge, Mass.: Schenkman Pub-
         lishing Company. An essay in the sociology of knowledge, this book
         contains some differences with, and similarities to, theories discussed
         by Berger and Luckmann (1966).

HOWE, IRVING, AND LEWIS COSER
  1957   *The American Communist Party.* Rev. ed., 1962. New York: Praeger.
         These authors have produced the definitive history of this movement.

KRAMER, JUDITH
  1970   *The American Minority Community.* New York: Appleton. This valu-
         able text contains a discussion of minority groups as status com-
         munities.

KUPER, LEO, AND M.G. SMITH (EDS.)
  1969   *Pluralism in Africa.* Berkeley: University of California Press. This
         volume contains a series of papers presented at a colloquium on
         social pluralism in Africa. The various case studies included here
         provide an excellent starting point for the comparative examination
         of group pluralism and social change.

LENSKI, GERHARD
  1961   *The Religious Factor.* Paperback ed., 1963. Garden City, N.Y.: Dou-
         bleday. This Detroit Area Study remains the only major empirical
         attempt to demonstrate the importance of religious differences as inde-
         pendent variables in American society.

  1966   *Power and Privilege.* New York: McGraw-Hill. This text on stratifica-
         tion attempts to delineate the major types of societies in a context
         that combines both consensus and conflict theory.

LERNER, DANIEL
  1958   *The Passing of Traditional Society.* New York: Free Press. Lerner's
         study is a comparative examination of social change and modernization
         in several middle eastern countries. Clearly, it would require social

research of the scope of Lerner's fine study to answer the questions raised here concerning the kinds of social variables that interact to produce pluralistic societies.

LUBBOCK, JOHN

1870   *The Origin of Civilization and the Primitive Condition of Man; Mental and Social Condition of Savages.* Harlow, Essex, England: Longmans. This early anthropological treatise is an excellent example of the problems created by a one-sided, culture-bound view of things.

O'DEA, THOMAS

1957   *The Mormons.* Chicago: University of Chicago Press. A fine case study of one of America's most unique religious minority groups.

SCHERMERHORN, RICHARD

1970   *Comparative Ethnic Relations.* New York: Random House. This is one of the few important theoretical texts on the subject.

SCHUTZ, ALFRED

1957   "Equality and the meaning structure of the social world," in *Aspects of Human Equality,* pp. 33–78. Edited by Lyman Bryson et al. New York: Harper & Row. Schutz's work has only begun to receive the recognition that it deserves in American sociology. This essay is reprinted in Arvid Brodersen (ed.), *Alfred Schutz, Collected Papers, Volume 2* (The Hague: Martinus Nijhoff, 1964), pp. 226–273.

SCOTT, ROBERT A.

1969   *The Making of Blind Men.* New York: Russell Sage Foundation. This book represents a very significant departure, as it is the only major attempt to employ a sociological perspective in the study of the blind. The book contains some very important policy implications.

SEGAL, BERNARD E. (ED.)

1966   *Racial and Ethnic Relations.* Rev. ed., 1972. New York: T.Y. Crowell. This is one of many anthologies on the subject.

SHIBUTANI, TOMATSO, AND KIAN KWAN

1965   *Ethnic Stratification.* New York: Macmillan. A comparative text on minority groups.

SIMMEL, GEORG

1908   "Superordination and subordination," in *The Sociology of Georg Simmel.* Translated and edited by Kurt H. Wolff, 1950. New York: Free Press. Simmel wrote several essays on this subject. Wolff's translation is based upon Chapter 3 of Simmel's 1908 opus *Soziologie.*

SIMPSON, GEORGE, AND J. MILTON YINGER

1953   *Racial and Cultural Minorities.* Rev. eds., 1958, 1965, 1972. New York: Harper & Row. This has become one of the most frequently used college texts on the subject. The central focus is upon prejudice and discrimination.

TUMIN, MELVIN M.

1953   "Stratification: A critical analysis," in *American Sociological Review,* Volume 18, pp. 387–394. This well-known essay was originally written in response to Kingsley Davis and Wilbert Moore's essay, "Some Principles of Stratification" (1945). Tumin attacks the view that stratification is functional and raises a number of objections to functional analysis.

VAN DEN BERGHE, PIERRE L.

1967   *Race and Racism.* New York: Wiley. This comparative study of racism in four countries contains some useful theoretical insights.

WALKER, WILLISTON

1918   *A History of the Christian Church.* Rev. ed., 1959. New York: Scribner. This standard history of Christianity contains more than a few interesting examples of religious minorities.

WEBER, MAX

1904–1905   *The Protestant Ethic and the Spirit of Capitalism.* Translated by Talcott Parsons, 1958. New York: Scribner. Weber's essays of 1904–1905 concerning the genesis of Western culture have become one of the central documents of historical and sociological thought in the twentieth century.

1922   "Class, status and party," in *From Max Weber.* Translated and edited by Hans Gerth and C. Wright Mills, 1946. New York: Oxford University Press. This essay contains Weber's often-quoted definitions of class, status, and power.

WILSON, BRYAN

1963   "A typology of sects in a dynamic and comparative perspective," in *Archives de Sociologie de Religion,* Volume 16, pp. 49–63. Wilson's analysis of the different types of religious sects could provide a fruitful starting point for the analysis of religious minorities. A more extended treatment will be found in Wilson's book *Sects and Society* (1961).

WIRTH, LOUIS

1945   "The problem of minority groups," in *The Science of Man in the World Crisis.* Edited by Ralph Linton, 1945. New York: Columbia University Press. This well-known essay has been reprinted in numerous anthologies.

YINGER, J. MILTON

1960   "Contraculture and subculture," in *American Sociological Review,* Volume 25, pp. 625–635. Yinger's stimulating essay attempts to show that there can be important differences between the types of societal groups that vary from the norms.

1970   *The Social Scientific Study of Religion*. New York: Macmillan. This volume, which is a revision of Yinger's earlier text, *Religion, Society and the Individual* (1957), contains a useful discussion of the three types of religious sects.

YOUNG, DONALD

1932   *American Minority Peoples*. New York: Harper & Row. This is one of the first textbooks on the subject.

PART II
THE SOCIAL PROCESSES OF PLURALISM

CHAPTER 3
Theories of Social Pluralism

The Meaning of Theory

The first part of this book has addressed problems of definition. The purpose has been to formulate some sensitizing concepts about social groups and human societies. As was previously noted, the purpose of all scientific concepts is to emphasize the most important or significant aspects of the phenomena being studied. If these concepts have been well aimed, they have helped to formulate the sociological problem of minority groups in a more useful manner. The second part of this book is addressed to problems of a theoretical nature. Having defined the basic characteristics of minority groups and pluralistic societies, the structures and processes of intergroup relationships in American society may now be examined.

In this regard, it is important to understand the purpose and nature of theory. Perhaps the most common misunderstanding about theories is the notion that they answer the question "why?" In the final analysis most answers to the question "why?" are ontological or theological. For instance, biologists have learned a great deal about the substances RNA and DNA. Few readers can help but be excited by James D. Watson's book *The Double Helix* (1968), in which he tells the story of the discovery of these important "secrets" of genetic reproduction.

Yet what are these discoveries really about? What kinds of questions were being asked by Watson, Linus Pauling, and the others who worked on this problem? Their discoveries were both structural ("What do these proteins look like?") and functional ("What do they do?"). In a functional sense the question "Why do DNA and RNA exist?" has been answered. These substances exist because the genetic transmission of information must occur for reproduction to happen. But the questions of why DNA and RNA exist in the first place and why it is that these and not some other substances perform this task remain unanswered. These kinds of "whys" are beyond the pale of science.

Questions about the "essence" of either natural phenomena or social life are not the stuff of scientific theories. In this sense, any answer to the question "Why do prejudice and discrimination exist?" would most probably be teleological, theological, or ideological, but not scientific. What, then, is the domain of theory in the sciences and, especially, in the social sciences?

A theory is a set of related propositions that may explain how a phenomenon has arrived historically, how it works or what its meaning is empirically, and, under given circumstances, what one may expect in the future. A theory may do one or any number of these things. Clearly, the sciences do not possess a crystal ball. As historian Edward Hallett Carr suggests (1961), science is very much a probabilistic game. Scientists are in the business of calculating what parts of the past will be reproduced in the future and under what circumstances. Beyond this, theories may reveal what kinds of structures and processes characterize the events that are studied and what their consequences are likely to be. At the simplest level, theories reveal the relationships between different parts of experienced reality. *Questions of process, structure, and relationship constitute the domain of sociological theory.* Even though science does not explain the ultimate meaning of life, it is not totally irrelevant in the face of social problems. History seems to have proven Karl Mannheim correct in his presumption that the highly industrialized nations of the West would more and more attempt to employ rational planning as a means for solving social problems (1950). The problems of human engineering have become the problems of our time. In this context, the need for sociological theories about intergroup relationships has never been greater. One returns to the maxim that social problems require sociological understanding. While sociological theories may not explain the essence of life, they can provide a valuable understanding of the structures, processes, and relationships in human affairs, as well as a tentative knowledge of the probable consequences of social policies. These, then, are the limits, potentials, and meanings of sociological theories.

Ideology and Sociological Theory

Historically, American sociologists have employed three distinct theoretical interpretations of social pluralism. The theories of assimilation, amalgamation, and cultural pluralism have each, in turn, provided answers to the question: What kind of long-term social process emerges in a pluralistic society? Yet the intriguing thing about these three theories is that they did not originate in the halls of science. Rather, as both Nathan Glazer (1954) and Milton Gordon (1961) have shown, social scientists adopted and modified these three theories after they had first enjoyed wide popularity as social doctrines in the United States. Assimilation, amalgamation, and cultural pluralism have appeared as successive ideological interpretations of the meaning of American history. Each of the three views has served, to use Walter Lippmann's apt phrase, as "pictures in our heads" (1922) of where America is going and how she is going to get there.

The question of what distinguishes scientific theories from ideologies is an important issue in the branch of sociology that examines the relationship between ideas and society: the sociology of knowledge. Both Weber (1904) and Mannheim (1929) were correct in arguing that complete objectivity is rarely, if ever, possible in the sciences. Both men realized that science is an institution in society and that the scientific act, like any other social act, involves choices and values. Every interpretation of social life is "one-sided" to the extent that it is formulated according to the scientist's class position and interests, to his social values and life-style, or to whatever happens to interest him as an individual.

It is for this reason that Mannheim and Weber speak of "approximate truth" and "meaningfulness" as the goals of social science. Mannheim implies that the pragmatic test of utility, the degree to which social theory assists men in shaping their world and solving their social problems, is the ultimate test of social science (1929). Weber, on the other hand, contends that the scientific point of view is characterized by the conscious attempt by the scientist to rid himself of his biases once he has selected his problem (1904).

While the intentional goal of the investigator to be objective is an important earmark of science, it is not the only one. All science is also based upon the principle of replication or reproducability, the ability of different men to arrive independently at the same conclusions. Finally, scientific propositions, unlike ideologies, can be subjected to rigorous testing. A true scientific theory is testable.

In contrast, ideological formulations, whether they be unconscious expressions of group interests or, as Marx contended, conscious lies about the nature of reality, are recognizable because of the congruence between ideas and the social groups, structures, or societies in which they emerge. *Ideologies may be defined as any set of ideas that explain or legitimate social arrangements, structures of power, or ways of life in terms of the goals, interests, or social position of the groups or social collectivities in which they appear.*

Another way of expressing the difference between a scientific theory and an ideology is to suggest that a theory is a descriptive statement about what "is." It is an attempt to predict on the basis of available descriptive information. In contrast, ideologies or doctrines attempt to say what "ought" to be and contain a distinguishable evaluative, judgmental element. A full investigation of all the important issues that emerge in the distinction between science and ideology is beyond the scope of this book. Yet in the context of this study, it is important that the ideologies of amalgamation, assimilation, and cultural pluralism be distinguished from their corresponding formulations as sociological theories. These three ideological interpretations of American pluralism appeared in the context of a changing structural situation in American society.

It has only been within the past several decades that sociologists have moved beyond these three traditional theories in search of a more comprehensive understanding of American pluralism. Most notably, Nathan Glazer and Daniel Patrick Moynihan in their landmark study *Beyond the Melting Pot* (1963) and Milton Gordon in his stimulating work *Assimilation in American Life* (1964) examine new approaches to the problem. The three traditional theories, as well as these two more recent studies, may be viewed as five distinct theoretical positions.

The remainder of this chapter addresses several related tasks. First, the ideologies of assimilation, amalgamation, and cultural pluralism must be understood in the context of the social conditions that precipitated them and the social groups that endorsed them. To this extent, the following analysis is a study in the sociology of knowledge, for it is an attempt to understand the relationship between social groups and structures, and the social doctrines that emerge within them. Second, these three ideologies must be distinguished from their reformulations as theories in American sociology. Since all theories are testable, it will be useful to assess the degree to which sociological research has either validated or refuted each of these theories as accurate explanations of what is occurring in American society. Finally, in the context of this test of the theories, it will be possible to understand how the theoretical perspectives offered by Glazer and Moynihan (1963) and Milton Gordon (1964) represent important additional theoretical alternatives for understanding social pluralism in the United States. In a larger sense this entire chapter is an attempt to trace and assess the history of the study of minority groups in American sociology. By focusing upon both the theoretical gains and weaknesses of the five existing theories, this chapter provides the groundwork for understanding the thrust of the theoretical departure offered in Chapter 4.

Assimilation: A Majority Ideology

The first of the five theories considered is the theory of assimilation. This theory of majority-minority relationships may be expressed in the formula $A + B + C = A$, where A, B, and C represent different social groups and A represents the dominant group. Regardless of the number of groups involved, the theory of assimilation is a theory of majority conformity. The basic contention is that, over time, all groups will conform to the mores, life-style, and values of the dominant group. As Cole and Cole (1954) have suggested, the American case may be called "Anglo-conformity." The major difference between the ideology of assimilation and the sociological theory of assimilation is the reason offered for why a particular group becomes the majority group. The ideological version of the concept is examined first.

It has just been suggested that an understanding of why particular social ideologies arise at given times and places may be acquired if ideologies are examined in the context of the social environment in which they appear. While it is indeed difficult to determine exactly when a distinct national consciousness first emerged in the United States (Merritt 1965), there can be little question that the doctrine of assimilation arose in American society after the first quarter of the nineteenth century. Here, for the first time in the American experience, major social groups and movements began to declare that a dominant culture existed and that incoming groups would be expected to conform to this majority culture.

The reasons for the emergence of these new groups and the doctrine of assimilation that they endorsed can be explained, in part, in the context of the immigration statistics for the United States during the years 1820–1940, shown in Figure 2. During these years, as a result of successive waves of immigration, the social structure of the United States changed in two important ways. First, the number of different social groups (both ethnic and religious) increased greatly. Second, the geographical distribution of the different groups became more heterogeneous.

While, from its inception, the United States was a pluralistic society composed of numerous different groups, the structure of American pluralism changed greatly during this period. A distinction between *segregated pluralism* and *integrated pluralism* will help to conceptualize these changes. *The term "segregated pluralism" may be used to refer to a society in which there are many different groups, but in which each group inhabits its own geographical area. "Integrated pluralism" may be used to refer to a society in which there are many different groups that are also geographically intermixed.* The term "integrated pluralism" is not meant to imply that social groups in the United States have become integrated in every sense and, especially, not in terms of residential integration. It is, of course, well known that the great waves of immigration resulted in the formation of so-called ethnic neighborhoods in most, if not all, American cities. It is this pattern that Robert Park called "a mosaic of segregated peoples"

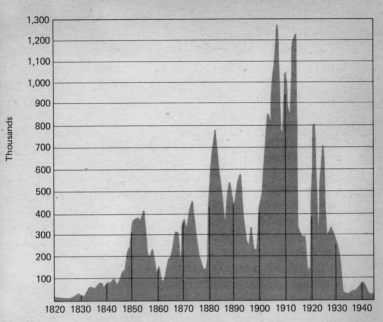

FIGURE 2. Immigration into the United States: 1820–1940. From Maurice R. Davie, *What Shall We Do About Immigration?* (New York: Public Affairs Committee, Inc., 1946, Pamphlet No. 115, p. 3.) Used with permission.

(1928/1952:99–100). The argument here is that a society in which the pattern of a segregated mosaic is repeated over and over again in every part of the country is structurally different from a society in which groups are segregated from each other on a broad geographical scale. Even though one may encounter both voluntary and forced residential segregation within the overall pattern of integrated pluralism, such a society still provides day-to-day contact between members of different social groups. This kind of pluralism "in the streets," so to speak, is not found in a society in which segregated pluralism exists on a grand scale. The terms "integrated pluralism" and "segregated pluralism" refer to the geographical distribution of different groups on a grand scale and to the patterns of social contact and interaction between group members resulting from that distribution.[1] Switzerland represents one of the most interesting contemporary examples of segregated pluralism. Each of the Swiss cantons possesses its own unique subculture. Some political theorists maintain that the geographical segregation of different ethnic groups is one of the keys to the success of Switzerland's federated form of democracy.

A situation of segregated pluralism first emerged in the United States during the colonial period. Most of the English-speaking peoples resided in New England and Virginia. The Dutch and Swedes occupied the Hudson and Delaware river valleys. The German population was almost exclusively located in Pennsylvania. Even after the first great wave of immigration, between 1820 and 1860, a pattern of segregated pluralism still prevailed. By 1860, two-thirds of the Irish had settled in New York, Pennsylvania, and New England. Over half the German population had settled in the Mississippi and Ohio valleys, while virtually no Germans settled in New England. Two-thirds of the Dutch were contained within the four states of New York, Michigan, Iowa, and Wisconsin. Norwegian immigrants settled only in Wisconsin and Minnesota (Jones 1960:117–146).

Contemporary American society still possesses some residues of its earlier pattern of group regionalism. Wilbur Zelinsky (1961) has shown that there are no truly national churches or denominations in the United States. Rather, each religious group holds a dominant position in only one part of the country. In essence, the United States consists of numerous distinct religious regions. The contemporary pattern of religious regionalism can, of course, be traced to earlier patterns of ethnic regionalism and religious revivalism (Sweet 1939, Hudson 1965).

As shown in Figure 3, the "old immigration" between 1820 and 1860 differed greatly from the "new immigration" between 1860 and 1940. Prior to the Civil War, most of the immigrants came from the countries of northern and western Europe: England, Wales, Scotland, and Germany. The new immigrants who entered the United States after the war were predominantly from the countries of eastern and southern Europe and Eurasia: Italy, Austria, Russia, Hungary, and Poland. The

---

[1]The existence of residential segregation within the overall pattern of integrated pluralism is an important topic and will be discussed at length in Chapter 4.

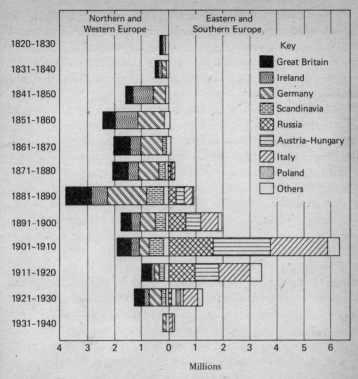

FIGURE 3. Immigration into the United States, according to countries of origin: 1820-1940. From Maurice R. Davie, *What Shall We Do About Immigration?* (New York: Public Affairs Committee, Inc., 1946. Pamphlet No. 115, p. 5.) Used with permission.

situation resulting from the second wave of immigration (1860–1940) may be described as integrated pluralism in two senses. First, it created a much more diverse mixture of cultures. The number of different ethnic and religious groups increased greatly. Second, the old pattern of rigid sectional boundaries between groups was lost. Particularly in the fast-growing cities of the Northeast, sizable groups of different ethnic and religious traditions lived side by side. The distribution of different populations became structurally integrated.

As is the case with most sociological distinctions (ideal types), the difference between segregated and integrated pluralism is a matter of degree and is not absolute. As has already been noted, the United States still possesses some features of a segregated pluralistic society. This is not only evident in the realm of religion (Zelinsky 1961, Niebuhr 1929) but even more so in the matter of American race relations. American blacks are located predominantly in the inner cities of both the North and the South. But between 1860 and 1940 the American social structure changed dramatically in the direction of an integrated pluralism in which different ethnic and religious groups became geographically intermixed.

It would be entirely misleading to suggest that immigration figures alone tell the complete story of the reshaping of American society in the late nineteenth century. Social, political, and economic factors in both the United States and Europe must be examined if one is to understand the human meaning of the great migration. Just as political turmoil, economic crisis, and crop failures in Europe explain why the immigrants left their homelands, so the emergence of urbanization and industrialization in the United States explains why the immigrants came here rather than going elsewhere and why their arrival produced new social structures. The unprecedented growth of American capitalism and industry, the need for new labor forces, and the concentration of American manufacturing in the cities all must be considered (Hansen 1940). The plight of the immigrants in the "promised land" is another important part of this story. While Oscar Handlin's work *The Uprooted* (1951) is one of the best accounts of the experiences of the European immigrants, there have been innumerable sociological studies of the different groups. W. I. Thomas and Florian Zanecki's classic study *The Polish Peasant in Europe and America* (1918) proved to be the first of many such studies. In spite of the predominant interest of contemporary sociologists in the experience of black and Spanish-speaking minorities, studies continue to appear in the sociological literature on the subject of the European immigrants.

While the reactions of the immigrants to their new surroundings will be considered later, the concern for the moment is the way in which the existing majority group responded to the immigrants in terms of new social movements and new social doctrines. The ideology of assimilation was a majority response to a changed situation.

It is generally agreed among American historians that ethnic and religious conflicts were a significant element in American life even during the colonial and revolutionary periods. While this part of the American saga is perhaps too infrequently told, it is known that violent outbreaks between Germans and Englishmen, Protestants and Catholics, and Congregationalists and Presbyterians were not uncommon. Yet it was not until the early nineteenth century that group conflicts became couched in assimilationist ideologies of broad popular appeal.

While the "old immigration" between 1820 and 1860 originated primarily in western and northern Europe, it did involve sizable numbers of one new group, Irish Catholics. Accordingly, the ideology of the American Nativist Movement of the 1830s and 1840s, as well as that of the "American" or "Know-Nothing" party of the 1850s, was ardently anti-Catholic. Two representative documents of the period were authored by Samuel F. B. Morse, inventor of the telegraph, and the prominent New England clergyman Lyman Beecher. While Morse's essay *A Foreign Conspiracy Against the Liberties of the United States* (1834) warned that Irish immigration was part of a papal conspiracy to gain control of the United States, Beecher's tract *A Plea for the West* (1835) suggested that all Catholic immigrants be segregated to the then undeveloped and undesirable western section of the country. Although the roots of the Nativist Movement were ostensibly religious and social, economic factors also played a part. Particularly after the economic panic of 1837, numerous labor groups began requesting that American workingmen be protected from competition by incoming cheap "foreign" laborers. Since many of the new immigrants came to the United States fleeing from starvation and poverty, pauperism was rapidly becoming a problem, especially in the cities. To the already existing anti-Catholic fears of the Protestant majority population, complaints about the pauperism and alleged criminality of the "foreigners" were added. While the Nativist Movement prior to the Civil War appears meek when compared to the excesses of bigotry and prejudice that arose between the Civil War and the early 1900s, several important features of the ideology of assimilation were already in evidence.

The central tenet of the assimilationist position was that new groups must conform to the cultural tradition of the majority or dominant group. But two important corollary notions were involved. First was the contention that the culture of the dominant group was in some way superior. Conversely, the ideology also maintained that minority cultures were inferior. In sociological terms, this ideology contains specific social definitions of the in-group and the out-groups. Prior to the 1860s these ideological group definitions were based upon religious, political, and social criteria. The dominant culture (primarily German, English, and Protestant) was viewed as freedom-loving, clean, honest, and industrious. The culture of the newcomers was viewed by the majority as inferior because of alleged dishonesty, poverty, uncleanliness, and subversive political goals stemming from allegiance to the pope.

Understandably, both Nativism and immigration diminished with the onset of the Civil War. Yet the period between the end of the war and the early 1900s was marked by unprecedented waves of immigration. As has already been noted, the "new immigration" brought new groups from eastern and southern Europe, not to mention increasing numbers of Chinese who were imported to assist in the building of the railroads. In the context of the "new immigration," Nativism was reborn, and the ideology of assimilation came to full maturity.

Even during the years of the "old immigration" several states had passed anti-immigration laws. All of these laws were invalidated by the Supreme Court in 1876 on the grounds that they violated the constitutional powers of the federal government. Yet contrary to the Court's ruling, demands for immigration restrictions could be heard throughout the land. As John Higham (1955) has shown, the most important restrictionist organization of the era was the American Protective Association, which was founded in 1887. While the APA began as an anti-Catholic organization, it won broad popular support on an "anti-foreigners" platform. In addition to arguing for immigration restrictions, the APA also advocated the use of literacy tests as a criterion for voting rights in the United States. To some extent, the goals of the APA were thwarted in 1896 when President Grover Cleveland, in the last days of his administration, vetoed a literacy-test law that had been passed by both houses of the Congress. Various laws that were passed at the federal level did somewhat restrict the "Atlantic migration" by forbidding the immigration of paupers, anarchists, persons with criminal records, and persons afflicted with a wide assortment of illnesses. All of these laws were consolidated in 1907 by a law that placed a then-expensive head tax on immigrants of four dollars each. Even prior to this, the Chinese Exclusion Acts of 1882, 1892, and 1902 had all but halted immigration from the Asian continent.

As Thomas F. Gossett (1963) explains in his fine history of the subject, the appearance of the concept of race was the most important ideological development in the growth of the assimilationist doctrines of the late nineteenth and early twentieth centuries. The adoption of Charles Darwin's theory of human evolution into the realm of social science and social philosophy in the form of social Darwinism provided new grist for the ideological mills.[2] In short, if human history was to be understood as a process of successive evolutionary phases, then clearly one race had to represent the last phase in that process. As Madison Grant proclaimed in his book *The Passing of a Great Race* (1916), superior cultures were produced by superior races, and inferior cultures were produced by inferior races. The only way to keep America "pure" was to exclude inferior "races" such as blacks, yellows, Catholics, Jews, Poles, Slavs, and so on. Only members of the "Aryan" or "Nordic" (i.e., English and German) races were capable of assimilating. "Mongrel" peoples would only pollute the race. Grant's hideous book was, of course, not the origin of these ideas but, rather, their most elaborate exposition. As early as the 1890s such groups as the Daughters of the American Revolution, the Society of Colonial Dames, and the Sons of the American Revolution had championed the superiority of the white Anglo-Saxon Protestant "race." Yet no discussion of these groups would be complete without some mention of the most powerful of them all, the Ku Klux Klan.

Most Americans are apt to associate the initials KKK with the white-protectionist groups that appeared in the South immediately after the Civil War. But as David Chalmers reveals in his study *Hooded Americanism* (1965), the Klan was reborn as an unparalleled political and militia force between the years 1915 and 1924. While the old Klan was primarily antiblack, the new Klan was antiblack, anti-Catholic, anti-Jew, anti-Communist, antianarchist, and antiforeigner. It was not primarily a southern organization but it virtually controlled American political and

---

[2]The basic ideas of social Darwinism were really invented by Herbert Spencer, not Charles Darwin. See the discussion on p. 257ff.

social life in many states, with some of its strongest "klaverns" in the Northeast. Not surprisingly, it relied upon the leadership of politicians, law enforcement officers, and, most of all, white Protestant clergymen. The Klan must be viewed as an important force in the Red Scare and the Palmer Raids of 1919, when Attorney General A. Mitchell Palmer simply deported large numbers of Communists, Jews, anarchists, socialists, labor leaders, Seventh Day Adventists, and other "undesirables." The period climaxed in 1924 with the passage of the National Origins Quota Act, the first comprehensive immigration legislation in the nation's history.

This act provided a solution to the problem of America's recently acquired "unassimilatables." It allowed a yearly quota of over 127,000 immigrants from western and northern Europe, but an annual quota of less than 24,000 people from eastern and southern Europe. Immigration from all other parts of the world was limited to just over 3,000 per year. The ideology of Anglo-conformity had been institutionalized. The Quota Act had been based upon the findings of a congressional commission created in 1907, the Dillingham Commission. It provides an interesting case study in the uses of social science. Its report, elaborately documented with social statistics, was slanted to "prove" that the "new immigrants" were predominantly unskilled, illiterate, and undesirable. More recent examinations of the commission's report have demonstrated that the statistics do not even support its findings.

To summarize, the ideology of assimilation first arose in the United States during the late nineteenth and early twentieth centuries as a majority reaction to severe structural changes in American society. The immigration of large numbers of new peoples and the distribution of these immigrants into a structural pattern that may be described as integrated pluralism provided the social context for the new ideology. While prior to the Civil War the doctrine of assimilation was based upon alleged social, religious, and political differences between peoples, the mythology of race was later used to specify which groups could and could not assimilate.

Both the ideology of assimilation and the sociological theory of assimilation maintain that group relationships in pluralistic societies evidence a tendency for minority groups to assume the culture of the dominant group. Yet the sociological theory does not rely upon race and cultural myths to explain why the majority prevails. There are no scientific criteria for determining whether a given culture is good, bad, inferior, or superior. These kinds of ideological assertions are not scientifically testable. No truly scientific theory can be based upon myths of group superiority. Rather, by definition, majority groups are power-holding groups in societies.[3] Hence, the sociological theory of assimilation maintains that the distribution of social power plays a major role in determining the direction of assimilation, if and when it occurs. There are many different historical circumstances that may allow a particular group to become the majority or dominant group in a society. Possession of an advanced technology or of superior military strength may insure a position of social power and dominance. While history is replete with examples of indigenous groups that were conquered by invaders, invaders have often acquired control of the land and wealth in a society and thereby maintained dominance over future immigrants and invaders. Of course, for assimilation to occur it is presumed that the majority wants minority groups to assimilate and that minority groups will not resist. Neither of these conditions are guaranteed in any situation, least of all in the United States. But the question of whether or not the theory of assimilation accurately describes what has happened or is happening in America will be addressed later in this chapter. Several additional theories must first be examined.

Amalgamation: A Minority Utopia

The central proposition of the theory of amalgamation may be expressed in the formula $A + B + C = D$, where A, B, and C represent different social groups and D represents an amalgam, a synthesis of these groups into a distinct new group. In terms of American society, the theory of amalgamation maintains that Englishmen, Germans, Italians, Irishmen, and Russians, over time, all become Americans, a new group that is different from any of the original groups but is also a hybrid or combination of them all.

Again, social doctrine must be distinguished from sociological theory. While the ideology of assimilation began as a majority interpretation

[3]See the discussion on pp. 17–24.

of American history, the idea of amalgamation was a minority response to the meaning of the "Atlantic migration." The doctrine of amalgamation is frequently expressed in the term "the melting pot," taken from the title of a play written in 1909 by the Jewish immigrant Israel Zangwill. The basic idea is that the different cultures will eventually merge and create a new social and cultural phenomenon.

As Nathan Glazer has noted (1954), the emergence of this ideology is somewhat ironic for, by the time it caught on, the Congress had already passed the National Origins Quota Act of 1924, virtually eliminating immigration except from those nations that represented the majority cultural stocks in the United States: northern and western Europeans. While this irony is an interesting one, it is perhaps more revealing to consider this social doctrine from the standpoint of those minority groups for whom it was meaningful. As Handlin (1951) and others have shown, the experience of being "uprooted" was at best chaotic and difficult.

In this respect, the ideology of amalgamation shares certain common features with all ideologies that emerge in the context of severe social-structural changes. Man's perception of time and history is most susceptible to drastic change when all that is familiar and taken for granted suddenly changes. As was already seen in the ideology of assimilation, even when society must be reinterpreted, there is a tendency for redefinitions to be cast in the framework of past experience. While in the late nineteenth and early twentieth centuries America's majority population realized that society was changing, these changes were forced to "make sense" in the context of past experience through the ideology of assimilation. The majority viewed these changes as temporary, lasting only until the recent immigrants had time to assimilate and the tide of unassimilatables could be stopped. After assimilation, it was presumed that American society would look very much as it always had. The taken-for-granted world would return.

Of course, the more severe the changes in man's social environment the more difficult it becomes for the future to make sense in the context of the past. For instance, during both the French and Russian Revolutions, definitions of time and history changed greatly. In the year 1793, the Gregorian (Christian) calendar was eliminated. It was no longer A.D. 1793 but "Year 1 of the Republic" and "Year 1 of Liberty."

The old calendar was not reinstituted until 1801 by Napoleon, as a gesture to the pope. While there is a tendency, then, for men to define the present and the future in terms of the past, some experiences may be so severe as to require an entirely new understanding of history. This was unquestionably the case for the European immigrants, for they had left their pasts behind them.

The ideology of the melting pot was one way in which the immigrants were able to impart positive meaning to an otherwise chaotic and unpredictable situation. But dramatic new social meanings are rarely viewed as meaningful only for the moment. Rather, redefinitions of the present point in different ways to both the past and the future. To the European immigrants, the Atlantic crossing meant not just a new historical moment for them but a new historical epoch for all mankind. The idea of amalgamation meant that human history had set out on a new path.

The doctrine of amalgamation is a fine example of what Karl Mannheim has called a *utopia* (1929). It is a definition of social reality that departs from the actual state of affairs in a new way. Utopian doctrines describe societies that have not yet happened. In contrast, Mannheim used the term *ideology* to refer to those doctrines that also depart from the real situation in society but that are based upon old, rather than new, perceptions. Ideologies are doctrines that describe societies that have already passed from the scene. Mannheim readily admitted that it is often difficult, if not impossible, to know whether a particular set of social doctrines should be labeled as an ideology or a utopia. In order to determine this, one must be able to distinguish the doctrine from the real situation of the society it claims to describe. This is always easier to do in retrospect. Yet Mannheim's two concepts, ideology and utopia, do help to emphasize the fact that the doctrine of assimilation was the majority's way of interpreting the present and the future through the past. The doctrine maintained that immigration would not greatly change the nature of American society. The Quota Act of 1924 was designed to guarantee that immigrants who would precipitate change would be kept out. On the other hand, the utopian doctrine of amalgamation forecasted a new future for the nation and, particularly, for the immigrants who had been severed from their pasts.

For the sake of clarity, Mannheim's distinction between ideologies and utopias will not be stressed beyond this point. Due to the problems inherent in distinguishing these two types of doctrines from one another, it will be simpler to use the term ''ideology'' in a broader sense that encompasses both of Mannheim's ideal types. As was previously noted, an ideology may be viewed as any social doctrine that explains, interprets, or legitimates social realities from the standpoint of the groups that produce or endorse it.

It should not be assumed that the ideology of amalgamation is a totally inaccurate description of what may occur in a pluralistic society. There are some indications that some instances of amalgamation have occurred in the United States to some degree. But for the moment the more important question is how the ideology of amalgamation may be distinguished from its corresponding formulation as a sociological theory. As was the case with the idea of assimilation, these two kinds of formulations differ according to the reasons offered for the occurrence of the phenomenon.

While the doctrine of amalgamation argues that different cultural stocks will blend into a new culture, it also contains the important corollary proposition that the new amalgam will represent only the ''best'' qualities and attributes of the different cultures that contribute to it. This part of the ideology is understandable in terms of the interactions between different groups. Just as a majority group may develop prejudices and antagonisms toward minorities, so minority groups may develop stereotypes about both the majority and other minorities. While group prejudices and stereotypes emerged on all sides in the United States, it is also true that every group has been recognized, if not admired and envied, for its own distinctive cultural values and achievements. The ideology of amalgamation resolved these crosscurrents very nicely. While no group would remain the object of prejudice, all groups would be able to boast of their unique contributions to the new cultural stock. Similarly, all the desirable attributes of the different groups would be shared in the new culture.

In this regard, it is ironic that the minority group doctrine of the melting pot is based upon the same social Darwinist assumptions as the majority group ideology of assimilation. While the doctrine of assimilation contends that the dominant group's culture is the ''best,'' and that all other groups will conform to it for this very reason, the minority group doctrine of amalgamation assumes that the "best" cultural traits of each group will be selectively contributed to the new amalgam. In both instances it is assumed that one can justifiably speak of "good" and "bad" in the realm of cultural differences.

Just as the sociological theory of assimilation rejected the specification of superior and inferior cultures, so the theory of amalgamation rejects the specification of desirable and undesirable aspects of cultures. There are no scientific criteria with which one can evaluate the cultural attributes of groups, nor are there any laws of social causation that can guarantee that so-called better attributes will become the basis for a cultural or racial amalgamation. It is every bit as likely that an amalgamation will produce a blending of the "worst of the lot," whatever that may be. Rather, a sociological study of amalgamation focuses upon those historical and situational factors that produce an affinity between the cultural traits of the different groups that are combining. Some of the basic elements of the theory of amalgamation will be discussed shortly. But first the doctrine of cultural pluralism must be examined.

Cultural Pluralism: Another Minority Utopia

The meaning of the phrase "cultural pluralism" may be expressed in the formula $A + B + C = A + B + C$, where A, B, and C represent different social groups that, over time, maintain their own unique identities. Cultural pluralism is often viewed as a "peaceful coexistence" between groups. The theory contends that after some (unspecified) period of adjustment, different groups will make their peace with one another and live side by side.

While the theories of assimilation and amalgamation began as social ideologies and were later modified by scholarly students of American society, the theory of cultural pluralism has followed a somewhat different path. The author of this third view of American pluralism was a Harvard-educated philosopher of Jewish immigrant stock named Horace Kallen. While the actual phrase "cultural pluralism" did not appear until the publication of a collection of his essays in 1924, Kallen had enunciated the basic ideas of his theory in a series of articles that appeared in the magazine *The Nation* in 1915. This is not to suggest that Kallen was the only spokesman for this position. By the early 1900s many Americans had already recoiled from the majority ideology of assimilationism and pure Americanism. As Milton Gordon observes (1964:138), the well-known settlement house worker Jane Addams became an eloquent spokeswoman for the richness of America's newly acquired immigrant cultures. In her book *Twenty Years at Hull-House* (1914), she entered a plea for the preservation and appreciation of the positive contributions of America's many ethnic cultures. Yet, as will be seen, Kallen's work must be viewed as the focal point for the idea of cultural pluralism.

The dates 1915 to 1924, which frame the appearance of Kallen's early writings, are of immense social significance. It will be recalled that these are the very dates Chalmers (1965) used to mark the resurgence and dominance of the Ku Klux Klan in the United States. Similarly, these dates encompass the frantic Red Scare and the Palmer Raids. Ironically, Kallen's book *Culture and Democracy in the United States* (1924) was born in the wake of the Dillingham Commission and the National Origins Quota Act of 1924. The ideology of cultural pluralism must be understood in this social context. As Karl Mannheim suggests, all ideologies may be recognized by the fact that they are carefully designed to do battle with opposing ideas (1929/1936:57). Kallen's sophisticated and erudite philosophy of cultural pluralism was, on the one hand, aimed at the majority ideology of assimilationism and pure Americanism. On the other hand, Kallen wished to refute the doctrine of the melting pot, which had gained great currency, especially among the liberal intellectuals of the day.

While many immigrants endorsed the doctrine of amalgamation and its distinctive way of looking to the future, Kallen's notion of cultural pluralism was based upon a philosophical examination of the American past. His ideas involve at least three central propositions, the first of which contains a cogent sociological observation. First, he argued that while there are many kinds of social memberships and identities that man may choose voluntarily, no one may choose his ancestry. The doctrine of assimilation is unrealistic, for it is unlikely that even after long periods of time a man will forget his family was once German, Italian, Jewish, Russian, or Irish. In this sense Kallen anticipated Louis Wirth's contention that minority groups, by definition, are composed of people who have a conscious identification with some distinctive group trait.[4] In terms of Erving Goffman's poetic phrase, Kallen was suggesting that a person's social origins become an important part of his "identity kit" (1959).

A second part of Kallen's argument was that each of the minority cultures has something positive, something of value, to contribute to American society. This proposition is understandably shared by both minority ideologies, amalgamation and cultural pluralism. Finally, Kallen maintained that the idea of democracy, in the words of the Constitution, of "all men being created equal," carries an implicit assumption that there are ostensible differences between men and groups that can be viewed as "equal." Without the presumption that differences existed, the statement in the Constitution about all men being equal in spite of their differences would be meaningless. In this way Kallen maintained that cultural pluralism had always been an important part of the American tradition. The results of the "Atlantic migration" represented a continuation of the American heritage. In the face of the majority ideology of assimilation, Kallen attempted to prove that cultural pluralism, freedom, and unity through diversity was the real meaning of American history.

The idea of cultural pluralism was later adopted and further popularized by another immigrant writer, Louis Adamic (1938, 1940, 1944). Throughout the 1930s and 1940s, Adamic employed the poet Walt Whitman's phrase "a nation of nations" to underline the significance of America's multicultural composition. It must be remembered that while Kallen was correct in asserting that American society has always been pluralistic, this argument is of greater ideological than sociological significance.[5] While it is always scientifically useful to know the origins of a phenomenon, it can often be misleading and inaccurate to explain or understand a phenomenon in terms of its origins alone. This tendency was one of the great errors of the nineteenth century school of philosopy known as "historicism" and has been properly criticized by Karl Popper in his book *The Poverty of Historicism*

[4]See the discussion on pp. 15–17.
[5]Kallen's argument might also be refuted through the distinction discussed earlier between integrated and segregated pluralism. See the discussion on pp. 54–56.

(1957). Rather, a sociological theory of cultural pluralism must focus upon those social forces that contribute to the maintenance of distinctive group traits in any society. Similarly, such a theory must be testable in terms of historical as well as empirical research.

Finally, it may be noted that the doctrine of cultural pluralism corresponds to what Karl Mannheim has called a *conservative utopia* (1929/1936:206–215). In contrast to "ideologies" which view history through the recent past, and "utopias" which interpret history in terms of the near future, "conservative utopias" interpret the present and future through the distant past. As is shown in Table 6, the doctrines of assimilation, amalgamation, and cultural pluralism differ greatly in terms of the ways in which they approach the problem of meaning in history.

Three Theories: Their Sociological Uses

It has been shown that the ideologies of assimilation, amalgamation, and cultural pluralism emerged as alternative majority and minority interpretations of American society during the late nineteenth and early twentieth centuries. It will be useful to pause here and examine the ways in which these three ideas have been used in sociological investiga-

TABLE 6. Assimilation, Amalgamation, and Cultural Pluralism Viewed as Ideology, Utopia, and Conservative Utopia

Social doctrine	Group that creates or endorses the idea	Karl Mannheim's descriptive term[a]	Way in which the doctrine interprets the present
Assimilation ("majority-conformity")	Majority	Ideology	Through the recent past
Amalgamation ("the melting pot")	Minority	Utopia	Through the near future
Cultural Pluralism ("a nation of nations")	Minority	Conservative utopia	Through the distant past

[a]These terms are employed in Karl Mannheim's *Ideology and Utopia* (1929).

tions of American society. A brief review of some of the major studies of minority groups in American sociology will make possible a deeper appreciation of the contributions of Glazer and Moynihan (1963) and Milton Gordon (1964).

Most of the literature on American minority groups has, until very recently, focused upon three variables: race, religion, and ethnicity. Most studies also suggest that the theory of amalgamation does not explain majority-minority relationships in the United States. Rather, the theories of assimilation and cultural pluralism have alternately enjoyed the theoretical spotlight. Before turning to the uses of these two theories in American sociology, several aspects of the theory of amalgamation should be discussed. Amalgamation is the least frequently encountered of these three phenomena. There are several important reasons why this is the case. First, both amalgamation and assimilation require that majority groups allow and encourage minority groups to assimilate or amalgamate, and that minority groups will either voluntarily or involuntarily (through some form of coercion) attempt to assimilate or amalgamate. While both of these conditions may prevail in some situations, this is rarely the case. Moreover, for amalgamation to occur majority groups must relinquish their position of dominance in society. From our earlier discussion of stratification, it will be recalled that the emergence of dominant and subordinate groups is an all-but-universal phenomenon in human societies.[6] For complete amalgamation between groups to take place, this basic feature of social life must be overcome or counteracted. Few dominant groups in the history of mankind have voluntarily relinquished power.

This is not to suggest that amalgamation is impossible. In his study of Hawaii, Ramanzo Adams maintains that when Captain Cook arrived in the islands in the late 1700s the indigenous Hawaiian populations had already undergone complete amalgamation (1937:39). Another example of nearly complete amalgamation is that of the mestizo in Mexico. Following the conquest of Mexico by the Spanish under Cortez, two parallel processes of amalgamation began to occur. One type of mestizo resulted from the mating of Spanish and Indian populations, while a second type of mestizo represented the mixing of Indians and

[6]See the discussion on pp. 16, 25.

blacks. Initially the mestizo were assigned a low position in Mexican society, but the successive amalgamation of the various amalgamated peoples of Mexico produced a new racial and cultural mainstream. Today the bronze peoples of Mexico constitute better than 85 percent of the population and many, though not all, of the previous status differences between different ethnic and racial groups have faded into the background (van den Berghe 1967:42–58).

Both of these examples suggest a number of conditions that may promote amalgamation, if and when it occurs. First, amalgamation does not typically involve a large number of groups at one time. Rather, the melting pot evolves in successive stages over long periods of time. Second, as was the case in Spanish-Indian amalgamation in Mexico, a sexual imbalance in the population distribution of at least one of the two amalgamating groups is an important factor. The absence of Spanish women in Mexico increased the probability of intermarriage and amalgamation. Finally, the Hawaiian case suggests that severe isolation from outside groups may lead to social and/or economic interdependency and, subsequently, to amalgamation between groups that live in close proximity over long periods of time. This condition, of course, is becoming more and more unlikely in the modern world. An alternative to the severe isolation of certain groups may be the existence of a common enemy and a common life-style for two amalgamating groups, even within a pluralistic society. The concentration of blacks and Puerto Ricans in American urban ghettos has produced some degree of amalgamation between the two groups. Yet, as Piri Thomas reveals in his autobiography *Down These Mean Streets* (1967), while blacks and Puerto Ricans share a common enemy, "Whitey," an individual of mixed parentage may find it difficult to be at home in either of the two minority communities.

Moreover, while it may be accurate to use intermarriage as a measure of racial amalgamation between groups, intermarriage does not necessarily produce a cultural amalgamation between two ethnic or religious groups of the same race. For instance, marriages in the United States between Irish Catholics and Italian Catholics or between white Anglo-Episcopals and white Norwegian Lutherans is not likely to produce a new ethnic-religious amalgamation. Rather, these kinds of intermarriages usually produce "trade-offs" in which the members of the mixed marriage choose between one of the two ethnic-religious communities. Nor can the marriage between an American Jew and an American Methodist be viewed as amalgamation if they subsequently join the Unitarian Church. All instances of intermarriage do not produce amalgamation, and there may be significant differences between situations of racial and cultural amalgamation.[7]

To summarize, amalgamation is a relatively unique occurrence and tends to appear under special circumstances. The number of amalgamating groups at any one time is usually limited to two, and complete or nearly complete amalgamation in any society requires a long period of time. While some degree of amalgamation does occur between groups in pluralistic societies, it is not often a total societal process. Intermarriage should not be viewed as being synonymous with amalgamation. While the theory of amalgamation has been employed by students of comparative sociology and anthropology, it has not been widely used to interpret American society. Rather, the theories of assimilation and cultural pluralism have most often been used to describe the experience of racial, religious, and ethnic groups in the United States.

While the study of minority groups did not enjoy wide popularity in American sociology until after World War II, studies of ethnic groups did begin to appear in the early 1920s. There are at least two ostensible reasons why ethnic groups drew the interest of some sociologists during this period. First, as has already been shown, the nation as a whole became preoccupied with the question of immigration. While many sociologists during this era were attempting to disengage themselves from the field of social work and the study of social problems, it is understandable that those sociologists who maintained an interest in social problems would turn to the question of ethnic groups. More importantly, the 1920s and 1930s saw the rise of an influential trend in American sociology known as the "Chicago School." Those sociologists who either taught or studied at the University of Chicago during these years are credited with having originated, among other things, the field of study now known as urban sociology. It will be recalled

---

[7]Intermarriage is frequently treated as a measure of assimilation as well. As will be seen in Chapter 4 (pp. 162–164), existing research findings on intermarriage in the United States suggest that neither assimilation nor amalgamation is occurring but that there is, as has been suggested here, simply a pattern of trade-offs between groups.

that the concentration of American industry in American cities drew large numbers of diverse immigrants to the cities. Thus, the study of city life required a study of the new patterns of ethnic pluralism that were emerging.

Three of the better-known studies of this period are W. I. Thomas and Florian Zanecki's *The Polish Peasant in Europe and America* (1918), Louis Wirth's *The Ghetto* (1928), and Harvey Zorbaugh's *The Gold Coast and the Slum* (1929). While all of these writers recognized that the different immigrant groups shared a common problem of assimilating or acculturating into American society in some manner, the central focus of their works was cultural pluralism, not assimilation. As the late Judith Kramer has shown (1970), Everett V. Stonequist's phrase "marginal man" (1937) best captures the findings of these early studies of ethnic groups in America. Many authors observed that the immigrants had been forced into a marginal existence in American society, captured, as it were, within the secluded enclave of the ethnic community. Other students of the subject took a more optimistic view of the new cultural pluralism by suggesting that the ethnic community served as a protective shelter for the immigrants during the difficult period of adjustment to the new society. Regardless of how sociologists interpreted the ethnic community, they were unanimous in their perception that the European immigration had not resulted in assimilation but, instead, in Robert Park's words, in "a mosaic of segregated peoples" (1928/1952:99–100), a situation of cultural pluralism.

This interpretation of American society was further reinforced in the late 1930s and 1940s when American sociologists began to study race relations. As the late black sociologist E. Franklin Frazier has shown, while all of the founders of American sociology—Ward, Sumner, Giddings, Cooley, Small, and Ross—wrote occasionally on the subject of race, none of these early sociologists contributed greatly to the analysis of race relations in the United States (1947). To some extent this is understandable in terms of the fact that almost all of the founding fathers of American sociology were social Darwinists. Since they subscribed to the biological notion of racial superiority, social differences between the races did not represent a sociological problem.[8] It is for this reason that such relatively recent studies as Gun-

[8]See the discussion on pp. 258–261.

nar Myrdal, et al.'s *An American Dilemma* (1944) and John Dollard's *Caste and Class in a Southern Town* (1937) may be viewed as pioneering studies. These and subsequent studies of black-, Mexican-, and Asian-Americans have stressed the ways in which cultural pluralism has resulted from the prejudices and discrimination of America's majority population.

While studies of America's racial minorities were adding more plausibility to the idea that the nation was essentially pluralistic, new studies of second-generation ethnic groups pointed in the opposite direction. The third volume of Lloyd Warner's famous "Yankee City Series" of community studies was focused entirely upon the problem of ethnic communities. While the existence of ethnic enclaves is the starting point of the study, the real theme is the way in which ethnic groups emerge from their separate communities into the mainstream of American society. In this sense assimilation, not cultural pluralism, is the characteristic process for the second generation (Warner and Srole 1945). Both Irvin L. Child's study *Italian or American?* (1943) and P. J. Campisi's study of Italian-American family life (1948) demonstrated that the structure of immigrant families evidenced a number of assimilative changes. These changes are often viewed as a class-related phenomenon as well. As second-generation ethnic groups were able to obtain a higher social class position in American society, their members often moved out of the old ethnic neighborhoods, changed or anglicized their names, and generally established new patterns of social relationships, breaking the old European pattern of extended families. Occupational and class groupings seemed to be replacing ethnic cohesiveness. The inner structure of the second-generation immigrant family changed as well. Women acquired a greater degree of freedom and autonomy. The old father-dominated family became a typically American, middle-class, child-centered family. These are only a few of the changes in the life-style of second-generation immigrants that led sociologists in the 1940s to argue that assimilation was occurring.

An even more complicated answer to the assimilation or cultural pluralism question was suggested by historian Marcus Lee Hansen in 1938. Hansen, whose study *The Atlantic Migration* (1940) has already been noted,[9] suggested that "what the son wishes to forget, the grandson

---

[9] See the discussion on p. 58.

wishes to remember'' (1937:15). *Hansen's law* stipulates that while assimilation characterizes the second generation, cultural pluralism is typical of the third generation. It is argued that after the second generation throws off its immigrant skin, the third generation suffers an identity crisis. In a truly pluralistic society it is not enough to be just an American. The question ''What kind of American are you?'' must be answered. Accordingly, the third generation falls back upon the social identity of its grandfathers. Hansen's law, then, depicts a threefold pluralism-assimilation-pluralism sequence.

Turning to the role of religious differences, the earliest major study of American religion was H. Richard Niebuhr's *The Social Sources of Denominationalism* (1929). Niebuhr attempted to demonstrate that social factors such as race, class, ethnicity, and regionalism had produced the uniquely diverse array of American Protestant denominations. In this sense the latent theme of his work is cultural pluralism. Yet, as was the case with studies of ethnicity, studies of religion done at different times revealed different findings. Ruby Jo Reeves Kennedy conducted two successive studies (1944, 1952) that suggest that ethnic intermarriage is taking place, but only within the three major religious communities. She argues that American pluralism is actually a *triple melting pot*, with assimilation or amalgamation occurring *within* the Protestant, Catholic, and Jewish groups, but with cultural pluralism remaining characteristic of the relationships *between* the three communities. This interpretation was later supported by Will Herberg in his essay *Protestant-Catholic-Jew* (1955). Herberg maintained that with the disappearance of ethnic differences, religious groups have become America's major communities of belonging and identity. Finally, in a study of the unusually large number of organizational mergers between American Protestant denominations in the twentieth century, Robert Lee supports the view of Kennedy and Herberg. Lee's study *The Social Sources of Church Unity* (1961) argues that the very social factors that Niebuhr (1929) believed had produced an ethnically divided Protestantism are now receding. Lee's theme is assimilation, for he contends that ethnic churches are a thing of the past.

Just as urban sociologists during the 1930s and 1940s looked to the cities for an understanding of American pluralism, sociologists of the 1950s and 1960s have turned to the new suburbs for information about the shape of the emerging society. Similarly, while studies of race, ethnicity, and religion have depicted different trends depending upon when the studies were conducted, the literature on suburban America has vacillated between the pictures of assimilation and cultural pluralism. Earlier studies such as William H. Whyte's *The Organization Man* (1957), John Seeley, et al.'s *Crestwood Heights* (1956), and Gibson Winter's *The Suburban Captivity of the Churches* (1961) echo the theme of the great American melting pot. Suburbs were depicted as ethnically and religiously heterogeneous enclaves populated by the conservative and conformist-oriented sons of the middle class. Sociologists seemed convinced that differences in ethnicity and religion that had survived at least three, if not four, generations were now giving way to a new monotonous, suburban, middle-class life-style.

One of the first writers to explode this "myth of the suburbs" was William M. Dobriner in his study *Class in Suburbia* (1963). While he clung to the Kennedy-Herberg hypothesis that ethnicity was fast disappearing, he still maintained that religion and economics created important divisions in the suburbs. His central theme is that suburbs are not class homogeneous. Rather, religion and class differences are producing a pluralistic pattern in the suburbs. Other studies such as Bennett Berger's *Working Class Suburbs* (1960) and Herbert Gans' *The Urban Villagers* (1962) and *The Levittowners* (1967) not only supported the contention that the suburbs reveal class pluralism but have further shown that both ethnic and religious differences remain significant. Marvin Bressler summarizes this revised view of the suburbs as a pluralistic entity in the following manner:

> People bring to the suburbs the material, intellectual, spiritual, and political furniture of their previous residences. The special fact of living between an urban and rural locale does not necessarily produce anything uniform, monolithic, distinctive or distinguishable (1968:98).

In simple terms, the ethnic, racial, and religious enclaves of the city have not entirely disappeared. To a large extent they have simply been transported to the suburbs and further intersected by differences in social class.

To summarize, successive studies of race, ethnicity, religion, cities, and suburbs have provided conflicting themes about the nature of intergroup relationships in the United States. While studies of second-generation ethnic groups pointed toward assimilation, research on both first- and third-generation ethnic groups reveals a pattern of cultural pluralism. Studies of race and religion indicate cultural pluralism with some degree of assimilation or amalgamation occurring within the major religious and racial groups. While the early studies of cities depicted a pattern of majority group-enforced pluralism, more recent studies of suburbs reveal voluntary pluralism between racial, religious, ethnic, and class-homogeneous groups. It is against the background of these various types of studies that Glazer and Moynihan's *Beyond the Melting Pot* (1963) and Milton Gordon's *Assimilation in American Life* (1964) may be considered.

"Beyond the Melting Pot": Attempting a Synthesis

Prior to the publication of *Beyond the Melting Pot,* the sociology of minority groups evidenced two outstanding limitations. First, there was a relative absence of comparative studies. No major study had attempted to analyze at the same time the experience of different ethnic, religious, and racial groups in the United States. Second, and very much related to the lack of comparative studies, there remained no unified theoretical perspective for explaining American pluralism. Nathan Glazer and Daniel Patrick Moynihan attempted to address both of these problems. The book is in every sense a synthesis. While it builds upon past theories, it also offers some important new insights. Although the authors recognized that the theories of assimilation, amalgamation, and cultural pluralism each failed to explain American society, they also attempted to salvage the more accurate parts of the three theories. For the sake of convenience, Glazer and Moynihan's theory may be referred to as "modified pluralism."

Beyond the Melting Pot was not intended to explain everything about majority-minority relationships in the United States. Rather, it was an exploratory case study based upon the history of several groups in that remarkable human-relations laboratory, New York City. While the study did not encompass all of the minority groups in New York, it did compare some of the larger ones, specifically blacks, Puerto Ricans, Jews, Italians, and the Irish. Since New York City is the nation's largest commercial and industrial center as well as the port of entry for most immigrant groups, it seemed reasonable to expect that such a study could offer some basic insights into the nature of American pluralism.

Glazer and Moynihan's major hypothesis is best stated in their own words:

> The assimilating power of American society and culture operated on immigrant groups in different ways, to make them, it is true, something that they had not been, but still something distinct and identifiable. . . . *The ethnic group in American society became not a survival from the age of mass immigration but a new social form*[10] (1963:13–14, 16).

This theory may be expressed in the formula $A + B + C = A_1 + B_1 + C_1$, where A, B, and C represent different groups and A_1, B_1, and C_1 represent groups that are distinct from one another but also different from A, B, and C. In other words, an Italian in Italy is different from an Italian-American. An Austrian Jew is different from an American Jew of Austrian origins. A black African is different from an Afro-American. Glazer and Moynihan explain how it is possible for both assimilation *and* cultural pluralism to have occurred in the United States. Each ethnic, racial, and religious group assimilates into American society at different rates and times. On the other hand, ethnic, racial, and religious differences remain distinct but also assume new social meanings. Glazer and Moynihan stress two important ways in which existing group differences acquire new meanings. First, each minority group becomes a community of membership, but not in the manner that Stonequist (1937) and others had observed. Minority group membership is not so much a marginal existence removed from the larger society but, rather, a form of social identity, a way of knowing who you are, within the larger society. Second, each of the so-called hyphenated-American minorities (Italian-Americans, Irish-Americans, etc.) represents a political interest group. Each group, in its own time and place, becomes politically organized in order to acquire its share of society's rewards.

Beyond the Melting Pot moves from this general theoretical perspective to a detailed examination of the differences and similarities between the major racial, ethnic, and religious minority groups in New York City. Glazer and Moynihan discuss the various cultural, economic,

[10]Italics in original.

social-structural, and political differences between the several groups as well as those forces and events in the history of the city that have shaped group life generally. In the last chapter of *Beyond the Melting Pot,* the authors attempt to predict what the future will bring. Their predictions take the form of two major assertions. First, they argue that while ethnicity provided the most important dividing lines between groups prior to the 1960s, race and religion will dominate the 1960s and 1970s. Second, they predict that blacks and Puerto Ricans will "climb the ladder of success" in the same way that the European immigrants have done before them. To what extent have these two predictions proved true?

While Glazer and Moynihan were correct in predicting that racial and religious differences would predominate over previously important ethnic differences, these ethnic differences have not disappeared. Rather, as Glazer and Moynihan now suggest in their revised edition (1970), ethnic factors still play a part in the life of New York City. The original edition of *Beyond the Melting Pot* seems to err in the direction of the triple melting pot hypothesis of Kennedy (1944, 1952) and Herberg (1955). While Glazer and Moynihan were correct in predicting a diminished role for ethnic differences, their analysis clearly does not provide for the reemergence of ethnicity as a divisive factor between groups. Thus, their theory provides little understanding of the way in which the ethnic communities of the city have been transplanted to the suburbs or of the way in which ethnic conflicts have gained renewed prominence in American life in the late 1960s and 1970s. Similarly, their prediction that blacks and Puerto Ricans would "climb the ladder of success" has also not proved true. How could the insightful theoretical framework with which they began produce such erroneous predictions? It is important that a precise answer to this question be found. For if the purpose of this study is to offer an alternative theoretical perspective, it must be one that does not repeat the errors of past theories.

While Glazer and Moynihan discuss various cultural, economic, social-structural, and historical aspects of the different groups, their central focus is upon minority groups viewed as political interest groups. Most importantly, their predictions are based upon the assumption that each minority group creates the same kind of political organization and enters into the same basic political process. In terms of Louis

Wirth's typology of minority groups,[11] they seem to have assumed that all minority groups are of either the pluralistic or assimilative types and that the goals of assimilation or group pluralism will be sought through the existing political institutions and techniques available in the society. Conversely, they provide little understanding of minority group militancy or of the conditions that dispose minority groups to act out their goals through channels other than the routine political institutions in the society. As is frequently the case, there is an important connection between the theoretical framework of *Beyond the Melting Pot* and the methodology employed. Since the authors have assumed that all groups enter into the same basic political process at different times and at different rates, they have focused upon the internal life of the different groups in order to understand why they have attained social and political advancement to differing degrees. Assuming that over time the various cultural differences between groups can be in some sense equalized, the critical variable becomes time itself. The internal structure of the minority community is examined in order to find those factors that have retarded the groups' entrance into the mainstream of the political process. In other words, the emphasis of Glazer and Moynihan is more upon minority groups than majority-minority relationships. Even during the early 1960s there were other sociologists who adopted a more relational perspective and arrived at very different conclusions from those of Glazer and Moynihan. For instance, Lewis Killian and Charles Grigg in their book *Racial Crisis in America* (1964) focused upon black-white relationships and especially upon the probable success of blacks in overcoming white prejudice and discrimination. Unlike Glazer and Moynihan, Killian and Grigg quite accurately predicted increased socio-economic cleavage between the races and increased social conflict. Moreover, since Killian and Grigg gave a balanced emphasis to both sides of the majority-minority relationship, they were able to see that the emerging situation would produce not only increased conflict but also the type of conflict that would move more and more outside the routine political processes.[12] Finally, it should be noted that Glazer and Moynihan erred in assuming that reduc-

[11]See the discussion on pp. 15–17.
[12]This topic is treated in Chapter 4 (pp. 124ff.). It must also be stressed that, unlike Glazer and Moynihan, Killian and Grigg do not attempt to provide a general theory.

tions in the economic gap between the white and black communities that appeared in the post-World War II period could be taken as indications of a general trend. Given the status of blacks prior to the war, the economic fruits of the war and the postwar period could not have helped but reduce the economic gap between blacks and whites. But from the present vantage point it is now clear that the temporary bridging of this gap in the 1950s did not continue into the 1960s.

In summary, *Beyond the Melting Pot* offers both an important theoretical departure as well as some serious theoretical limitations. The central contribution of the study is the theme that both assimilation and pluralism have prevailed in different ways. The process through which minority groups gain new Americanized identities represents a form of cultural assimilation. The emergence of minority groups as political interest groups represents a pluralistic trend. On the other hand, the assumption that all minority groups enter the political arena in the same way is a serious shortcoming. It provides little understanding of groups like the Black Panthers, the Young Lords, the Black Power Movement, and the Jewish Defense League. While *Beyond the Melting Pot* still retains the limited focus upon racial, religious, and ethnic minorities, it is the first major attempt at a comparative study of these kinds of minority groups. In the context of Glazer and Moynihan's contribution, Milton Gordon's *Assimilation in American Life* may now be examined. While Gordon's analysis echoes some of Glazer and Moynihan's themes, it also provides some important new concepts for the study of majority-minority relationships in the United States.

Cultural and Structural Assimilation

Milton Gordon's work *Assimilation in American Life* (1964) represents a fifth approach to the study of American pluralism. While Gordon's primary concerns are prejudice and discrimination, he also argues that majority-minority relationships require a scrutiny of the problem of "*the nature of group life itself* within a large, industrialized, urban nation composed of a heterogeneous population"[13] (1964:1). Gordon's work is one of the first major attempts to connect the study of minority groups with the study of society per se.

[13]Italics in original.

What kind of name is "Golab", anyway?

Racial, religious, and ethnic groups all possess "subcultures" that are to some extent couched within "subsocieties." While assimilation is depicted as taking place within economic, political, and educational institutions, subsocieties are maintained in the institutional areas of religion, family, and recreation. In this sense Gordon sees both assimilation and cultural pluralism occurring. Moreover, while race, religion, and ethnicity are important determinants of these subsocieties, these three variables are intersected by three others: social class, urban-rural residence, and sectional residence. The various combinations of these six variables create what Gordon calls "ethclasses." Examples of such groups include southern, lower-class, Protestant, rural blacks; northern, upper-class, white, urban Jews; and northern, lower-class, white, urban Catholics (1964:18–54).

The central theme of *Assimilation in American Life* is that assimilation is not a single social process but a number of different subprocesses or dimensions. The two most important forms of assimilation are *cultural assimilation* and *structural assimilation*. Cultural assimilation refers to the fact that all incoming minority groups must to some degree learn the appropriate and required modes of action, dress, language, and other day-to-day norms of the culture. It may be useful to think of cultural assimilation as another way of describing what Glazer and Moynihan (1963) viewed as the process by which group differences take on new meanings in a new host society. Cultural assimilation is the process through which Italians become Italian-Americans, Poles become Polish-Americans, and the Irish become Irish-Americans. Gordon contends that while some degree of cultural assimilation always occurs, the process may continue indefinitely and may never be complete (1964:77).

Structural assimilation refers to the degree to which minority groups attain entrance into the major institutions of society, especially on a primary-group level. In addition to these two important types of assimilation, which may occur at very different rates, Gordon presents five other ways of measuring assimilation. They are (1) group intermarriage or amalgamation, (2) identificational assimilation, or the degree to which minority groups think of themselves as Americans, (3) the absence of prejudice, (4) the absence of discrimination by the majority group, and (5) the absence of a power or value conflict between groups. In summary, there are at least seven different measures of assimilation in pluralistic societies. Amalgamation is, in effect, viewed as one particular aspect of the overall assimilation process (1964:70–71).[14]

As might be expected, this approach has both advantages and shortcomings. The claim that the three traditional forces of religion, race, and ethnicity are intersected by the additional factors of social class, urban-rural residence, and regionalism is an important insight. Those groups that are the object of the most extreme forms of prejudice and discrimination vary according to sectional differences: blacks in the South, both blacks and Puerto Ricans in the North, Mexican-Americans in the Southwest and West, and, during an earlier era, Asians in the West. While Gordon's concept of the ethclass has not enjoyed wide usage, his introduction of the variable "social class" into the field of minority group studies was an important way of updating the field to account for the research of Dobriner (1963), Berger (1960), and others. Subsequent studies have shown that both race consciousness and class consciousness are involved in intergroup conflicts (Mack 1963, Leggett 1968). Finally, Gordon's claim that majority-minority relationships must be examined in the larger context of the prevailing social structures marks an important turning point in the field.

Yet there are several inadequacies inherent in Gordon's work. *Assimilation in American Life* shares with *Beyond the Melting Pot* the limited focus upon race, religion, and ethnicity. This theoretical framework provides little, if any, understanding of groups like the handicapped, American Indians, and such religious sects as Hasidic Jews and Quakers that either by choice or because of majority group discrimination fail to become either culturally or structurally assimilated. Further, while Gordon is correct in contending that assimilation may never be complete, he inaccurately assumes that cultural assimilation is a one-directional, linear process. In other words, the Italian-American Civil Rights League, the Polish-American Civil Rights League, Afro-American culture groups, hippie communes, and groups extolling the dignity of Chicano culture do not support the theory of ongoing cultural assimilation. These

[14]Gordon equates the terms "intermarriage" and "amalgamation" and views amalgamation as a subprocess of assimilation. This, of course, is not consistent with the meaning of the term "amalgamation" as it has been discussed here (pp. 63–67). As was noted earlier (p. 73), there are many instances of intermarriage that do not produce either cultural amalgamation or assimilation. They simply represent "trade-offs" between different groups.

are groups that after some period of acculturation have reversed the process of cultural assimilation by placing great emphasis upon the distinctiveness of their group.

Yet the most important issue arising from Milton Gordon's approach is the question of structural assimilation. Gordon contends that *"Once structural assimilation has occurred, either simultaneously with or subsequent to acculturation all other types of assimilation will naturally follow"*[15] (1964:81).

Gordon readily admits that structural assimilation has not yet occurred in American society on any grand scale. He specifically argues that parallel structures characterize family, religious, and recreational institutions in the United States. In this context he asks whether it is likely that prejudice and discrimination will be eliminated in a society where cultural but not structural assimilation has occurred (1964:81). But the more important question is whether the theoretical notion of assimilation is an appropriate one for studying a society in which the most important form of assimilation, structural assimilation, has not occurred. It is not until the very last chapter of *Assimilation in American Life* that the author comes to grips with this nagging question (1964:223–265). The question is never answered. Finally, it may be asked whether Gordon is correct in presuming that structural assimilation will automatically produce all other forms of assimilation as well as the elimination of prejudice and discrimination. This important question will be addressed in the following chapter. In summary, although Gordon's work has deservedly become a modern classic in the literature on American minority groups, his focus upon the processes of assimilation leaves a number of issues unresolved, the most critical of which is whether or not any theory of assimilation adequately depicts American society.

Retrospect and Prospect

Five successive theories of American pluralism have been examined. The theories of amalgamation and assimilation both depict a linear process through which different social groups will combine. While the idea of amalgamation has not been widely employed to describe

[15]Italics in original.

American society, the theory of assimilation has been one of the central themes in the literature on minority groups in the United States. In contrast to the theory of assimilation, the theory of cultural pluralism contends that, over time, groups will maintain their differences. Studies of different minority groups conducted at different points in time have alternately supported either the assimilation or pluralism theory. But it has become more and more apparent that the various groups in the United States are neither retaining all their cultural differences nor discarding them all. In other words, the theories of assimilation and cultural pluralism both seem to be extreme descriptions of the situation. Both Glazer and Moynihan in *Beyond the Melting Pot* and Milton Gordon in *Assimilation in American Life* attempt to deal with the inadequacies of previous theories. Glazer and Moynihan argue that minority groups pass through an initial phase of assimilation in which they acquire new Americanized identities. The different Americanized minority groups existing alongside each other represent a new form of social pluralism. Yet this new form of pluralism becomes a launching pad for further assimilation through the routine political processes. While Glazer and Moynihan refrain from predicting any ultimate outcome of this process, they do maintain that each group will, to a large degree, become economically and socially assimilated into American society through their participation in the normative political institutions of the society. It is here that their theory begins to lose its utility. All minority groups do not remain within the existing political institutions in society. Thus the Glazer-Moynihan hypothesis does not allow for minority groups that depart from the Americanized value system, groups that reassert their differences from the basic cultural system. Nor does their theory explain those groups that decide to compete socially and economically, but not through the routine political processes.

The fifth theory examined, that of Milton Gordon in *Assimilation in American Life,* is similar to that of Glazer and Moynihan. Gordon sees assimilation occurring at different times and in different ways. Like Glazer and Moynihan, Gordon suggests that cultural assimilation, Americanization, is a linear process. While it may never be complete, the theory does not allow for its reversal. In other words, Gordon does not allow for significant value conflicts that will pull minority groups away from the basic values and life-style of American society.

In contrast to Glazer and Moynihan, Gordon does claim that once structural assimilation occurs, the process of group assimilation will move toward an ultimate outcome—for he contends that all forms of assimilation follow from structural assimilation. As has just been noted, Gordon's theory loses its utility when it is realized that large-scale structural assimilation has not occurred in the United States. Moreover, as will be seen in the next chapter, there is actually little reason to suspect, as Gordon does, that structural assimilation will produce a greater degree of group integration in America or any other pluralistic society.

Since the purpose of the next chapter is to offer an alternative theory of American pluralism, it will be useful here to summarize the shortcomings of previous theories. First, whether assimilation or cultural pluralism is occurring in American society, it should not be presumed that the process is linear. Different groups at different times may move in either pluralistic or assimilative directions depending upon various factors. Second, it should not be assumed that all groups seek the same type of assimilation or pluralism in the same way. Rather, it is necessary to study the goals of different groups, as well as the social structures in which different groups are located, in order to understand why they do or do not gravitate toward the routine political processes, social values, and institutions of the society. The focus of previous studies upon the experiences of certain racial, religious, and ethnic groups has obscured the fact that there are different types of minority groups and that the experience of the European immigrants may represent only one possible model for group relationships in a pluralistic society. Different kinds of minority groups may elect different social goals and different social arrangements. The next chapter of this book represents an attempt to provide a theory of American pluralism that avoids these previous theoretical errors.

FOR FURTHER READING

ADAMIC, LOUIS
1938 *My America*. New York: Harper & Row. In this and the other two works cited below, the author stresses the idea of cultural pluralism

and its positive benefits. While Adamic emphasizes cultural pluralism for the immediate future, there are also indications that he anticipated a melting pot in the distant American future.

1940   *From Many Lands*. New York: Harper & Row. See annotation for Adamic, 1938.

1944   *A Nation of Nations*. New York: Harper & Row. See annotation for Adamic, 1938.

ADAMS, ROMANZO

1937   *Interracial Marriage in Hawaii*. New York: Macmillan. This study maintains that the Hawaiians, prior to the arrival of Captain Cook, represented a mixed race. The study examines further evidence of amalgamation through intermarriage statistics. See also Kuykendall and Day (1948) and Lind (1955).

ADDAMS, JANE

1914   *Twenty Years at Hull-House*. New York: Macmillan. This well-known American describes her work in one of the most famous urban settlement houses. She defends the value of America's multinational cultures.

BEECHER, LYMAN

1835   *A Plea for the West*. New York: Leavitt, Lond and Company. This prominent New England clergyman argued that Catholic immigrants should be sent to the West, presumably to prevent their capturing the civilized eastern states for Rome. The book is a revealing historical document.

BERGER, BENNETT M.

1960   *Working Class Suburbs*. 2nd ed., paperback, 1968. Berkeley: University of California Press. Like Dobriner (1963), Berger challenged the notion that the suburbs were a new phenomenon. Rather, he depicts them as transplanted cities, with all the social divisions between groups that exist in the cities.

BRESSLER, MARVIN

1968   "To suburbia with love," in *The Public Interest*, Number 10 (Winter), pp. 97–103. In this review essay of Herbert Gans' book *The Levittowners* (1967), Bressler describes some of the major shifts of interpretation in the field of suburban sociology.

CAMPISI, P. J.

1948   "Ethnic family patterns: The Italian family in the United States," in *American Journal of Sociology*, Volume 53 (May), pp. 443–449. Campisi studies the effects upon family patterns of second-generation attempts to assimilate.

CARR, EDWARD HALLET

1961   *What Is History?* New York: Random House. A prominent historian reflects on some important methodological problems in the social sciences.

CHALMERS, DAVID M.

1965   *Hooded Americanism.* Garden City, N.Y.: Doubleday. Paperback ed., 1968. Chicago: Quadrangle Books. This excellent study of the Ku Klux Klan focuses upon the period 1915–1921. The study was compiled, in large part, from the many doctoral dissertations written about the Klan in the various states.

CHILD, IRVIN L.

1943   *Italian or American?* New Haven: Yale University Press. Like Campisi's study (1948), this one focuses upon the problems created when second generations attempt to assimilate.

COLE, STEWART G., AND MILDRED WISE COLE

1954   *Minorities and the American Promise.* New York: Harper & Row. This book introduced the term "Anglo-conformity."

DOBRINER, WILLIAM M.

1963   *Class in Suburbia.* Englewood Cliffs, N.J.: Prentice-Hall. Dobriner was one of the first authors to challenge the popular notion that the suburbs contain only middle-class inhabitants.

DOLLARD, JOHN

1937   *Caste and Class in a Southern Town.* New York. Harper & Row. This pioneering study depicts the castelike segregation of American blacks.

FRAZIER, E. FRANKLIN

1947   "Sociological theory and race relations," in *American Sociological Review,* Volume 12 (June), pp. 265–271. Frazier shows that the founders of American sociology contributed relatively little to the study of race. This black sociologist, who taught at Howard University, contributed a number of important studies of black Americans, including *The Negro Church in America* (1963), *The Negro Family in the United States* (1939), *Black Bourgeoise* (1957), *The Negro in the United States* (1949), and *Race and Culture Contacts in the Modern World* (1957).

GANS, HERBERT

1962   *The Urban Villagers.* New York: Free Press. This study, based upon research in the West End of Boston, demonstrates the continued role of both class and ethnic factors in American community life.

1967   *The Levittowners.* New York: Pantheon. This study of Levittown,

Pennsylvania, essentially shows that the image of the suburbs as a boring monolithic climate is a myth. While Gans focuses primarily upon the political life of the community, his study reveals the continued force of traditional group differences.

GLAZER, NATHAN

1954   "Ethnic groups in America: From national culture to ideology," in *Freedom and Control in Modern Society*. Edited by Morroe Berger, Theodore Abel, and Charles H. Page. New York: Van Nostrand Reinhold, 1954. This essay describes the social setting of the two ideologies, amalgamation and cultural pluralism. For another treatment, see Gordon (1961, 1964).

GLAZER, NATHAN, AND DANIEL PATRICK MOYNIHAN

1963   *Beyond the Melting Pot*. Rev. ed., 1970. Cambridge, Mass.: M.I.T. Press. This is a classic study of blacks, Puerto Ricans, Jews, Italians, and the Irish in New York City.

GOFFMAN, ERVING

1959   *The Presentation of Self in Everyday Life*. Garden City, N.Y.: Doubleday. Goffman offers a rich array of concepts and insights in this book, which has become a basic source on social psychology and the study of identity in society.

GORDON, MILTON

1961   "Assimilation in America: Theory and reality," in *Daedalus*, Volume 90 (Spring), pp. 247–285. Gordon analyzes the three ideologies: assimilation, amalgamation, and cultural pluralism. He stresses themes that are treated in more detail in his larger work *Assimilation in American Life* (1964). These two essays may be compared with Glazer (1954).

1964   *Assimilation in American Life*. New York: Oxford University Press. Gordon's book is a theoretical study of race, religion, and ethnicity in the United States.

GOSSETT, THOMAS F.

1963   *Race: The History of an Idea in America*. Dallas, Tex.: Southern Methodist University Press. This standard work on the subject contains important findings concerning the relationships between racism, science, and religion in the late nineteenth and early twentieth centuries.

GRANT, MADISON

1916   *The Passing of a Great Race*. New York: Scribner. This is the American version of *Mein Kampf!* While there have been equally racist writings in the United States, Grant's is probably the most well known and most influential.

HANDLIN, OSCAR
1951   *The Uprooted.* New York: Grosset & Dunlap. This book, which won a Pulitzer Prize, is a dramatic historical interpretation of the plight of the European immigrants. Handlin has contributed a number of other important works on minority groups.

HANSEN, MARCUS L.
1937   *The Problem of the Third Generation Immigrant.* Rock Island, Ill.: The Augustana Historical Society. This work contains Hansen's law, which stipulates that the third-generation immigrant identifies strongly with the ethnic culture that the second generation attempts to reject.
1940   *The Atlantic Migration 1607–1860.* New York: Harper & Row. Hansen's book is viewed as the authoritative source on this period of immigration to the United States.

HERBERG, WILL
1955   *Protestant-Catholic-Jew.* Garden City, N.Y.: Doubleday. Herberg argues that with the loss of ethnic communities in the United States, a religious triple melting pot has become the foundation of social pluralism. The book also makes a controversial contribution to the sociology of religion, for it attempts to explain how it is possible for both church membership and secularization to be increasing at the same time. Herberg's view of ethnicity is based upon Kennedy (1944, 1952).

HIGHAM, JOHN
1955   *Strangers in the Land: Patterns of American Nativism 1860–1925.* New Brunswick, N.J.: The Trustees of Rutgers College in New Jersey. (Paperback ed., 1963. New York: Atheneum.) This volume does for the "new immigration" what Hansen (1940) did for the "old immigration." Higham's work is the most comprehensive treatment of the rise of assimilationist groups and "pure Americanism."

HUDSON, WINTHROP
1965   *Religion in America.* New York: Scribner. This is a comprehensive treatment of the history of religion in America. In many ways it updates Sweet (1939).

JONES, MALDWYN ALLEN
1960   *American Immigration.* Chicago: University of Chicago Press. This study encompasses both of the historical periods treated in Hansen (1940) and Higham (1955). It contains a particularly useful bibliography.

KALLEN, HORACE M.
1915   "Democracy versus the melting pot," in *The Nation,* Volume 100

(February 18, 25), pp. 190–194, 217–222. This series of essays introduced Kallen's claim that the majority assimilationist view was counter to the American tradition of democracy. It is reprinted in Kallen (1924).

1924   *Culture and Democracy in the United States*. New York: Liveright. This collection of Kallen's essays stresses his notion of the democratic character of cultural pluralism. The latter term first appeared in this volume.

KENNEDY, RUBY JO REEVES

1944   "Single or triple melting pot? Intermarriage trends in New Haven, 1870–1940," in *American Journal of Sociology*, Volume 49 (January), pp. 331–339. This study put forth the thesis that cultural pluralism was occurring within religious groups but not between them. This theme is developed in Kennedy (1952) and Herberg (1955).

1952   "Single or triple melting pot? Intermarriage trends in New Haven, 1870–1950," in *American Journal of Sociology*, Volume 58, pp. 56–59. A restatement of her theme (1944) based upon new data. Together, these two essays are an excellent example of the value of "follow-up" studies in sociology. While a given trend may appear during a particular historical period, that trend may change with time. In this instance the researcher uses new information to demonstrate that her earlier interpretation is still valid.

KILLIAN, LEWIS, AND CHARLES GRIGG

1964   *Racial Crisis in America*. Englewood Cliffs, N.J.: Prentice-Hall. Contrary to the trend of analysis in Glazer and Moynihan (1963), Killian and Grigg predict increased cleavage between racial groups in the United States and increased social conflict. Their analysis points in the direction of that offered here in Chapter 4.

KRAMER, JUDITH

1970   *The American Minority Community*. New York: Appleton. This valuable text was written just prior to the author's untimely death. While various themes are stressed, particular emphasis is placed upon the meaning of minority status for the various groups discussed.

KUYKENDALL, RALPH S., AND A. GROVE DAY

1948   *Hawaii: A History*. Rev. ed., 1961. Englewood Cliffs, N.J.: Prentice-Hall. This volume supports Adams' (1937) view that amalgamation had already occurred prior to Captain Cook's arrival. Both authors have written extensively on Hawaii.

LEE, ROBERT

1961   *The Social Sources of Church Unity*. Nashville, Tenn.: Abingdon.

While Niebuhr (1929) has argued that American denominationalism resulted from social factors, including ethnic differences, Lee maintains that the diminishing of ethnic differences after the early 1900s has contributed to the movement toward church unity and organizational mergers between American Protestant denominations. In this regard, his interpretation is consistent with Herberg (1955).

LEGGETT, JOHN

1968   *Class, Race and Labor*. New York: Oxford University Press. Like the various essays in Mack's collection (1963), this study demonstrates the connection between race and class consciousness.

LIND, ANDREW W.

1955   *Hawaii's People*. Honolulu: University of Hawaii Press. This demographic study of the Hawaiian population covers the years 1778–1950. Lind concludes that amalgamation has not occurred at the rate that Adams (1937) and others thought it might. Lind sees ethnic stratification as well as amalgamation.

LIPPMANN, WALTER

1922   *Public Opinion*. New York: Macmillan. Lippmann observes that men react as seriously to social fictions as they do to social facts. In this context, one must understand the ''pictures'' in people's heads in order to understand human conduct. A brief section of Lippmann's work is reprinted in C. Wright Mills' collection (*Images of Man*. New York: Braziller, 1960).

MACK, RAYMOND (ED.)

1963   *Race, Class and Power*. 2nd ed., 1968. New York: Van Nostrand Reinhold. A collection of essays depicting the importance of both race consciousness and class consciousness in intergroup relationships.

MANNHEIM, KARL

1929   *Ideology and Utopia*. Translated by Louis Wirth and Edward Shils, 1936. London: Routledge & Kegan Paul. (Paperback ed., 1936. New York: Harcourt Brace Jovanovich.) Mannheim's essay was a pioneering work in the sociology of knowledge. In addition to studying different types of ideologies, Mannheim also attempted to deal with the issue of value-bias as a methodological problem in the social sciences.

1950   *Freedom, Power and Democratic Planning*. Edited by Ernest K. Bramsted and Hans Gerth. London: Oxford University Press. In these collected essays, Mannheim argues that rational planning is an essential tool in protecting democracy in mass societies. To a large extent Mannheim believed (with Veblen) that the scientific technocrats would be the salvation of modern societies. The argument seems less plausible today.

MERRITT, RICHARD

1965   "The emergence of American nationalism: A quantitative approach," in *The American Quarterly*, Volume 17, pp. 319–335. Merritt examines those terms that the American colonists used to refer to themselves in newspapers in order to answer the question, "When did the notion of American nationality first emerge?" He finds that this new identity emerged slowly. The essay is reprinted in Seymour Martin Lipset and Richard Hofstadter (eds.), *Sociology and History: Methods* (New York: Basic Books, 1968).

MORSE, SAMUEL F. B.

1834   *A Foreign Conspiracy Against the Liberties of the United States.* 6th ed., 1855. New York: American Foreign and Christian Union. Morse's essay, like Beecher's (1835), is an example of the early Nativist opposition to Irish-Catholic immigration. (Originally published in the *New York Observer*.)

MYRDAL, GUNNAR, ET AL.

1944   *An American Dilemma.* New York: Harper & Row. This was the first major study of the effects of racism and discrimination in the United States. A shorter presentation of the findings was later published by Myrdal's co-worker, the late Arnold Rose, in *The Negro in America* (Boston: Beacon, 1959).

NEIBUHR, H. RICHARD

1929   *The Social Sources of Denominationalism.* New York: Holt, Rinehart & Winston. (2nd ed., 1954. Hamden, Conn.: Shoe String.) This was the first sociological interpretation of the making of American denominationalism. As Lee has shown (1961), the factors which Niebuhr depicted were changing even as Niebuhr was writing the book.

PARK, ROBERT E.

1928   "Forward," in Louis Wirth's *The Ghetto,* pp. ix–xi. Chicago: University of Chicago Press. In this brief foreword to Wirth's classic, Park used the poetic phrase "a mosaic of segregated peoples." Park, who was a leading figure in the Chicago school movement, provided an early, though deterministic, theory of race relations. In his cyclical theory, racial groups passed through continuing phases of competition, conflict, cooperation and accommodation. The similarities between Park's approach and that of Wirth (1945) are obvious and some sociologists even refer to the Park-Wirth school of race relations. This foreword was reprinted in Everett C. Hughes, et al. (eds.), *Human*

Communities: The Collected Papers of Robert Ezra Park, Volume 2 (New York: Free Press, 1952), pp. 99–101.

POPE, LISTON

1942   *Millhands and Preachers.* New Haven: Yale University Press. Written by the dean of Yale Divinity School, this is one of the earlier studies of religion in American life. With the exception of discussions of religion in some community studies, no major sociological study of religion appeared between this and Niebuhr's book (1929).

POPPER, KARL

1957   *The Poverty of Historicism.* Boston: Beacon. This is a collection of essays that attack various forms of "deterministic" interpretations of history. While Popper describes many things with the label "historicism," it is clear that he rejects the notion that a thing can be understood in terms of its origins alone.

SEELEY, JOHN, ET AL.

1956   *Crestwood Heights: A Study of the Culture of Suburban Life.* New York: Basic Books. While this is actually a study of a Canadian suburb, it had a major impact on American sociologists who viewed the suburbs as an assimilated, middle-class phenomenon.

STONEQUIST, EVERETT

1937   *The Marginal Man.* New York: Scribner. This work may be viewed as a summary statement on the early studies of ethnic communities in the United States.

SWEET, WILLIAM WARREN

1939   *The Story of Religion in America.* New York: Harper & Row. This is one of a number of histories of American religion written by Sweet.

THOMAS, PIRI

1967   *Down These Mean Streets.* New York: Knopf. (Paperback ed., 1968. New York: Signet Books.) A revealing autobiography written by an American of black and Puerto Rican parentage.

THOMAS, WILLIAM I., AND FLORIAN ZANECKI

1918   *The Polish Peasant in Europe and America.* Chicago: University of Chicago Press. This is the first major study of the immigrant experience and its consequences.

VAN DEN BERGHE, PIERRE L.

1967   *Race and Racism.* (Paperback ed., 1970. New York: Wiley.) A comparative study of race relations in four countries.

WARNER, LLOYD, AND LEO SROLE

1945   *The Social System of American Ethnic Groups.* New Haven: Yale University Press. This is the third volume of the well-known "Yankee City Series" of community studies. It depicts a transition from cultural pluralism to assimilation by second-generation ethnic groups in the United States.

WATSON, JAMES

1968   *The Double Helix*. New York: Atheneum. An excellent study in the human dimension of the sciences, this volume tells the story of the discovery of the structure of DNA and RNA.

WEBER, MAX

1904   " 'Objectivity' in social science and social policy," in *The Methodology of the Social Sciences*. Translated and edited by Edward Shils and Henry Finch, 1949. New York: Free Press. This essay contains Weber's thinking on the nature of social scientific inquiry.

WHYTE, JR., WILLIAM H.

1957   *The Organization Man*. Garden City, N.Y.: Doubleday. This well-known essay presented a monolithic and pessimistic picture of American suburban life.

WINTER, GIBSON

1961   *The Suburban Captivity of the Churches*. Garden City, N.Y.: Doubleday. Winter attempted to depict the suburban, middle-class captivity of American Protestantism. His theological assessment of both the life-style and the religious habits of suburbanites is severe.

WIRTH, LOUIS

1928   *The Ghetto*. Paperback ed., 1958. Chicago: University of Chicago Press. This is one of the better-known early studies of ethnicity in the United States. Wirth has contributed several valuable essays on minority groups and city life.

ZANGWILL, ISRAEL

1909   *The Melting Pot*. New York: Macmillan. Zangwill's play is the source of this popular phrase, which is used to describe the alleged cultural amalgamation of America's peoples.

ZELINSKY, WILBUR

1961   "An approach to religious geography of the United States: Patterns of church membership in 1952," in *Annals of the Association of American Geographers*, Volume 51 (June), pp. 139–193. Zelinsky employs some twenty-six maps to illustrate the regionalization of American religious groups into a pattern that has been described here as "segregated pluralism."

ZORBAUGH, HARVEY

1929   *The Gold Coast and the Slum*. Chicago: University of Chicago Press. An early study of the nature of ethnic communities in the United States.

CHAPTER 4
A Theory of Social Conflict

Social Order and Social Change

It was suggested in Chapter 2 that one cannot adequately study majority-minority relationships without considering the very nature of the societies in which they occur. It was shown, for instance, that the configurations of elite-mass and majority-minority only become meaningful when it is realized that they characterize different types of societies, that they occur in very different kinds of social contexts. It has been shown that the study of majority-minority relationships must be connected with the study of total societies. Far from being an isolated area for sociological inquiry, majority-minority relationships must be viewed as an occasion for general theory building.

Milton Gordon makes this same point when he argues that majority-minority relationships must be understood in terms of the very *"nature of group life itself* within a large, industrialized, urban nation"[1] (1964:1). As was noted earlier, group relationships are at once contextually set within, as well as important sources of, the basic structures of society. A general theory about group relationships is in effect a social theory. It is a general theory about the nature of society.

[1]Italics in original.

The purpose of this chapter is to offer a general social theory about group relationships in pluralistic societies and to apply that theory to the study of majority-minority relationships in the United States. It has already been shown that the five theories discussed in Chapter 3 provide some useful insights but that each of these theories is inadequate. Most of these theories assume that all minority groups move in a single, linear, assimilative direction. In other words, these theories do not provide an understanding of the diversity of minority groups or of the different kinds of majority-minority relationships found in pluralistic societies. Yet it is necessary to examine these five theories further, not just in terms of what they have to say about majority-minority relationships but in terms of how they may be characterized as general social theories. For as will be seen, each of these theories contains important assumptions about the very nature of society and the nature of group life within society. In order to understand these theoretical assumptions, one must turn to one of the overriding issues in social theory—the relationship between social order and social change, or group consensus and group conflict. Sociologists have long disagreed over which aspect of social reality, change or order, is more important. One camp has argued that social order is the paramount feature of society and has focused upon the way in which group relationships contribute to the maintenance of social order and stability. The other camp has contended that social change is the more important aspect of society and has placed great emphasis upon the way in which group interactions, especially conflicts, contribute to social change. In order to understand the genesis of these two alternative perspectives in social theory, one must look to the "classic tradition."

As C. Wright Mills has observed, the outstanding contribution of the so-called classical theorists of the nineteenth and early twentieth centuries was that each of them—Comte, Marx, Weber, Durkheim, Pareto, Simmel, and others—attempted to depict the "main drift" of modern societies (Mills 1960). While there are some great similarities in the works of these writers, there are also some striking differences between them (Nisbet 1966, Aron 1965, Zeitlin 1968). One of the overriding differences is the respective emphasis of the various theorists upon social order and group consensus as opposed to social change and group conflict. As contemporary sociologists have refined and extended the insights of the classical thinkers, two opposing schools of thought have emerged. Both of these schools draw upon the insights of their respective patron saints from within the classic tradition.

The issue that divides these two perspectives in social theory hinges upon the following question: Are the complex societies of the twentieth century best understood in terms of a tendency toward a consensus of social values, an inherent stability and order of social institutions, and a gradual integration of social groups; or are these societies more appropriately comprehended in terms of group conflicts, divergence, and social change? Consensus theorists have traditionally emphasized social order as the most important aspect of societies. This approach typically involves studying the ways in which social institutions function to maintain social equilibrium. As John Horton has observed (1966), consensus theories stress the processes by which groups adjust to society. Conflict, nonconformity, and deviance are viewed as resulting from the inadequate socialization of groups and individuals. Consensus theories depict order and stability as the paramount feature of social reality and as the eventual outcome of group interactions in society. In short, once the need for social order has been defined as the most important problem for societies, social research becomes fixated upon processes of group integration, adjustment, adaptation, and consensus.

On the other hand, conflict theorists maintain that change, rather than order, is the ubiquitous feature of modern societies. Rather than viewing deviance and group conflict as dysfunctional, these phenomena are interpreted as important sources of social change. In some instances, conflict theorists view prolonged periods of order and stability as signs of social paralysis. In simple terms, what one type of theory interprets as the norm, the other type of theory sees as problematic in society. The question of whether social order or social change constitutes the paramount feature of societies may be better understood by briefly examining some of the classical statements from which these two positions have emerged.

Those theorists who stress conflict and change often point to Karl Marx, whose best-known pronouncement on the ubiquity of group conflict is found in his coauthored work with Frederick Engels, *The Communist Manifesto*: "The history of all hitherto existing society is the history of class struggles" (1848:1).

Other conflict theorists turn to Max Weber, who maintained that "Conflict cannot be excluded from social life . . . peace is nothing more than a change in the form of conflict, or in the antagonists, or in the objects of conflict, or finally in the chances of selection" (1917/1949:26–27).

On the other hand, those theorists who view social order and the integration of groups and institutions as the most significant aspect of modern societies draw upon that part of the classic tradition that begins with Auguste Comte and reaches its zenith in the works of Emile Durkheim. Here, in a nutshell, is Durkheim's argument from his seminal work *The Division of Labor in Society*:

> The totality of beliefs and sentiments common to average citizens of the same society forms a determinate system which has a life of its own; one may call it the collective or common consensus. . . . Moreover it does not change with each generation, but, on the contrary, it connects successive generations (1893/1933:79).

In Durkheim's view, societies represent organisms that exhibit ordered continuity over long periods of time. The American social theorist Talcott Parsons has followed the teachings of both Durkheim and Pareto in arguing that societies are social systems in which the various social institutions are functionally related to the whole of society (1951). In short, while conflict theorists argue that peace, order, and stability are nothing more than temporary lapses in the ever-present stream of social conflicts and change, consensus theorists contend that conflict and disruptions are nothing more than momentary shifts and realignments in the inherent order of social reality.

There are, of course, a wealth of substantive and methodological differences between (and within) these two schools of thought. At even the most elementary level of analysis, theories that overemphasize the importance of change in society often fail to explain how societies manage to stay afloat. Given the pervasive existence of change and group conflict, how do societies manage to hold themselves together? On the other hand, an overemphasis on order and stability provides few insights into how and why societies change. While there is little need here to review all of the relative advantages and shortcomings of these two perspectives, the study of intergroup relationships does require a theoretical perspective concerning the main drift of modern, pluralistic societies. Which tendency best characterizes the American scene, conflict or order; or, in the words of Kenneth Burke (1935), "permanence or change?" Which of these two views of social reality offers the more salient clues about intergroup relationships in the United States?

Clearly, the answer is neither. In lieu of making an either/or choice between these two perspectives, the analysis of group relationships requires a dialectical view of change and order in society. As will be seen, such a perspective does more than simply admit that both order and conflict are inherent in social reality. It seems fair to conclude that previous theorists have realized that both of these aspects of society exist. What separates these two schools is the degree of importance that is attached to one of the two phenomena. A "dialectical"[2] perspective grants that *both* change and order are ubiquitous and examines the ways in which these two aspects of society are essentially interrelated. The need for a perspective that depicts the relationship between social change and social order was clearly seen by the German theorist Georg Simmel. Simmel argued:

> A more comprehensive classification of the science of the relations of men should distinguish, it would appear, those relations which constitute a unit, that is, social relations in the strict sense, from those which counteract unity. It must be realized, however, that both relations can usually be found in every historically real situation. . . . There probably exists no social unit in which convergent and divergent currents among its members are not inseparably woven (1908a/1955:14).

Simmel's contention that both change and order, conflict and consensus, are elements that characterize all societies and group relationships in societies has more recently been endorsed by both Ralf Dahrandorf (1959) and Lewis Coser (1956). In Dahrendorf's view:

[2]Unfortunately, the term "dialectic" has a number of complex philosophical connotations. The term is used here only to mean that the two phenomena of change and order are interrelated and interdependent aspects of social reality. Where one is found, so is the other. Neither is more important than the other. The task is to understand their relationships.

> For sociological analysis, society is Janus-headed and its two faces are equivalent aspects of the same reality. . . . . Neither of these two models can be conceived as exclusively valid or applicable. They constitute complementary, rather than alternative, aspects of the structure of total societies as well as of every element in this structure (1959:159, 163).

Simmel's approach, as well as those of Ralf Dahrendorf and Lewis Coser, represents both an extension of, and a departure from, the classic tradition. While these writers have retained some of the basic teachings of the classical theorists about social change and social order, they have also rejected an either/or approach to the study of these two phenomena in society. Yet it must be remembered that each of the classical theorists had important reasons for stressing his side of that two-sided coin called society. Their respective interests in social change and social order, group conflict and group consensus, may be understood in the context of the problems and audiences to which their works were addressed.

Durkheim, for instance, was greatly concerned with establishing the viability of the sociological perspective in a time and place when biology and psychology provided the dominant scientific explanations of human conduct. Durkheim's strategy was to demonstrate that sociology has a subject matter distinct from the other sciences. Rejecting the notion that society is nothing more than a product of the inner psychic states of individuals' minds or thoughts, he insisted that there are "things" called "social facts" that are external to individuals. In his book *The Rules of Sociological Method* (1895), Durkheim observed that social institutions evidence continuity over long periods of time. They are external to individuals in that they have "historicity" and live longer than either individuals or generations. In this context Durkheim's interest in group consensus and order in society is meaningful.

Much the same may be said of the work of the contemporary American theorist Talcott Parsons. In his major works, most notably *The Structure of Social Action* (1937) and *The Social System* (1951), he was attempting to demonstrate that sociology is capable of producing a highly generalized theoretical framework for the study of societies. Accordingly, his "systems theory" approach focuses upon comparative features of those social institutions that most societies have in common. These more permanent features of societies tend to be essentially consensual or ordered in nature. They are the central focus of structural-functional analysis.

Turning to the conflict side of the classic tradition, Karl Marx's works stem from within several schools of thought, all of which reveal a conflict orientation. Several of the so-called classical economists, notably Ricardo and Smith, had already written on conflict and specifically, class conflict. Similarly, the immediate audience for Marx's writings, those philosophers known as the "Young Hegelians," had already studied the role of conflict and alienation in society. Marx's genius lies not so much in his ability to create new categories of analysis but in his synthesis of previous philosophical and economic studies of conflict into a sociological view of social change. To this extent, in spite of their differences, both Marx and Durkheim were involved in the very same task of establishing a uniquely sociological approach to the study of society. Even Marx, who is championed as one of the founders of conflict theory, realized the importance of social order and group consensus. In another coauthored work with Frederick Engels, *The German Ideology* (1845–1846), Marx contends that the very source of social conflict is the mutual cooperation of men in human labor.

After Marx, most German sociologists continued to study the problems of capitalist society and social conflict. Weber, Mannheim, and even Simmel follow this trend. The respective interests of these various theorists in order or change should not be viewed as instances of naiveté. As Lewis Coser has shown (1971), each author must be understood in the context of his historical time and place. Each provided important insights about the nature of modern societies.

The value of referring to the classical theorists, or any previous theorists for that matter, is lost if one follows in their footsteps too closely. As Weber himself remarked, all scientists must live with the knowledge, indeed the hope, that new investigators will develop new problems and new tools of analysis that will eventually replace older perspectives (1917/1949:105). Continuing to interpret society through the two mutually exclusive perspectives of change and order would essentially leave social theory in the position of the three blind men and the elephant. While each of the blind men obtained an accurate impression of some part of the elephant, none of them gained an accurate impression of the whole animal. Although no scientific concept or theory will ever encompass all aspects of the phenomena under study, this inherent limitation should not prevent scientists from attempting to view important aspects of a phenomenon in relationship to one another.

In summary, there are two important criteria for assessing a theory of majority-minority relationships. First, such a theory must, in the last analysis, be adequate as a general theory of group relationships in society. As will be seen, even when theories appear to be restricted to the problem of majority-minority relationships, they contain implicit general theoretical assumptions about the nature of group life in society. Second, any general social theory must offer a balanced understanding of social change and social order, group conflict and group consensus. Theories that either implicitly or explicitly grant a more important status to the problem of either change or order are at best distorted half-theories. Both social change and social order, group conflict and group consensus, are endemic to societies and must be understood in relationship to one another. Given these two criteria, how successful are the five theories of majority-minority relationships discussed in Chapter 3? Are they adequate general theories of group interaction? Do they provide an understanding of both order and change in society?

Five Theories Reexamined

The theories of amalgamation and assimilation both reveal a bias in the direction of an order theory of society. Both theories assume that minority groups will want to be absorbed into the dominant group and that the majority will want or allow minority groups to merge with them. In terms of Louis Wirth's typology, these two theories view all minority groups as assimilative in nature.[3] Consistent with the theme of all order theories, the theories of assimilation and amalgamation view group conflict as a temporary phenomenon resulting from the need for social adjustment on the part of different groups. In the final analysis, it is argued that groups become integrated with each other to provide an ordered state of social equilibrium. Little if any understanding is provided concerning the ubiquity of social change and the nature of group conflicts.

[3]See the discussion on pp. 38–40.

While the theory of amalgamation has not been widely employed *(static theories)* in the study of American society, there have been many sociological studies of the process of assimilation. Social conflict between groups is usually viewed as resulting from either an insufficient time allotted for minorities to acculturate or from the inability of majority groups to allow minority groups to take their place in society. But the thoroughgoing implication of both theories is that after some period of adjustment, group relationships in society will stabilize, social groups will integrate in some manner, and social order will prevail. While the theories of amalgamation and assimilation may be accurate interpretations of the process of interaction between specific groups at some point in time in a given society, they fail as general theories of society. Both theories understand social change and conflict as temporary dislocations in the normal ordered state of society. If it is granted that both change and order are ubiquitous, the explanatory power of an exclusively consensus-oriented theory is greatly reduced. Change and stability are viewed as alternative situations rather than as interrelated processes. Most of all, such theories fail to explain the reemergence of conflict involving so-called assimilated minority groups as well as the very nature of those groups that simply do not wish to assimilate and therefore remain apart from the larger society. The theories of assimilation and amalgamation are extremely one-sided views of group relationships.

The theory of cultural pluralism, though a more complex view of pluralistic societies, is nonetheless an order theory. Not unlike the two theories just discussed, the theory of cultural pluralism argues that conflict is a temporary phase in group relationships. "Unity through diversity" and "peaceful coexistence" are merely metaphors for social consensus and order. In short, the three traditional theories of amalgamation, assimilation, and cultural pluralism are all consensus theories of society. In each theory the problem of social order provides the overriding framework for analysis, with social change and conflict being viewed as temporary phenomena. As conflict disappears, order and consensus reappear.

Perhaps another way of viewing the central error of these kinds of theories is to note that they are static rather than dynamic theories of society. In each instance it is presumed that society reaches a static point characterized by a particular set of ordered social structures. But just as conflict and consensus are ever-present in society, so the metaphors of structure and process are interrelated ways of viewing society. Societies are in a continual process of change, with each point in that process being described as a set of ordered structural arrangements. Social theories that project social order as the eventual outcome of social interaction between groups tend to emphasize society as an ordered structural phenomenon. Such theories provide little understanding of the diverse processes through which societies and the groups within them pass from one structural situation to the next.

Nathan Glazer and Daniel Patrick Moynihan's interpretation of American pluralism in *Beyond the Melting Pot* is a more sophisticated form of order theory. Their observation that religious, racial, and ethnic group traits take on new social meanings is an important insight into the process of adjustment or assimilation. Once groups have assimilated and acquired a new understanding of their distinctiveness in society, they engage in social conflict as political interest groups. But, as Glazer and Moynihan now suggest in their revised edition, it is erroneous to presume that there is only one type of minority group and that all minority groups will compete for self-advancement through the prescribed social and political institutions in the society (1963/1970:xiii). The overriding consensus orientation of this theory is revealed in the authors' presumption that all social conflict will be conflict within the existing political system. The rules for social conflict and the legitimate political institutions designed to accommodate conflict in society constitute an ordered, integrated system in which conflict occurs. As will presently be explained, this type of conflict, which is strongly bounded by consensual norms, is only one possible form of intergroup conflict. Thus, while Glazer and Moynihan allow for change and conflict, these phenomena are always within an integrated, ordered social context. In a sense, it is always change *within* society, not change *of* society. While Glazer and Moynihan have acknowledged this basic shortcoming of *Beyond the Melting Pot*, they have not attempted to pursue its theoretical implications. Ordered conflict within the system is only one of several possible forms of social conflict. Unlike the three theories already discussed, the theory offered in *Beyond the Melting Pot* does not make the error of predicting some ultimate form of social integration between groups as the outcome of majority-minority relationships. But the authors do maintain that conflict tends to occur only within an ordered framework. To this extent, theirs is a consensus theory of society.

Like the other four theories, Milton Gordon's approach in *Assimilation in American Life* stresses the ordered side of social reality. But as is the case with *Beyond the Melting Pot,* Gordon's study is much more than a simple one-dimensional consensus theory. Gordon's concept of "behavioral or cultural assimilation" conveys the same notion as Glazer and Moynihan's observation that group traits take on new meanings consistent with the contextual framework of the host society. In Gordon's view, minority groups merge into the everyday meanings of the host society. While Gordon does not examine different types of social conflict per se; he does offer seven institutional measures or "assimilation variables" for studying the process of minority group integration into society. As previously noted,[4] they are (1) cultural assimilation, (2) structural assimilation, (3) intermarriage between groups, (4) identificational assimilation on the part of minority groups, (5) the absence of prejudice, (6) the absence of discrimination, and (7) the absence of value and power conflicts (1964:71–83). By suggesting that the first four variables represent a normative pattern and that the last three variables may be measured against a scale in which their absence is the end point, Gordon's theory points toward an order theory of society. His model of the process of intergroup relationships suggests a consensus-conflict-consensus progression. Cultural assimilation is followed by group conflict, which, in turn, is followed by structural and all other forms of assimilation.[5] But as long as assimilation is the measure against which group relationships and social structures are studied and as long as structural assimilation is viewed as the ultimate end product, an order theory of society is the dominant image.

In summary, each of the five theories discussed places greater emphasis upon the ubiquity of social order than of social change. None of them provides a balanced understanding of group consensus and social order, group conflict and social change. Each sees social order as the normative state of society and interprets change and conflict as temporary lapses in that order. At best, Glazer and Moynihan acknowledge the existence of intergroup conflict, but this conflict is understood only as long as it takes place within the established, routine

[4]See the discussion on pp. 82–85.
[5]In this context, Gordon's model is just the reverse of that suggested by Hansen's law. (See the discussion on pp. 75–76.)

political institutions of society. Thus, in their theory, social conflict is an essentially ordered phenomenon.

It was noted earlier that the five theories discussed here evidence two critical errors at the level of group analysis.[6] They maintain that the process of group interaction in society is linear, moving in one assimilative direction with no reversals. They also assume that there is only one type of minority group and one inevitable set of assimilative goals that are acted out at different rates by all groups. These two assumptions about the nature of group relationships are clearly related to several important underlying assumptions about the nature of societies. The first assumption is that social order, and not social change, is ubiquitous. Groups move in a linear, one-directional assimilative process because societies move in a one-directional path toward social order. The second assumption is that social conflict is an adaptive mechanism that disappears once social integration between groups is attained. In other words, ongoing intergroup conflicts are not consistent with the inherent order of society. All of the five theories, with the exception of Glazer and Moynihan's position, predict a static condition of society as the eventual outcome of group interactions. The original theories of assimilation and amalgamation predict alternative final outcomes. Either all groups are absorbed into the majority (assimilation), or all groups, including the majority, create a new, ordered synthesis of cultures (amalgamation). In the same way, cultural pluralism is assumed to reach a point of equilibrium, peaceful coexistence. While Milton Gordon surely demonstrates that the process of assimilation is multifaceted, his concept of structural assimilation provides a turning point in the social process through which an end state, all forms of assimilation, will be attained. Again, the theme is an ordered end product. Even though it is achieved through a more complex set of social processes, complete assimilation, social consensus is the result.

The theory presented in the remainder of this chapter rejects the notion that any process of group relationships is ever complete in terms of an ultimate end point. Just as society at any given point in time may be described in terms of a set of ordered group relationships and social structures, so, too, societies are always in the process of change.

[6]See the discussion on p. 87.

Order and change are ubiquitous aspects of social reality. While the focus of the theory to be presented is the phenomenon of social conflict per se, it will be shown that even social conflicts exhibit both unitive and disunitive elements. Group conflicts, then, may be viewed as mechanisms for achieving both social order and social change. Yet, as will be seen, there are important reasons for viewing group conflict and not group agreement and consensus as the essential form of social interaction between groups in pluralistic societies.

Social Conflict and Types of Societies

Social conflict theory.

Having examined the shortcomings of previous theories, the remainder of this chapter presents an alternative theoretical perspective. The central argument is that social conflict theory provides a useful and meaningful general framework for understanding majority-minority relationships in pluralistic societies. As is the case with all theoretical enterprises, the ultimate goal is to provide a related set of empirically testable propositions that bring meaning to the events being examined. In this case, the experience that demands understanding is American society and the group relationships within it. As has just been suggested, such an analysis must give equal weight to the problems of social order and social change and must also recognize that all social phenomena, even social conflicts, contain elements of both social unity and social disunity. In view of the shortcomings of previous theories, the theory presented here must provide an understanding of the diversity of types of minority groups and majority-minority relationships that are found in pluralistic societies. The task, then, is to construct a general theory of social conflict and then to employ this theory in the study of majority-minority group relationships.

The first step in constructing a theory of social conflict involves three basic questions. First, how is the subject at hand to be defined: What is social conflict? Second, under what conditions do social conflicts between groups typically occur? Finally, to what degree is social conflict a frequent or normative occurrence in societies and, particularly, in the pluralistic type of society being studied? In other words, why is a theory of social conflict the appropriate frame of reference for understanding pluralistic societies and the group relationships within them?

Turning to the first of these questions, *social conflict may be defined as a form of group relationship (or interaction) involving a struggle over the rewards or resources of a society or over social values, in which the conflicting parties (in this case, groups) attempt to neutralize or injure each other* (Coser 1956:8). There are several important components of this definition.

First, as Simmel contends, social conflict is a form of "sociation" or social relationship (1908/1955:15). As with any form of social interaction, the conflicting parties have reciprocal expectations about each other's goals and actions. Simply because these expectations exist does not mean that they are accurate. As Gustav Ichheiser observes (1970), social relationships may be sustained by reciprocal misunderstanding as easily as by reciprocal understanding. This point is humorously, though graphically, illustrated in Robert Grover's novel *One Hundred Dollar Misunderstanding* (1961), which describes the relationship between a young white college student and an even younger black prostitute. Throughout the entire novel, Kitten presumes that their relationship is a pecuniary one, while the male protagonist assumes that she is interested in him because of his male prowess and other "sterling qualities." The book provides a continuous view of how a social relationship may have very different meanings for the parties involved. Social conflict, then, is a social relationship, a form of interaction, involving reciprocal, though not necessarily common, expectations.

Second, social conflict is a struggle between parties over either social rewards and resources or over social values. Societies may be viewed as "distribution systems" for the allocation of resources. As Weber has shown (1922), these rewards are of three basic types: class (material rewards, wealth, and property), status (honor, privilege, and prestige), and power. As was previously noted,[7] social power is the ability of groups or individuals to determine their own as well as others' actions, regardless of the desires of others. Intergroup conflicts revolve around the unequal distribution of these three kinds of rewards in society. It is for this reason that it was argued in Chapter 2 that majority-minority relationships must be viewed in terms of social stratification. The very definitions of majority, minority, mass, elite, and deviant groups are

---

[7]See the discussion on p. 16.

based in part upon variations in the distribution of two resource variables: power and status. The terms "dominant" and "subordinate groups" call attention to the fact that groups in societies are ranked (stratified) differently in terms of social power. On the other hand, the degree to which a group exemplifies or varies from the norms and archetypes of a society is a status variable. Minority status is a positional rank involving both power differences and differences in honor, prestige, and privilege. There are, of course, many possible ways of allocating the available resources in any society at any given point in time. Group conflicts are further generated by the fact that people tend to view one group's gain as another group's loss. As will be seen, the relative positions of groups in the stratification system is an important factor in determining the kinds of resources over which they will fight and the kinds of social conflicts that become the vehicle for those fights.

In addition to conflicts over class, status, and power resources, social values may also provide the focal point for social conflicts between groups. As Gordon suggests (1964), each minority group constitutes to some degree a "subsociety" possessing a "subculture." As was just noted, in one sense the norms of that subculture represent status factors that locate the group in society in terms of honor, prestige, and privilege. Yet there is another sense in which the norms of groups, such as social, political, and religious ideologies and goals, may be viewed as differences in social values. Groups may engage in social conflict over the social positions that they occupy as well as over the goals and ideals that they choose to value. Status conflicts and value conflicts are very similar, and it is indeed difficult to make a clear empirical distinction between the two in many instances. The important point is that not all social conflicts are over resource systems in the strict sense of the term. Value disagreements are an equally important source of social conflicts.

A third aspect of social conflict is that it typically entails the neutralization and injury, rather than the destruction, of social groups. Situations in which the destruction of groups is the goal or outcome of conflict are not normative in societies and, at best, represent extreme instances of one particular type of social conflict.[8] Even war, which is the most

[8]See the discussion of *rigid-means* conflict, on pp. 124–128.

destructive form of social interaction, does not usually result in the complete destruction of groups. Rather, warfare ceases when one group is convinced that it has successfully neutralized the other. Moreover, war, like any other form of social interaction, evidences both unitive and disunitive elements. Even as groups engage in warfare, they have agreements about the object of their conflict and about what weapons are "fair game" (for instance, agreements on germ warfare, nuclear warfare, etc.). The injury and neutralization of groups is the immediate goal of social conflicts.

Having examined the basic elements of the phenomenon of social conflict, the next important question is: Under what social conditions do group conflicts typically occur? Here it is necessary to distinguish between competition and social conflict. The term "competition" refers to any situation in which social groups evidence mutually opposed attempts to acquire the same social resources or reach the same goals. Unlike social conflict, competition does not require that group members be conscious or aware of their mutual opposition, nor does competition involve interaction between groups. For instance, college seniors at the University of Connecticut and at the University of California may be competing with each other for job positions. Neither group may be aware of this fact; the two groups do not interact and conflict does not occur. Competition is an objective state of affairs and does not involve either subjective awareness or interaction between group members. Competition may be viewed as an important prerequisite or condition under which conflict occurs. But competition does not automatically produce social conflict (Park and Burgess 1921). Rather, social conflict results when different groups view each other as competitors or threats. The relationship between the subjective awareness of a threat and the occurrence of social conflict may be stated in terms of a general theoretical proposition.

Proposition 1: The frequency of intergroup conflict in societies is directly proportional to the degree to which different social groups view each other as competitive threats to their social resources, to resources that they wish to obtain, or to their basic social values.

As the subjective awareness of competitive threats becomes greater, the probability of social conflict occurring becomes greater. As Shibutani and Kwan have observed (1965), there are a wide variety of specific social factors that may contribute to a heightened awareness of threat and competition between groups. Technological change in societies represents one such factor. Numerous analysts have argued that a spiral of rising expectations created the increased pace of black protest in the United States during the 1960s, and that this new perception on the part of blacks was made possible by the diffusion of a new technology, especially television and other mass media. Demographic shifts may also lead to increased group awareness of competition and subsequent social conflict. As was seen in Chapter 3, immigration into the United States by various European national groups combined with urbanization and industrialization to create social conflict. The geographical distribution of populations and changes in those distributions were an important element in the transition of the United States from a situation of segregated pluralism to one of integrated pluralism.[9] This, of course, does not mean that new contacts between groups always lead to conflict. In the American case, the fact that the new groups were "uninvited" was certainly an important element. In this context, Richard Schermerhorn (1970) has called for greater attention to the different types of migration and contact. Some of the types he discusses are forced migration, voluntary migration, contracted labor, slavery, colonization, and annexation.[10] In Schermerhorn's view these different sequences of intergroup contact may be understood as important variables that influence the creation of different kinds of dominant-subordinate relationships. Even such general social factors as technological change and demographic change, which lead to group perceptions of threats, must be examined in careful detail if the diversity and complexity of these factors are to be understood. In any case, the emergence of conflict may be viewed as a function of the degree to which various kinds of social conditions heighten the perception of threat and competition between groups. While it is difficult to generalize about those conditions, the relationship stated in Proposition 1 between the degree of threat-awareness and the probability of social conflict occurring provides a starting point for a general theory of social conflict.

While Proposition 1 provides some understanding of why conflict

---

[9]See the discussion on p. 54ff.
[10]For a further discussion of these forms of group contact, see pp. 152–156.

happens and when it happens, it does not explain why social conflict is more prevalent in one type of society than another. For if social conflict theory is to be viewed as an appropriate framework for studying majority-minority relationships in American society, it must be shown that conflict is indeed a normative occurrence in this society. In order to explore the connection between social conflict and pluralistic societies, one must return to certain considerations discussed in Chapter 2. It will be recalled that a central assumption of this study is that group relationships cannot be understood without examining the context in which those group relationships occur. In this framework, it was asked: How do societies differ? Following van den Berghe's study of race relations (1967), it was suggested that there are at least two polar types of societies, pluralistic and nonpluralistic (monadic or dyadic). It was further argued that the configuration of group relationships is related to the types of social structures in these different types of societies. Specifically, majority-minority relationships, as opposed to elite-mass relationships, are characteristic of pluralistic societies, those societies that exhibit open stratification systems, a high degree of overall social differentiation, and a high degree of internal social, political, and economic differentiation.[11] If social conflict is a frequent occurrence between majorities and minorities, it must be shown that the same structural conditions that precipitate the majority-minority configuration also precipitate frequent social conflict.

It was stated in Proposition 1 that the probability of social conflict occurring is directly proportional to the degree to which social groups view each other as threats or as competitors. What structural features of pluralistic societies increase groups' consciousness of competition and thereby increase the occurrence of conflict? Of the several structural features of societies examined in Chapter 2, the stratification system seems to provide a meaningful answer to this question. To use van den Berghe's terms, the open stratification systems of pluralistic societies contain a competitive rather than a paternalistic ethos. In nonpluralistic societies with closed stratification systems, the social ethos implies that social rewards are paternalistically given to the subordinate group by the dominant group. But the achievement ethos of pluralistic societies

[11]See the discussion on pp. 24–33.

demands that social rewards and resources be earned. Competition and achievement are prescribed norms. This ethos must be viewed as the connecting link between an objective state of competition and the emergence of frequent social conflict.

It may be argued that since the stratification system is probably best viewed as an outcome, or dependent variable in society, the competitive ethos of pluralistic societies is better understood as a dimension of large-scale political and economic differentiation. To pursue this line of argument would only result in resurrecting the time-honored Marx-Weber debate. While Marx argued that the economic basis of society was the most important factor in understanding social relationships between groups, Weber attempted to show that the ethos of social competition and achievement, regardless of its source, is an important intervening variable affecting social relationships and social structures. The position argued here is clearly that of Weber (1904–1905). The degree to which overall differentiation, economic, social, and political differentiation, interact to produce pluralistic societies and a competitive ethos is an open question that can only be answered on the basis of more comparative social research. It is not possible here to answer the question of how one ethos rather than the other emerges. The important point is that the social norms of societies differ and that the competitive social ethos of pluralistic societies is an important explanatory link between the existence of an objective state of competition and the frequent emergence of social conflict. The relationship between the ethos of competition and the frequency of conflict is described in Proposition 2.

Proposition 2: The degree to which different social groups view each other as competitive threats, and therefore the frequency of social conflict between them, is directly proportional to the degree to which competition and achievement are prescribed norms in society.

It must be cautioned that this proposition does not imply that conflict will not occur in nonpluralistic societies possessing elite-mass configurations. But it does suggest, all other things being equal, that conflict will be less frequent in nonpluralistic societies. Conversely, in a pluralistic society with a majority-minority configuration, as stated in Proposition 1, group conflict will be frequent. This is because the competitive ethos of pluralistic societies increases the probability that objective conditions will become subjectively real. In order for conflict to become less frequent in a competitively oriented society, there would first have to be a high degree of parity in the distribution of rewards between groups. Such a distribution of rewards does not mean that conflict will cease. Rather, as Weber predicted (1922/1946:193–194), as class resources are more evenly distributed between groups, conflict, when it occurs, will take the form of status conflict. And even if class, status, and power resources were somewhat evenly distributed between groups, this would not rule out the emergence of value conflicts. As was previously noted, the kinds of rewards possessed by groups greatly influence the kinds of conflicts in which the groups engage. While black Americans may be involved in a struggle for their very existence in terms of material resources, the so-called middle-class white minority groups in the United States are more likely to fight over status or social values.

The two theoretical propositions discussed thus far are summarized in Figure 4. Conflicts are struggles over resources and values. Conflicts increase as groups view each other as resource and value threats. The probability that groups will develop a consciousness of their opposition and that the groups' awareness will result in conflict increases when the social norms or ethos of a society prescribe competition. In this context, social conflict becomes a phenomenon of central importance for understanding intergroup relationships in pluralistic societies.

It should not be concluded from these first few general propositions that conflict pervades all majority-minority relationships. This is far from the case. As will be seen, even social conflict has ordered elements; and social conflicts may contribute to social order, internal group consensus, and coalitions between groups. But for the moment, these first few propositions call attention to the fact that social conflict is a frequent occurrence in pluralistic societies. Contrary to the five theories previously discussed, conflict is more than just a passing phase of group relationships that fills the gap until a minority group can adjust or assimilate. Rather, the competitive ethos of pluralistic societies makes competition and conflict prescribed techniques for individual and group advancement in society. There is, then, an important theoretical justifica-

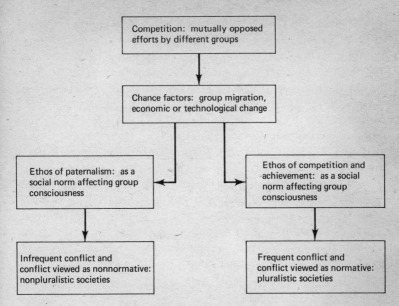

FIGURE 4. Pluralistic societies: From competition to conflict.

tion for focusing a general theory of group interaction upon the very phenomenon that previous theories have so greatly overlooked—social conflict.

The two theoretical propositions presented thus far address questions of a very broad nature. Under what conditions do social conflicts occur and why are intergroup conflicts more frequent in one type of society than the next? From this point, the focus of our inquiry may be narrowed to questions about intergroup conflicts in pluralistic societies. Before additional propositions may be formulated, it is first necessary to examine previous studies of social conflict. These studies may provide important concepts and useful predictions that may be incorporated into future theoretical propositions offered in this chapter. The next two sections of this chapter consist of an assessment of previous theoretical studies of social conflict. The different types of social conflict are examined first.

Types of Social Conflict:
Assessing Previous Studies

One of the most widely employed distinctions between types of social conflict is that between *conflict within the system* as opposed to *conflict about the system*. The central thrust of this typology is to distinguish situations in which social conflicts remain within the ordered framework of the existing social institutions and social norms, as opposed to situations in which conflicts are aimed at changing the very nature of the system and its norms. As Ralf Dahrendorf observes (1959:210), this typology has the clear ring of a consensus or integration approach to the study of social groups and societies. In practice, consensus theorists, particularly structural functionalists, have argued that social conflicts that aim at changes of the social system are ultimately dysfunctional and therefore implicitly undesirable. In other words, once the theorist has assumed that the need for order rather than the need for change is the paramount problem in societies, conflict within the system becomes more important and more desirable socially and more interesting sociologically. The analytical thrust of consensus theory has been to show that group conflict within the system is functional for societies because, either directly or indirectly ("manifest" or "latent"),[12] these social conflicts reaffirm the institutions and norms of society. On the other hand, structural-functional theory fails to explain how conflicts about the system contribute to social order. At best, such theorists, when faced with instances of conflict about the system and faced with the desire to show that all social phenomena are in some way functional, shift their level of analysis. Basically, they contend that conflict about the system is only functional in that it promotes internal consensus and cohesion within the conflicting groups. Lewis Coser's study *The Functions of Social Conflict* (1956) is perhaps the best-known example of this type of analytical strategy. Obviously, if this approach is maintained, the implicit theme is that only certain kinds of conflicts contribute to consensus and order at the societal level. Conflicts that transcend

---

[12]Robert Merton's terms "manifest" and "latent functions" (1949/1957:19–82) carry essentially the same distinction as Max Weber's terms "intended" and "unintended consequences." In both cases, the thrust of the distinction is to show that the meanings or outcomes of people's actions are not always that which they intended and that the social scientist must often look beyond people's intentions in order to grasp the significance of events.

the existing institutional order are viewed as disruptive and undesirable. Particularly in the field of minority group studies, such a theme is both ideologically and theoretically unsupportable. As John Horton suggests (1966), such a theoretical stance places the theorist in the position of defending the existing order, the status quo, and condemning those groups that attempt to change it.

Yet the distinction between these two kinds of social conflicts has some degree of utility if the consensus framework from which the distinction emerges is discarded in favor of one that grants equal status to the problems of social order and social change, a framework that depicts the unitive and disunitive elements in all forms of social interaction at a consistent level of analysis. This may in part be achieved by redefining the distinctions at hand. The terms *consensus-bounded conflict* and *consensus-projecting conflict* will be employed here. While this distinction, like the one it replaces, relies ultimately upon the decision of the theorist to make distinctions of degree between different instances of social conflict, the typology does offer some analytical utility. *Any instance of social conflict may be viewed as consensus-bounded when that conflict by and large remains within the prescribed institutional framework for conflict of the society and within the norms embodied in those institutions.* In other words, even conflicts about the system may take place within the prescribed institutions and norms of the system and thereby reinforce basic social norms. In contrast, *consensus-projecting conflicts transcend the routine channels for conflict in the society.* Contrary to the assertion of some theorists, it would be entirely inaccurate to view consensus-projecting conflicts as socially dysfunctional. Conflicts that transcend or disrupt the existing social order are more meaningfully viewed as attempts to reorder society. Rarely do groups attempt simply to destroy society. The socially significant aspect of consensus-projecting conflict is the degree to which it represents an attempt to redefine the social order, to reach a new, changed social consensus.

As is the case with all sociological analysis, the distinction between consensus-bounded and consensus-projecting conflict relies upon the ability of the social scientist to discern what strategies of action are actually normative, and for what groups, at any given point in time. There are several factors that make this a very difficult task. First, just as societies are always changing, so their internal institutions and norms are continually changing. While a particular strategy of conflict may constitute a deviation from the norm at one point in time, it may later become institutionalized as part of the accepted, socially approved norms. Work strikes by labor unions and the very existence of labor unions provide examples of this point. For initially, both the formation of labor unions and the subsequent use of work strikes were viewed as radical departures from the normal course of labor-management relationships. Second, as Gunnar Myrdal observed in his important study *An American Dilemma* (1944), that which people say is normative may be at variance with the norms that actually guide people's actions. Myrdal called attention to the fact that the American ideology of "freedom and equality for all" is not consistent with the actual norms by which Americans act toward minority group members, especially blacks. In other words, the social scientist must distinguish between what people do and what people say. Finally, a given strategy of action that is normative and socially approved for one group may not be so for another. In spite of these analytical problems, the distinction between consensus-bounded and consensus-projecting conflicts may still provide some fruitful avenues of analysis.

For instance, politics in the streets, mass marches, sit-ins, physical attacks upon public and private property, and numerous other forms of group protest have occurred at various times in American history. While majority groups have always had an easier time of employing these forms of social conflict without paying a high cost for doing so, few of these forms of social conduct have come to be viewed as normative in the public mind. On the other hand, the formation of group self-defense organizations (NAACP, American Jewish Committee, Italian-American Civil Rights League, and others), the emergence of legislative lobbies, block voting, and other similar conflict techniques have become institutionally normative in the United States.

The Civil Rights Movement provides a relevant example of consensus-bounded social conflict. The predominant technique of this movement in the 1950s and 1960s was to effect social change through the courts and through legislative social reform. Even when Martin Luther King and his associates violated the law, they subsequently accepted punishment under the law and thereby reaffirmed their willingness to fight within the rules of the system. To some degree, having served a jail term became a badge of social honor within the movement. This very aspect of the Civil Rights Movement, its commitment to the system, must be viewed as an important factor in the transition from civil rights to Black Power. As one long-time leader of the Student Non-Violent Coordinating Committee complained:

> I'm tired but so is the whole movement. We're busy worrying about our position or our finances, so we don't do anything. . . . We're becoming lifeless just like all revolutions when they lose their momentum and become more interested in preserving what they've won than going on to new challenges (Luae 1965, quoted in Matusow 1969).

It is precisely this kind of perception on the part of many younger blacks in the United States, that the old movement is too committed to what it has won, too committed to the rules of the system, that has made the difference between the courtroom battles of the Civil Rights Movement and the confrontations in the streets of the Black Power Movement. The degree to which these two movements within the black community differ in terms of their assessment of the plight and position of blacks in American society is graphically depicted in the very language they use. While one camp perceives "discrimination" and fights for "equality of opportunity" and "equality before the law," the other camp perceives "racism," "oppression," and "colonization" and fights for "liberation." While one segment of the black community has engaged in consensus-bounded conflict, the other has stressed consensus-projecting conflicts outside the normative institutional framework that they inherently distrust.

These observations suggest the general proposition that *the greater the degree to which a social group shares in the rewards of a society or views itself as part of that society, the greater the likelihood that when such a group initiates social conflict it will be of the consensus-bounded type.* Groups that share in the resources of a society have a greater opportunity to use the existing political machinery. They also have a large material and cognitive investment in the existing institutional order by virtue of the rewards that they have reaped through it. Conversely, groups that possess an extremely low stock of social resources will be less able to use the existing institutions, will have less to lose by going outside the existing institutions, and will subjectively see themselves as disconnected from those institutions. The importance of these observations for understanding majority-minority conflict will be discussed in greater detail a bit later.

From the foregoing discussion, it should be clear that simply because a group in a given instance violates a law does not mean that it is engaging in consensus-projecting conflict. There are few, if any, groups that have not violated the law in the United States when they felt that the stakes were high enough or that they were able to risk the penalties. Just as civil rights leaders have violated the law but subsequently paid the penalty under the law, various public-employee unions such as public school teachers have followed the same strategy of action. In practice, violation of the law is often a prescribed and necessary way of having the validity or constitutionality of a law tested in the American legal system. The criterion for the distinction between consensus-bounded and consensus-projecting conflict is the degree to which conflict occurs outside the normative institutional settings, the degree to which new tactics and strategies that transcend the socially approved ones are employed.

Simply because consensus-bounded conflicts remain within the existing prescribed institutional techniques for conflict does not mean that they are a less effective form of social conflict or that they contribute more to social order than social change. For instance, it has taken more than a decade to produce the changes in southern school systems that were ordered by the Supreme Court in the case of *Brown v. Board of Education*. Yet the many attendant changes in southern society that have occurred since, and as a result of, that case would have been difficult to imagine in 1954. Consensus-bounded conflicts do produce major structural changes in society, but they are likely to be achieved slowly. This type of social conflict occurs when both of the conflicting parties view the basic institutional structures as legitimate or valid.

In contrast, consensus-projecting conflicts occur when at least one of the conflicting parties either views the existing institutions as illegitimate or is convinced that success is unlikely as long as the prescribed institutional techniques for conflict are employed. The degree to which consensus-projecting conflicts transcend the routine channels for conflict can often have great symbolic value. The "capture" of a midtown Manhattan church by the Young Lords, a militant Puerto

Rican youth group, as well as the "capture" of some government-owned land in the states of California and Illinois by groups of American Indians, are examples of consensus-projecting conflict that have high symbolic value. In both instances it seems fair to conclude that the groups initiating these conflicts were well aware that their tactics would not produce immediate solutions to their problems. Instead, these two situations were attempts to stimulate public awareness and public opinion in the direction of a new consensus and a new public consciousness about the plight of the groups involved. Both groups deviated from the routine, prescribed techniques for conflict in order to dramatize the need for a new legitimate order. While consensus-projecting conflicts hold greater potential for more rapid social change than do consensus-bounded conflicts, they may also involve greater risks. Even if the tactics of conflict employed do not violate the law, the larger society may define the group's actions as deviant. Thus, while consensus-projecting conflicts may bring about a new social consensus, they may also reinforce an old social consensus through a so-called backlash.

In summary, these two forms of social conflict are distinguished in terms of the degree to which the conflicting groups employ the normative channels for conflict in the society. There is a general tendency for groups that see themselves as having a stake in the existing institutions and rewards of the society to remain within those institutional boundaries when engaging in social conflict. On the other hand, groups that have little share in those institutions will have a greater tendency to step outside the routine channels for conflict in seeking social change. Consensus-bounded conflicts, by definition, reinforce the existing social order even while they attempt to change it. Consensus-bounded conflicts can produce major institutional changes but typically do so over long periods of time. Consensus-projecting conflicts produce more rapid social change but may also result in a rigid backlash in favor of the existing order. Both kinds of conflict promote social change and social order in different ways. Since change and order are equally important problems in societies, it would be inaccurate to view one type of conflict as any more functional or important than the other. The important point is that the position of a group in the social structure can have an important influence upon which form of conflict the group is most likely to initiate.

A second distinction between types of social conflict has been formulated by Georg Simmel (1908a) and Lewis Coser (1956) and will be referred to here as *variable-means conflict* and *rigid-means conflict*.[13] The important question for Simmel is whether groups are willing to vary the means or techniques of social conflict. *Rigid-means conflict refers to situations in which groups do not vary the means or techniques of conflict. Variable-means conflict refers to instances where the means or techniques of conflict are varied.* Turning again to the situation of American blacks, a variety of tactics have been employed. Legislative campaigns, court cases, boycotts, sit-ins, and black capitalism are different means for achieving the goals of equal rights and opportunities for black Americans. Obviously, groups that are willing to vary their tactics provide a fairly wide range of options for compromise and conflict resolution.

In contrast, rigid-means conflicts evidence no variance in the means of conflict. Simmel was particularly interested in instances of rigid-means conflict where the means of conflict itself becomes the only goal of the conflict. For instance, in Hitler's aggression against the Jews, elimination of the Jews from society became at once both the goal and the means. The term "rigid-means conflict" applies whenever one and only one strategy of social conflict is employed. Strikes, boycotts, and sit-ins are the most dramatic examples of rigid-means conflicts. It must be noted that the unit of analysis employed has a great bearing upon whether the distinction between these two forms of conflict is meaningful or useful. If the changing tactics of a given social group or movement over a long period of time are taken as the unit of analysis, the term "variable-means conflict" is appropriate. But if a shorter span of time is taken as the unit of analysis, during which the group or movement employs only one tactic, the term "rigid-means conflict" is appropriate.

Any social group may engage in either type of social conflict. *But the group's choice to engage in either rigid-means or variable-means*

---

[13]The actual terms employed by Coser (1956) and others are "realistic" and "nonrealistic." These are unfortunate terms because in fact both types are literally real instances of social conflict. In order to avoid the confusion stemming from the original terms, the more descriptive terms "variable-means" and "rigid-means" conflicts are being introduced here.

conflict is meaningful only in the context of the position of that group in the social structure, especially the stratification system. A group located near the bottom of the stratification system may engage in variable-means conflict because it does not possess the social resources or the social position in major institutions to severely affect society through rigid-means conflict. On the other hand, rigid-means conflict may emerge out of the failure of previously employed means of conflict. Rigid-means conflict may represent an act of desperation. To some degree, when groups are so positioned in society that they do not have access to a variety of institutional means, they are forced to employ rigid-means conflict. In this context, the terms "rigid-means" and "variable-means" conflict are useful devices for studying the processes through which the nature of group conflicts change, passing from one type to the next.

In contrast to groups that are positioned low in the social structure, groups that possess a large stock of class, status, and power resources may choose either form of social conflict precisely because they have those resources. Variable-means conflicts may be predicated upon the group's access to different institutional means and upon the fact that a failure of one means is not likely to severely injure the group. Since the group is already in a relatively high position in the society, it can afford to try alternative means of conflict. Similarly, a well-situated group may elect to engage in rigid-means conflict because, by virtue of its integration in the major institutional structures, it is capable of damaging those structures. The prime example is that of the labor union strike. Another example is that of black boycotts of businesses located in the black community that are viewed as unfair to that community. Here the relatively low socioeconomic position of blacks is overcome by geographical factors. Blacks represent the major source of livelihood for ghetto businesses. As will be seen later, there are several general propositions that may be constructed on the basis of the foregoing discussion of these two kinds of conflict.

It is important to note that, regardless of the group that engages in this type of conflict, there are distinctive requirements for, and consequences of, rigid-means conflict. Rigid-means conflict is more likely to produce a situation of polarization between groups. For if the particular single means of conflict employed is at all effective, the society must either adjust to a new definition of the situation and grant the demand of the protesting group or employ equally rigid means to resolve the conflict and reestablish a state of normalcy in society. In this context, both rigid-means conflict and consensus-projecting conflicts typically produce a high level of ideological debate between groups. In simple terms, if one is prepared to either transcend the existing social norms or refuse to negotiate or vary the means of conflict, strong ideological justifications are needed. These ideologies serve to strengthen the in-group solidarity as well as to intimidate the outgroup. As will be seen in Chapter 5, the phenomenon of prejudice may be viewed as an important aspect of in-group and out-group ideologies. Prejudice is a weapon of social conflict. Related to this is the fact that rigid-means conflicts require a high degree of social organization and in-group conformity within the conflicting group. Any deviation within the group becomes a threat to its success and a threat to its ability to convince the out-group that it means business. It is in this context that Coser (1956) has observed that social groups in conflict situations often aggress more violently against deviants and nonconformists within their own group than against members of the out-group with which they are in conflict. The individual who poses a threat from within undercuts the very morale of the group. During the conflict in Northern Ireland in the early 1970s, Catholic girls who dated British soldiers were tarred and feathered and subjected to other forms of public humiliation. It was believed that by "consorting with the enemy" those girls had injured the entire movement.

The in-group functions of social conflict are an important aspect of both Coser's (1956) and Simmel's (1908a) studies of social conflict. There are at least two ways in which social conflicts may help to create internal group solidarity and consensus. First, *groups organize in order to fight. Social conflict requires internal group cohesion for the sake of group advancement.* In this context it may be useful to view pluralism and assimilation, not as totally opposed modes of group interaction, but as reciprocally interrelated aspects of group relationships. For instance, the attempt of a minority group to enter the social, economic, and political mainstream of a society may be viewed as an assimilative process. But the very act of entering the social, economic, and political structures of a society that is competitively oriented requires organized group conflict and internal group cohesion. Thus, the very process of structural assimilation on the part of a minority group may promote internal group solidarity and may increase the group's awareness of its peoplehood and distinctiveness. In this framework Milton Gordon's attempt (1964) to distinguish different kinds of assimilative processes (cultural assimilation, structural assimilation, etc.) becomes all the more important. For these subprocesses of assimilation may be employed, not for the purpose of demonstrating total assimilation, but for the purpose of understanding the more discrete relationships between different forms of pluralism and assimilation among groups in society. It may indeed be the case that assimilation and pluralism, like social order and social change, are reciprocally related aspects of group relationships. In any case, as both Coser and Simmel suggest, groups typically organize in order to fight.

A second form of social consensus arising out of group conflict stems from the fact that *conflict often requires allies*. Groups often find it advantageous or necessary to form alliances with other groups similarly situated. Weaker minority groups may come together in order to wage conflict in their common interests against a majority group. On the other hand, majority and minority groups may form alliances in order to combat yet another minority group that is threatening their common interests.

Prior to the large-scale immigration of American Jews into the United States around the turn of the century, there were extreme status (ethnic) conflicts between eastern- and western-European Jews. Western-European Jews, primarily those from Germany, viewed their Polish and Russian cousins as "poor relations," a less "culturally sophisticated" lot. Yet majority group anti-Semitism in the United States was blind to these ethnic differences and conflicts. For all practical purposes, American Jews, regardless of their ethnic backgrounds, encountered the same patterns of prejudice and discrimination. The emergence of Jewish self-defense organizations like the American Jewish Committee and the Anti-Defamation League of B'nai Brith represent alliances in the face of social conflict. Such alliances may often overcome previous group differences and disputes. Common religious, ethnic, or racial bonds are not the only bases for group alliances. In fact, the very same factors that promote amalgamation between groups can be viewed as sources of group alliances in conflict situations. A common enemy, a common life-style, and common goals increase the probability that any two groups will form an alliance against a third group in a conflict situation. Cooperative efforts between blacks and Puerto Ricans in the United States during the 1960s were based upon a common life situation and a common enemy. Regrettably, this alliance could easily be shattered if one of the two groups advances faster than the other. Previous allies may later view each other as competitors.

In summary, four types of social conflict have been examined. Consensus-bounded and consensus-projecting conflicts both promote social order and social change in different ways and at different rates. The greater the degree to which a group shares in the existing institutions and resources of society, the greater the likelihood that conflicts initiated by such groups will be of the consensus-bounded type. Conversely, groups that are more detached from the rewards and institutions of society will tend to initiate consensus-projecting conflicts. Within this framework, it was noted that groups may engage in either rigid-means or variable-means conflict. In either case the social position of the group in the stratification system must be examined in order to understand the significance of these two types of conflict. These two forms of conflict have different meanings, depending upon whether they are employed from positions of strength or weakness. Different types of conflict affect society differently, with rigid-means conflict being more prone to polarization between groups. Similarly, rigid-means conflicts evidence a higher degree of ideological debate between groups and require, and sometimes produce, a higher degree of solidarity within groups. The various types of social conflict are best understood as situational alternatives for group interaction in pluralistic societies. It is extremely unlikely that all groups in a pluralistic society will continually move toward the same social values and goals over time. Rather, as social situations and group perceptions change, different forms of conflict are employed as the means to both social order and social change. The simplistic notion that assimilation and cultural pluralism are mutually exclusive occurrences, or that they are linear and nonreversible processes, belies the diversity and complexity of group relationships in pluralistic societies. From this standpoint, the structural arrangements within which groups interact are a second important factor in the kinds of group conflicts that emerge. Different groups occupy different positions in the social structure. This subject must be examined next.

Structural Variables Affecting Conflicts: Assessing Previous Studies

Regardless of the type of social conflict being studied, there are several important properties of all intergroup struggles. As Ralf Dahrendorf observes, conflicts vary in terms of their intensity (the degree of human energy or effort expended) and violence (1959:210–218). There may also be important variations in the relative frequency of occurrence of conflict for different groups. What kinds of structural aspects of group relationships affect these three dimensions of social conflict? While there are obviously many different ways of visualizing the structural arrangements between groups in societies, it is useful to conceive of societies as exhibiting two basic structural dimensions. One dimension is vertical and is composed of the stratification system through which social rewards and resources are allocated. To some extent this dimension of group relationships has already been discussed at various points in this book. Milton Gordon implicitly examines this dimension by grouping political, educational, and economic institutions together (1964:37). For the following analysis, economic institutions are viewed as the most important indicator of the vertical social relationships between groups.

The second dimension of the social structure is horizontal and consists of the allocation of social space between groups.[14] While Gordon's grouping of recreational, family, and religious institutions suggests this dimension (1964:37), clearly the most important indicator of social-space relationships between groups is residence. Residential *integration* and *segregation* are patterns for living in social space and are structural phenomena. Each of these two structural variables, vertical (social rewards) and horizontal (social space), has a direct bearing upon the intensity, frequency, and violence of intergroup conflicts. Horizontal group structure is examined first.

It was shown in Chapter 3 that the emergence of the ideology of assimilation and pure Americanism arose at a time when American society was passing from a situation of segregated pluralism to one

[14]The importance of group space or territory was an essential theme of the early Chicago school sociologists. This so-called ecological approach remains a major avenue of contemporary sociological theory. See, for instance, Kai Erickson's discussion in his fine study of social deviance *Wayward Puritans* (1966:9–12, 19–23, 68–70).

of integrated pluralism. The residential mixing of different groups, especially in the cities, produced more and more frequent contact and conflict between groups.[15] In this framework, some theorists, particularly structural functionalists, have argued that social segregation between groups functions to limit the frequency of conflict. While it is true that less frequent contact between groups reduces the possible number of occasions for conflict, it is questionable whether this function of social segregation is the most meaningful way of viewing the phenomenon. The proposition that segregation is functional because it limits conflict shows, again, the degree to which functionalists have understood social conflict only in terms of its contribution to apparent social stability and the existing order in societies. It is equally, if not more, important to note that segregation is an effective technique for institutionalizing social inequality. As Simmel observes (1908a), the absence of social conflict should not be viewed as an indication of social stability between groups. Socially segregated groups do engage in conflict less frequently than socially integrated groups; but conflicts between segregated groups tend to be extremely intense and are often violent. Conversely, social integration and closeness of relationships over time produce both a tolerance of conflict and a suppression of violence (Coser 1956:85).[16]

The traditional segregation between blacks and whites in the American South produced relatively infrequent conflict. But when conflict occurred it was typically intense and violent, including lynchings and murders. In a sense, men behave very much like the other forms of animal life described by Konrad Lorenz in his book *On Aggression* (1966). There is a pronounced tendency for other animals to establish territorial boundaries. The social segregation of space can operate in a similar way in human populations. The mere appearance of one of ''them'' on ''our'' turf produces aggression and violence. Thus, in the United States, blacks and whites refrain from invading each other's territory

[15]See the discussion on pp. 53–63..
[16]It should not be concluded here that contact between groups automatically produces greater tolerance or the reduction of group prejudice. Rather, the argument here is that contact between group members must be understood to have different consequences depending upon the social structures prevailing between the two groups and, as will be seen, upon the goals of groups.

after dark. In contrast, while there remains a high degree of residential segregation in the United States (both forced and voluntary), there are many suburban (usually class-homogeneous) communities in which different ethnic and religious groups live side by side. These communities evidence conflict that is frequent but neither violent nor intense. Group relationships are stable enough to permit the open expression of ethnic and religious jokes that are often something more than just jokes. In essence, the ethnic joke that is told over the back fence is a rather subdued form of conflict. Residentially integrated communities evidence on-going ordered conflict. Block voting and campaigns over school board elections are very different from lynchings, shootings, and riots. In an integrated situation, group differences, rather than disappearing, are manifested in frequent, though less violent and intense, forms of conflict. These relationships between the structure of social space and the frequency, intensity, and violence of conflict are depicted in Table 7.

On the basis of previous studies, then, one might be inclined to formulate a general proposition to summarize the information in Table 7. Such a proposition would contend that the greater the degree of social segregation between two groups, the greater the likelihood that conflicts between them will be relatively infrequent, though intense and violent. Conversely, it would stipulate that the greater the degree of social integration between two groups, the greater the likelihood that conflicts between them will be relatively frequent, though neither intense nor violent.

But there are at least two factors that militate against these formulations. First, it is widely recognized that segregation in the areas of residence, recreation, religion, and life-style may be either voluntarily

TABLE 7. Horizontal Social Structures and Social Conflict

Dimensions of conflict	Residential integration	Residential segregation
Relative frequency	+	−
Intensity	−	+
Violence	−	+

chosen or forced. In other words, a given social pattern may result from a number of different causes and may therefore have more than one social meaning. To assume that all instances of segregation between groups will have the same consequences for conflict or have the same social meanings, ignores the important difference between chosen and forced segregation. This factor will be explored more fully in the next section of this chapter. Second, and more importantly, it is extremely unlikely that the social-space arrangements in a society will run contrary to the basic system of social stratification between groups. In other words, vertical structuration between groups is an even more important prior area for investigation if the effects of social structures upon conflict are to be understood.

The vertical dimension of group relationships refers to the positions of different groups in the stratification system. Groups vary in terms of their possession of class, status, and power resources. Ralf Dahrendorf's study *Class and Class Conflict in Industrial Society* (1959) contains an examination of the relationships of resource distribution between groups and social conflict. There are several aspects of Dahrendorf's analysis that suggest that social class (economic position) may be viewed as the most important resource variable affecting group conflicts.

Dahrendorf observes that groups that are extremely deprived of economic resources are also typically deprived of social status and social power. He refers to this as a "total deprivation" of social resources. Whenever there is an extreme disparity between the resource positions of two groups, Dahrendorf predicts that conflicts between them will tend to be intense and more violent. This is because each instance of social conflict for the weaker group is an all-or-nothing situation in terms of gaining or losing all three kinds of social rewards. In contrast, as the social class position of a group increases, two things seem to happen. First, status and power resources also increase. But, more importantly, class, status, and power conflicts tend to disassociate. For members of groups above a minimal economic level (perhaps the lower-middle class), economic conflict does not usually entail status and power conflicts. Losses in one resource do not typically mean losses in others. Dahrendorf speaks here not of total deprivation but of "relative deprivation." For instance, a shop foreman who is a member of a given ethnic group may not possess the social status he desires, but at work he does participate in the authority and power structures, and he does earn a substantial salary. As different kinds of resource conflicts become disassociated, Dahrendorf contends that conflicts between groups will be less intense and less violent (1959:215–218).

A second factor examined by Dahrendorf is the question of how authority and power relationships are structured across different conflict situations. He employs the term "superimposition" when the members of two different groups engage in conflict in different institutional settings, and when it is always the members of the same group that are the underdog. Dahrendorf contends that where superimposition of conflict prevails, the different instances of conflict reinforce and resemble each other for the subordinate group. Again, high intensity of conflict and greater violence are predicted (1959:213–215). Yet even Dahrendorf admits that it is not probable that the different power and authority relationships in a society will countervene each other. Groups that possess power in one institutional sphere also do so in others, and vice versa. Moreover, as has just been noted, as the economic position of a group decreases, its access to, and participation in, authority and power structures also decrease. As is the case with American blacks, Indians, Puerto Ricans, and Chicanos, as economic deprivation increases, conflict superimposition also is more probable.

On the basis of the foregoing discussion, the vertical relationships between groups will be analyzed here primarily in terms of economic rewards. *Reward parity* will describe the position of a group that possesses a significant stock of economic and therefore other social resources. The term "reward parity" will also be used to describe a situation in which any two groups occupy similar positions in the stratification system. *Reward deprivation* refers to groups that possess a low stock of social resources. When referring to the relationship between a subordinate group extremely deprived of rewards and another group (majority or minority) that possesses a large stock of rewards, the term *disparity* will be used. On the basis of Dahrendorf's study, it may be stipulated that reward parity between groups produces less intense and less violent conflict. Reward deprivation or disparity between groups produces more intense and more violent social conflicts. Two additional points should be made here. First, violence in conflicts involv-

TABLE 8. Vertical Social Structures and Social Conflict

Dimensions of conflict	Reward parity	Reward disparity
Relative frequency	+	−
Intensity	−	+
Violence	−	+

ing groups that are deprived of social resources can easily be dominant-group-perpetrated violence. Since the subordinate group is extremely deprived of resources and has little access to power institutions, they are an easy target for dominant group violence. On the other hand, a subordinate group may opt for violence because of its lack of access to other means of conflict as well as the high degree of frustration and the intensity of conflict. Second, it seems likely that where reward deprivation is present, the minority will engage in conflict less frequently than in a situation where reward parity exists. This is because conflict itself is one way of expending scarce social resources and human energies, resources of which a deprived group possesses very little. The relationships between the distribution of resources among groups and the frequency, intensity, and violence of conflict are depicted in Table 8.

Again, it seems tempting to summarize the information in Table 8 in the form of a general proposition. It might be argued that the greater the degree of reward parity between two groups, the greater the likelihood that conflicts between them will be relatively frequent, though neither intense nor violent; and conversely, that the greater the degree of disparity of rewards between one group and another, the greater the likelihood that conflict between them will be relatively infrequent, though more intense and violent. While the position of groups in the stratification system is an extremely important determinant of the kinds of conflicts in which they will engage, the proposition suggested here will not suffice. For it has already been shown that the space relationships between groups are also a useful predictive measure. The larger task, then, is to consider both the space and stratification dimensions of group relationships together. Before doing so, there are already some aspects of our discussion of the effects of stratification upon group relationships that prompt a reconsideration of Milton Gordon's theory of structural assimilation.

Gordon contends that once the minority group has attained entrance into the major institutions of the society, all other forms of assimilation will follow (1964:81). But Gordon seems to assume that entrance into institutions will guarantee some degree of resource parity. The foregoing analysis suggests that this is not necessarily the case. Entrance into institutions is of little value to minority group members if it results in the institutionalization of reward deprivation. For instance, American blacks participate in the dominant institutions in American society but remain at the bottom of all of them. Forced segregation, coerced pluralism, results from this kind of structural assimilation. In contrast, the major European immigrant groups seem to have attained resource parity, as well as some degree of political and social assimilation, by constructing their own parallel, especially economic, institutions. Italian domination of the building trades, Irish domination of several trade unions as well as some civil service occupations, Jewish preeminence in garment manufacturing and retailing, and Greek and Chinese domination of some segments of the retail food industry, all represent parallel structuration within the realm of economics. In other words, structural assimilation may be a very poor measure of overall assimilation. The most assimilated minority groups in American society are those that have been able to create some degree of parallelism in the resource structures of the society. In this framework, prejudice and discrimination as well as status and value conflicts may be the more important areas of investigation for assessing the degree of assimilation between groups. This question is examined more fully later in this chapter.

Thus far, the probable effects of vertical and horizontal group relationships upon social conflicts have been examined. But the important question is what happens when these two aspects of the social structure are examined together. From the foregoing discussion it appears that there are four typical structural positions in which subordinate groups may be located: reward parity with integration, reward parity with segregation, reward deprivation with integration, and reward deprivation with segregation. As shown in Table 9, each of these four structural situations is occupied by different minority groups in American society. The major European religious and ethnic groups most closely resemble the position of reward parity with social integration. On the other hand, Asian-Americans and a variety of social and religious communes are in the position of reward parity with voluntary segregation. This also appears to have been the typical social position of many third-generation European immigrant groups. Reward deprivation with social segregation is the position occupied in the United States by a number of groups, including the aged poor, the residents of Appalachia, blacks, Puerto Ricans, American Indians, Chicanos, and migrant workers. Finally, reward deprivation with integration describes the position of the Women's Liberation Movement, the handicapped, and homosexuals. Each of these four situations depicted in Table 9 must be examined in detail. Moreover, these four kinds of group social locations and their relationships to different kinds of conflicts cannot be understood without considering the social goals and objectives of both the dominant

TABLE 9. Horizontal and Vertical Social Structures: Four Cases of Minority Group Social Location

Vertical structures	Horizontal structures	
	Integration	Segregation
Reward parity	Examples in United States: major religious and ethnic groups within class boundaries	Examples in United States: Asian-Americans, various religious or social communes and sects, and most third-generation immigrant groups
Reward deprivation	Examples in United States: the handicapped, homosexuals, and women's liberation movement	Examples in United States: blacks, Mexican-Americans, Puerto Ricans, aged poor, Appalachians, migrant workers, and American Indians

group and different kinds of subordinate groups. As was noted at the outset of this discussion, social structures are themselves expressions of group interaction and the desires of social groups. The next section of this chapter addresses two tasks. First, the previous studies of conflict just discussed must be tied together into an empirically testable set of related theoretical propositions about social conflict. Second, it must be shown how these general theoretical propositions may be applied to the study of majority-minority relationships.

Theoretical Propositions: Groups, Structures, and Conflicts

Two propositions about the occurrence of intergroup conflicts in societies have already been discussed earlier in this chapter. It will be useful to recall them here in order to provide a context for future propositions.

Proposition 1: The frequency of intergroup conflict in societies is directly proportional to the degree to which different social groups view each other as competitive threats to their social resources, to resources that they wish to obtain, or to their basic social values.

Proposition 1 does little more than express, in the form of a probability statement, the information that is already provided in the definition of social conflict discussed earlier. While it was noted that there are various chance factors such as technological change, economic change, and group migration that may produce a heightened sense of group awareness of competition and threat, these factors do not explain why intergroup conflict is a more frequent occurrence in one kind of society rather than the next. This question was answered in Proposition 2.

Proposition 2: The degree to which different social groups view each other as competitive threats, and therefore the frequency of social conflict between them, is directly proportional to the degree to which competition and achievement are prescribed norms in society.

Recalling the distinction between pluralistic and nonpluralistic societies, it was shown that the competitive open stratification systems in which majorities and minorities interact are indeed different from the closed, paternalistic systems in which elites and masses interact. The ethos of achievement and competition is an important intervening variable that produces frequent intergroup conflict in a pluralistic society. This, of course, is a corollary that may be derived from Proposition 2. *Societies that exhibit a competitive ethos, regardless of the source of that ethos, will exhibit more frequent social conflicts than societies that exhibit a paternalistic ethos.* Since intergroup conflicts are a frequent occurrence in such societies, a theory of social conflict becomes an appropriate frame of reference for understanding group relationships in pluralistic societies.

The previous two sections of this chapter have examined some earlier studies of social conflict. In retrospect, it may be noted that earlier theorists have followed two different avenues of analysis. One approach is to view different forms of social conflict as "given." Very little attention is paid to why one type of conflict rather than another emerges. Instead, the major question is how different forms of social conflict affect the social structure. For instance, structural-functional theorists rarely ask why "conflict within the system," as opposed to "conflict about the system," occurs. Their interest is in the social functions and dysfunctions of these different forms of conflict. To this extent social conflict is viewed as an independent variable.

The second avenue of analysis focuses primarily upon the structural determinants that shape social conflicts. For instance, Dahrendorf (1959) shows the way in which the structural positions of groups in the stratification system result in different degrees of intensity and violence of conflict. Similarly, Simmel (1908a) and Coser (1956), despite the latter's functionalist perspective, show that the very frequency of conflict is best understood in terms of structural arrangements, especially integration and segregation between groups. Conflict is treated, not as a given or as an independent variable, but as an outcome or a dependent variable.

Both of these approaches to the study of social conflict share one overriding shortcoming. Relatively little attention is given to the role of social groups, and especially the goals and desires of social groups, as the essential motor force in group conflicts. This is not to suggest that a structural approach to studying group conflict is not valuable. Quite to the contrary, social structures are extremely convenient and reliable measuring points for predicting the nature of intergroup conflicts. But there is a prior need to understand the way in which social structures are themselves the results of group interactions and group desires. A general theory of social conflict must first show how the very social structures in which groups are located have emerged. It is only on the basis of an understanding of the meanings of different structural arrangements that the conflicts within them may also be understood.

It was shown in Chapter 3 that the theories of assimilation, amalgamation, and cultural pluralism contain some major assumptions about the nature of majority and minority group goals and desires. Moreover, it was shown earlier in this chapter that those assumptions about the nature of group goals are related to some larger assumptions about the nature of societies. The theories of assimilation and amalgamation both assume that socially dominant groups (majorities and elites) will voluntarily relinquish their positions of dominance in order to either absorb new groups (assimilation) or merge with them (amalgamation). In the context of this central assumption, intergroup conflict is viewed as a temporary and nonessential aspect of the social order. Similarly, most previous theories have assumed that all minority groups possess the same set of assimilative goals and desires and that they all pass through the same kind of social processes as they are absorbed into the host society. Little attention is given to groups that do not wish to assimilate or to so-called assimilated groups that reassert their distinctiveness in society. These assumptions about the goals of dominant and subordinate groups overemphasize the tendencies for group consensus and produce an empirically invalid picture of what actually transpires between groups in society.

It is often the case that previous errors and mistakes provide as much information for new theory building as do previous theories that are confirmed by empirical testing. In this instance, the erroneous assumptions of the theories of assimilation and amalgamation provide some important information about the goals of socially dominant groups. This information is presented in Proposition 3.

Proposition 3: Socially dominant groups generally attempt to maintain or increase their position of dominance over other groups in society.

This statement underscores the importance of viewing majority-minority and elite-mass relationships in terms of social stratification (ranking). This avenue of analysis was, of course, suggested by the very way in which these different groups were defined in Chapter 2. It must be remembered that elite, mass, majority, and minority groups represent only one aspect of the ranking systems in societies. When studying majority-minority relationships, particular emphasis is placed upon the way in which distinctive cognitive, physical, and behavioral traits set the boundaries for ranking between groups. There are, of course, other, even broader, criteria for ranking that cut across or encompass majority-minority divisions. Social class and sex are two additional kinds of group differences that provide for dominance and subordination between groups in societies. Milton Gordon has stressed this point in his novel concept of the "ethclass," which draws attention to the intersections of different ranking criteria in societies (1964).[17] As was suggested earlier, majority-minority relationships are being viewed here merely as a case study in the larger phenomenon of social stratification. For this reason every attempt has been made to state the following theoretical propositions in terms of the general categories of dominance and subordination. It will then be shown how each proposition about the relationships between dominant and subordinate groups may be applied to the specific case of majority-minority relationships.

As stated in Proposition 3, socially dominant groups generally attempt to maintain or increase their positions of dominance in society. This basic goal of dominant groups provides an understanding of the social structures in which various dominant and subordinate groups are located. Since social dominance is a measure of the social resources or rewards which a group possesses, there is an important relationship between the goal of dominant groups to remain dominant and the resource positions of subordinate groups.

Proposition 4: The degree of success that a dominant group has in either maintaining or increasing its position of dominance will

---

[17]See the discussion on p. 82ff.

result in varying degrees of either reward deprivation or reward parity for subordinate groups.

In other words, while social structures provide a useful guide for understanding the kinds of future conflicts and coalitions that will probably occur between two social groups, those structures are already a historical record of previous relationships and interactions between the groups. As will be seen, this is as true of the social-space relationships between groups as it is of the distribution of social resources between them. Moreover, every specific majority-minority relationship in a given society may be structurally different from the next. That one minority is higher in the stratification system than the next indicates that the two groups have had different past relationships with the dominant group and that they are likely to have different interactions with the dominant group in the near future. The kinds of central tendencies that those interactions will exhibit are described in Propositions 5 and 6.

Proposition 5: The greater the degree to which a social group occupies a position of reward parity, the greater the likelihood that conflicts initiated by that group will be of the consensus-bounded type.

In terms of majority-minority relationships in pluralistic societies, Proposition 5 suggests that minority groups that reach some minimum level of parity with the majority (as was suggested earlier, probably the lower-middle class) will tend to initiate the kinds of conflicts that remain within the institutionally prescribed norms and techniques for conflict in that society. Even as they attempt to effect changes in social norms or a redistribution of the resources in society, they will do so through "the system." There are at least two reasons why this is the case. First, as groups develop material investments in a society, they develop cognitive investments as well. The more a group shares in the rewards of a society, the more group members are likely to see themselves, and be viewed by other groups, as part of that society. Second, most social conflicts for members of such groups are likely to be situations of relative, rather than total, deprivation. As was noted earlier, while ethnic or religious group membership may deprive the members of a group of social status, they may still derive enough wealth and power from the existing social institutions to legitimize them.

Proposition 5 describes not only the actions of certain minority groups but the actions of majority groups as well. Even where a number of minority groups attain a high degree of resource parity, the majority group remains the most equal among equals. In terms of the way in which the word "parity" is being used here, the majority group always has the highest position of parity. The majority group, as suggested in Proposition 3, attempts wherever possible to design the social order to its own best advantage. It has played the greatest role in defining the social norms and structures. Therefore, even when a majority group employs force or violence, it usually does so within the existing normative order, within society's rules of the game. This does not mean that "might makes right." But the majority group's might is usually institutionally legitimate, if not morally right. Proposition 5, then, stipulates the central tendency of conflict initiation for those groups that possess significant stocks of social rewards or resources. What about those groups nearer to the bottom of the stratification system?

Proposition 6: The greater the degree to which a social group occupies a position of reward deprivation, the greater the likelihood that conflicts initiated by that group will be of the consensus-projecting type.

Members of groups that are extremely deprived of social rewards are not likely to grant legitimacy to the very social norms and structures that have created and sustained their position of resource deprivation. Such groups, by virtue of their position in the social structure, typically, have relatively little access to the most important normative institutional channels for social conflict. As a radio advertisement for the Legal Aid Society explains, "You can't hire a lawyer if you haven't got a dime." In a sense, groups that are deprived of both social rewards and institutional access are forced to devise innovative alternative means for reaching their social goals.[18] In addition, consensus-projecting

---

[18]In his well-known essay "Social Structure and Anomie," Robert Merton employs the term "innovation" to refer to the actions of individuals who share society's goals but are thwarted from employing society's means for attaining those goals (1938).

majority-minority conflict is further predicated upon the fact that total deprivation of rewards makes each instance of social conflict with the majority appear as an all-or-nothing situation for minority group members. As the disparity of social resources between two groups increases, the greater the likelihood that conflicts will assume the pattern that Dahrendorf (1959) calls superimposition. The minority group encounters the same enemies everywhere. It must also be remembered that as one minority group attains the position of parity with the majority, that group holds a dominant position from the point of view of a minority at the bottom of the stratification system. As with most other things in life, the resource positions of groups in societies are always relative to each other.

In the context of Propositions 5 and 6, it is erroneous to view members of those groups that frequently initiate consensus-projecting conflicts as inherently disruptive. One frequently hears the complaints: "Why can't they be like the rest of us?" "Why are *they* always creating such a fuss?" It is frequently alleged that "those people" possess some sort of personality characteristic or collective cultural defect that causes them to break the rules of the game, to employ nonnormative conflict techniques. These kinds of complaints ignore the fact that the Irish were no less prone to initiate consensus-projecting conflicts in the nineteenth century than blacks, Mexican-Americans, and American Indians have been in the twentieth century. The affinity of groups for consensus-projecting conflicts is predicated upon their position in the social structure and their position relative to other groups with which they are in competition.

As the position of a social group changes in the social structure, its perception of the social order and its collective actions toward the social order are likely to change. This does not mean that once a group attains wealth, status, and power it will automatically abandon its distinctive cultural traits or that it will automatically assimilate into the majority group. But it does mean that the more a group's members share in the social resources of a society, the more they will employ consensus-bounded conflicts in attempting to redefine and change the social order.

It must be cautioned that Propositions 5 and 6 do not imply that groups that enjoy positions of reward parity never initiate consensus-projecting conflicts or that groups extremely deprived of social resources never initiate consensus-bounded social conflicts. Rather, Propositions 5 and 6, as well as the other propositions discussed here, are statements of central tendency. They specify, given stipulated conditions, what things are most likely to happen most of the time. Like all scientific theories, they are attempts to make probabilistic generalizations about future events based upon some understanding of past events. Like all such generalizations, they operate under the proviso "all other things being equal."

When variations from these central tendencies are encountered, it is advisable to examine those events for intervening variables not envisioned by the proposition. In this way it is possible to construct theoretical generalizations not only about normative tendencies but also about variations from those norms. For instance, groups that possess resource parity, and that experience only relative deprivation, fight from a position of strength in the social structure. It is indeed unlikely that such groups will initiate consensus-projecting conflicts when basic social resources are at issue. By definition, such a group's lack of a given social resource (class, status, or power) is relative to its possession of others. Even though social resources are involved in a given instance of conflict, the group still has more reason to support and work through the existing institutional structures than to violate the norms of those structures. It seems probable that such a group will resort to consensus-projecting conflict only if the basic social values of the group have been attacked or threatened or if status and value conflicts have become strongly superimposed for group members. The major purpose of this study is to specify the central tendencies of inter-group and especially, majority-minority conflicts. Just because variations from these central tendencies do not receive much attention here, it should not be assumed that they do not exist or that they are not important.

Thus far, Propositions 3 and 4 have explained the significance of the different positions that dominant and subordinate groups occupy in the stratification system. Propositions 5 and 6 have stipulated the way in which the positions of groups in the social structure are related to the initiation of consensus-bounded and consensus-projecting conflicts by different groups. It was noted earlier that any social group is as likely as the next to employ either rigid-means or variable-means conflict techniques. In other words, it is not possible to offer a statement of central tendency concerning the relative frequency of occurrence of these two kinds of social conflicts. Yet it was also stipulated earlier that a social group's use of either rigid-means or variable-means conflict techniques could best be understood in terms of the position of that group in the social structure, especially the stratification system. These two kinds of social conflicts may have very different social meanings. The next four propositions address the relationships between the positions of groups in the stratification system and their use of these two kinds of social conflict techniques.

Proposition 7: The greater the degree to which a social group occupies a position of reward deprivation, the greater the likelihood that its initiation of rigid-means conflict will be predicated upon its lack of alternative means and/or the failure of previously employed means of conflict.

It has already been noted that the nearer a social group is to the bottom of a stratification system, the more it is deprived of social resources in the strict sense (class, status, and power) as well as access to the prevailing institutional structures and means for social conflict. The use of rigid-means conflict by such a group is frequently an indication of its lack of meaningful and viable alternatives. Rigid-means conflict may represent, not the best of all possible courses of action, but the only plausible course of action. Rigid-means conflict may also signify the failure of previously employed means of conflict. It was noted earlier that there is often a progression from variable-means to rigid-means conflict. This is especially the case when a social group encounters repeated failures of various conflict techniques. Its members become at once more frustrated and more adamant about their demand for effective social change.

Lewis Coser has placed particular emphasis on the fact that rigid-means conflicts serve as a source of frustration and tension release for group members. Coser argues that this is especially the case when the particular conflict technique employed is really not aimed at the direct acquisition of goals or objectives (1956:49). Conflict itself appears to be the object. The best illustrations of Coser's point are acts of violence against property or symbolic demonstrations by group members. But in the context of the propositions offered here, Coser's observation would best be limited to rigid-means conflicts initiated by groups deprived of social resources. For, as is stipulated in Proposition 8, rigid-means conflicts initiated by groups possessing a high degree of reward parity are not so much acts of frustration and tension release as they are calculated tactics based upon the group's awareness of its ability to dramatically affect the social structure.

> *Proposition 8: The greater the degree to which a social group occupies a position of reward parity, the greater the likelihood that its initiation of rigid-means conflict will be predicated upon its ability to affect the social structure.*

It must be assumed that members of social groups that possess a high degree of parity of social rewards have received those rewards by providing either goods or services that the rest of society deems valuable. This, of course, is one of the central assumptions of "exchange theory" in sociology and economics (Homans 1961). Members of such groups either occupy functionally important positions in the key institutions of society (especially economic positions) or have been able to either capture or create their own in-group-controlled institutions upon which society relies for goods or services. They are therefore in a position to severely affect society by withholding goods and services (strikes and economic boycotts).

Organized labor threatens to strike or actually does strike, not because striking is the only means available or because union members are experiencing a high level of tension and frustration, but because it is known that the strike is a highly effective technique. It has severe consequences for the social order and for the dominant group with which union members are in conflict. Groups that remain marginal to the economy are rarely in a position to cause major dislocations in society by either withholding their services (refusing to work) or by withholding what little spending power they have. The work strike of grape pickers in California led by Cesar Chavez in the late 1960s is an excellent example. Even with members of more powerful groups assisting the grape pickers by boycotting grapes in the supermarkets, the strike had little major effect on the society as a whole. Even the grape growers were able to hold out for several seasons before a settlement was reached, a settlement that represented only partial victory for the striking workers. Groups that possess few social resources also control few positions in key social and economic institutions. The goods and services that they provide can frequently be foregone by the society, provided by other groups, or replaced by automation.

The differential meanings of rigid-means conflicts for groups located differently in the social structure also apply to conflicts that are other than economic in nature. In the case of status conflicts, the Italian-American Civil Rights League or the B'nai Brith are much more likely to affect the social structure through some sort of public demonstration, picketing, or publicity campaign than are groups representing blacks, American Indians, migrant workers, or Mexican-Americans. Higher social status means that the members of a social group are viewed as part of society. The use of dramatic kinds of rigid-means conflict techniques are essentially ways in which group members can reassert the importance of their "place in the sun." The social status that they possess lends credibility to their claims and protests. Groups that are marginal to the social structure do not possess enough social status to use that status effectively as a conflict resource.

Propositions 7 and 8 may also be considered in the light of the organizational aspects of rigid-means conflicts. As was previously noted, if group members are unwilling to vary their means of conflict, they must be able to rely upon a high degree of in-group solidarity. A strike is of little value if in-group members are willing to break that strike. An economic boycott is hardly effective if in-group members violate the boycott. Even such consensus-bounded techniques as a relentless struggle through the courts loses its effect if group members are not willing to finance such a campaign. Voter registration drives and the use of the political system are futile unless group leaders can count upon delivering the vote. It is extremely difficult to convince the enemy that one means business and that a given rigid-means tactic will injure him if the in-group members ignore the tactic. Since in-group organization for conflict is an expensive kind of activity in terms of the commitment of resources for the purpose of organization, there is again a greater likelihood that groups possessing resource parity will be able to engage in rigid-means conflict out of voluntary choice and organizational strength. Groups near the bottom of the stratification system can rarely count upon strong in-group organization as a motivating resource for rigid-means conflict.

In summary, as stipulated in Propositions 7 and 8, rigid-means conflicts have very different meanings depending upon the position of the group in the stratification system. In one instance, rigid-means conflict represents an act of frustration and desperation. It is something group members do because they have no other alternative or because other strategies of action have failed. Yet the more a group possesses resource parity, the more it will choose rigid-means conflict techniques, not out of frustration, but out of a calculated awareness of its ability to organize and deploy its existing resources in a way that will affect the social structure. Much the same may be said of variable-means social conflict.

Proposition 9: The greater the degree to which a social group occupies a position of reward deprivation, the greater the likelihood that its use of variable-means conflict techniques will be predicated upon its inability to employ effectively any single tactic.

While past failure and frustrations contribute to the use of rigid-means techniques by a group deprived of social resources, it should not be assumed that past failure and frustration automatically produce rigid-means conflict. Variable-means conflict may persist under these conditions precisely because the group does not possess the resources, social organization, and positions in key institutions to employ any single means of conflict with any degree of impact upon the society. In this case, variable-means conflict amounts to employing the means available rather than employing the means that are likely to work. Variable-means conflict may be a kind of grasping at straws. For groups possessing resource parity, the case is just the opposite.

Proposition 10: The greater the degree to which a social group occupies a position of reward parity, the greater the likelihood that its use of variable-means conflict techniques will be predicated upon the relative deprivation of conflict for group members.

It was noted earlier that for members of social groups that enjoy resource parity, most social conflicts are likely to be situations of only relative deprivation. Class, status, and power relationships tend to be disassociated from one another for group members. This important fact, coupled with the high availability of alternative means for such groups, explains why groups with resource parity are both willing and able to employ variable-means conflict techniques. Group members can afford to expend the resources required to fight on more than one conflict front and can afford to wait out the results of successive efforts. This is true whether several alternative means are employed simultaneously or whether they are employed in succession.

It must be stressed again that one group is as likely as the next to employ either rigid-means or variable-means conflict techniques. The factors that condition either form of conflict vary greatly according to the positions of groups in the stratification system. While groups with resource parity select either rigid-means or variable-means conflict techniques out of a position of strength and freedom of choice, groups that are deprived of resources are forced into one strategy or the other. The central tendencies for intergroup conflicts stipulated in Propositions 3 through 10 are schematically depicted in Table 10.

The theoretical propositions offered thus far have focused upon one of the two major structural dimensions of societies, the positions of groups in the stratification system. It has been shown that the position of a group in the stratification system is itself an outcome of group interactions and that the position of a subordinate group in the social structure is a measure of the degree of success that the dominant group has had in maintaining or increasing its position of social dominance. It has further been shown that once a group occupies a particular position in the stratification system, that position will have predictable consequences for the kinds of conflicts initiated by the group. The more a group is deprived of social resources, the more it is likely to initiate consensus-projecting conflict with a dominant group. The more a group participates in the social rewards of a society, the greater the likelihood that conflicts initiated by the group will be consensus-bounded. Similarly, the use of either rigid-means or variable-means conflict techniques are best understood in terms of the positions of groups in the stratification system.

Thus far, the second dimension of the social structure, the social-space

TABLE 10. Groups, Structures and Social Conflicts: Part 1

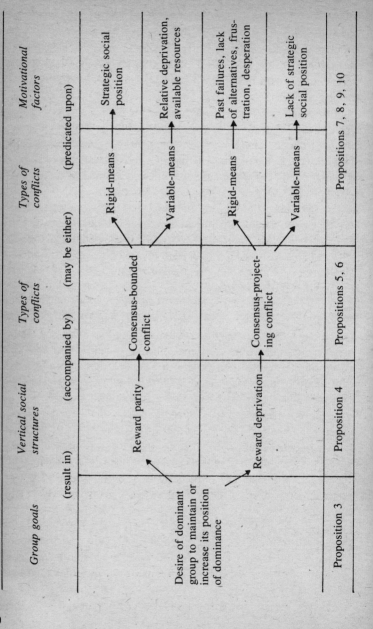

Group goals (result in)	Vertical social structures (accompanied by)	Types of conflicts (may be either)	Types of conflicts (predicated upon)	Motivational factors
Desire of dominant group to maintain or increase its position of dominance	Reward parity →	Consensus-bounded conflict	Rigid-means →	Strategic social position
			Variable-means →	Relative deprivation, available resources
	Reward deprivation →	Consensus-projecting conflict	Rigid-means →	Past failures, lack of alternatives, frustration, desperation
			Variable-means →	Lack of strategic social position
Proposition 3	Proposition 4	Propositions 5, 6	Propositions 7, 8, 9, 10	

relationships between groups, has not been examined. It will be recalled that there are two polar extremes, integration and segregation, and that these two space arrangements may combine with the distribution of social rewards to create four different social locations for minority groups: reward parity with integration, reward parity with segregation, reward deprivation with segregation, and reward deprivation with integration. Again, it must be remembered that these four cases represent ideal types or models to which empirical cases may be compared. Even within these four cases, empirical examples will exhibit differences of degree. But as is the case with any classification system or typology, the assumption here is that differences between the four cases are far more important than more minute differences between the social situations of groups within each category. What are the social meanings of these four types of subordinate group social locations, and what are the probable patterns of conflict between dominant groups and subordinate groups in these four situations?

Proposition 11: The greater the degree to which a subordinate group occupies a position of reward deprivation, the greater the likelihood that the social-space arrangements between it and the dominant group will represent the desires of the dominant group.

Proposition 12: The greater the degree to which a subordinate group occupies a position of reward parity, the greater the likelihood that the social-space arrangements between it and other groups will represent its own desires.

Propositions 11 and 12 bring together two points discussed earlier. First, it was noted that segregation and integration between social groups may occur for different reasons and may have different meanings. Either of these two patterns may be either forced or voluntarily chosen. Second, it was noted that the social-space relationships between groups are not likely to countervene the positions of those groups in the stratification system. In simple terms, groups that are deprived of social rewards are not in much of a position to implement their own choices for social-space arrangements, regardless of what those preferences may be. On the other hand, as a group acquires social resources, it is more able to implement its own preferences for living arrangements.

It may also be emphasized that Propositions 11 and 12 imply an empirically demonstrable point that is, so to speak, the Achilles heel of the theories of assimilation, amalgamation, and cultural pluralism. The theories of amalgamation and assimilation assume that all minority groups will seek the same sorts of social goals and policies. Even Glazer and Moynihan's theory of modified cultural pluralism (1963) depicts all minority groups as passing through the same basic social process in society. But Proposition 12 says nothing about the specific content of minority group goals regarding social-space arrangements. It only stipulates the conditions under which either segregation or integration will be minority group policies. But it is assumed here that either segregation or integration may be chosen and implemented by a minority group, provided it has the social resources to enforce its own choice. Moreover, simply because a social group has been assigned minority status in society and deprived of social rewards does not mean that it will automatically be segregated. Again, Proposition 11 grants the same alternative choices to the majority as Proposition 12 does to the minority. These points will be amplified as the four resulting majority-minority structural arrangements are examined. The first situation discussed is that in which the subordinate group occupies a position of reward deprivation and segregation.

Reward deprivation with segregation. It follows from Proposition 11 that, when a minority group is both socially segregated from the majority and deprived of social rewards, social segregation is an expression of the majority group's wishes. It matters little whether the minority group would choose segregation if given the opportunity to make such a choice. The point is that under these circumstances segregation represents, not a minority group technique designed to preserve its in-group solidarity or to preserve its distinctive cultural values or way of life, but a majority group technique designed to restrict and limit the social roles of minority group members and their collective impact upon the larger society. Whether at some future point in time the minority group later chooses voluntary segregation is yet another question. Black Protestant churches were not initially a voluntarily chosen phenomenon. But with the passing of time those segregated churches became the strongest self-controlled and self-help institutions in the black community (Frazier 1963). The social meaning of any institutional arrangement in society may change over time. For the moment the important point is that the greater the degree of social deprivation of a minority group, the greater the likelihood that segregation, if it appears, will have been forced upon it by the majority group.

It has already been suggested that the social-structural arrangements between a dominant and subordinate group are a historical record of the nature of their past relationship. Majority-minority relationships that exhibit extreme reward deprivation and social segregation for the minority group indicate that the majority views the minority as either a serious contracultural threat to its values or as a competitive threat to its resource position. It is for this reason that reward deprivation and segregation, both of which are essentially forms of social discrimination, have been employed by the dominant group. In other words, this particular structural arrangement reveals that some degree of social conflict has already occurred and that one group has felt the need to restrain the other and, in fact, has done so rather successfully.

Richard Schermerhorn has called attention to the fact that there are important differences in the sequences of contact through which social groups come to interact with each other (1970). In the American experience there have been at least four different sequences of group contact that have resulted in reward deprivation and social segregation for minority groups.

Blacks have experienced *forced migration*. Being brought here as slaves, they were easily deprived of social rewards and were socially segregated. As slaves, American blacks were, of course, functionally important to the economic system. But it is more important to see that the forced migrant, while functional to the economic system, is actually deprived of an active participation in that system. American Indians have been subjected to a process of *colonization*. In this instance, reward deprivation and segregation result, not from the migration of a minority group into a new host society, but from the conquest of an indigenous population by an immigrant group. Nor should it be assumed that the American Indian represents the only unique case of colonization in the United States. The Alaskan Eskimo as well as Mexican-American communities in various parts of the West and Southwest has also experienced colonization. Moreover, the United States still controls a number of other colonies, politely called possessions in our history books, such as Puerto Rico and the Virgin Islands.

These various cases of colonization and forced migration point to the limitation of Milton Gordon's theory of cultural assimilation (1964). First, Gordon's theory that all minority groups are in a continual process of cultural assimilation into the host society ignores instances in which the power positions between groups are reversed, as in the case of colonization. Moreover, neither colonization nor forced migration seem to provide much impetus, in and of themselves, for group assimilation or even amalgamation. This is particularly true when there are extreme cultural differences between the two groups. As was noted in Chapter 3, there are indeed a number of very special conditions, such as the existence of a common enemy or an imbalance in the sexual distribution in the population of at least one of the groups, that must be present to promote these processes. In most of the cases mentioned here, especially those of American Indians, Eskimos, and blacks, the majority group has neither encouraged the minority to assimilate culturally nor allowed the minority to maintain its own unique culture and life-style. While it may be granted that some minimal forms of cultural assimilation occur, such as the learning at some functional level of the majority group's language by the minority group, this is far from the cultural assimilation as a continual linear process envisioned by Gordon's theory.

A very different sequence of group contact is that of the *contracted laborer*. Asian-Americans first entered the United States in large numbers during the nineteenth century as contracted laborers to help in the construction of the great intercontinental railroad system. As was the case with colonization and forced migration, these contracted laborers first encountered both reward deprivation and social segregation. But there is an important economic difference between colonization and forced migration on the one hand and contracted labor on the other. Asian-Americans have traditionally been in a better position than either American Indians or blacks to acquire and accumulate social rewards. As a result, they have been able to choose between the alternative patterns of cultural assimilation with integration or cultural distinctiveness with segregation. These remarks should not be construed to mean that the economic position of a group in society is the sole determinant of its movement in the social structure. Every minority group, immigrant or indigenous, possesses its own unique kinds of cultural advantages and disadvantages for making its way in society. The degree of cultural congruity or discongruity between a minority and the host society can be a critically important factor in determining whether the minority group attains reward parity and how fast it attains that parity. It is simply being suggested here that, as was stipulated in Proposition 3, dominant groups generally attempt to maintain or increase their positions of dominance. Given the fact that dominant groups often attain this goal by segregating minority groups and depriving them of social rewards, there may be important differences in the sequences of contact through which this happens—differences that can affect the rate of movement of the minority group upward in the social structure.

The nineteenth century European immigrants represent an instance of *voluntary migration*. This is not to suggest that there were not compelling forces in their homelands that propelled them toward American shores. As was noted in Chapter 3, the great migration cannot be fully understood without considering the social, economic, and, in some instances, political turmoil in the various European countries during the period of mass out-migration. But the nineteenth century European immigrants chose to come to America rather than elsewhere. They were not forced to these shores under the yoke of slavery or of indentured servitude, as were the initial European settlers during the seventeenth century. As was also seen in Chapter 3, Irish Catholics and eventually all southern European immigrants were viewed as serious contracultural threats to American society. But like the contracted laborer, the voluntary migrant enjoys a degree of economic freedom that is denied to either the forced migrant or the colonized minority group.

There is, then, a diversity of kinds of sequences of intergroup contact that have produced reward deprivation and social segregation for minority groups in the United States. It should also be noted that the social segregation of a minority group into a clearly defined geographical space is not the only form of social segregation between groups. Migrant workers represent perhaps the most unique and devastating form of reward deprivation with social segregation in contemporary America. The migrant worker's economic position is second only to that of the slave in terms of the degree of deprivation involved. Moreover, perpetual mobility is an even more debilitating form of social segregation than that of restriction to a specific geographical area.

Most minority groups that have experienced forced segregation in the United States have been able, after differing time periods, to gain control of some of the institutions in their own communities. The recent history of American blacks, Indians, Mexican-Americans, and Eskimos all point to the unfolding process by which minority groups change their position in the social structure by creating strong self-defense institutions in their own communities. The need for minority groups to control the very institutions in their own midst was essentially the theme of the conflict in New York City in the late 1960s when blacks were demanding local control of their schools. Glazer and Moynihan (1963), as well as numerous other sociologists, have shown that this aspect of minority group ascendency was no less important for the European immigrant groups. A certain degree of self-autonomy within their own communities is a key aspect of the process through which each minority group makes its bid for its share in society.

But the migrant worker is socially segregated in an extremely unique manner. His continual mobility deprives him of the very basic social services and political rights of which most other minority groups are able to avail themselves. It may be granted that voter registration drives among blacks in the Deep South continue to be a long and hard-won battle. But the basic franchise is available. Migrant workers do not remain in any one location long enough to qualify under the residency laws for voting rights. Surely, members of all minority groups that have had to live in socially segregated ghettos have also had to live with the psychological handicap of knowing their "place." But the migrant worker knows that he has no place. Oscar Handlin has used the term "uprooted" to describe the experience of the European immigrants (1951). But the migrant worker is perpetually uprooted.[19] In summary, ghettoization is but one form, and perhaps not the most extreme form, of forced segregation.

Regardless of the specific sequence of group contact that results in reward deprivation and segregation for a minority group, and regardless of whether social segregation takes the form of either ghettoization or perpetual mobility, there are several predictable central tendencies in conflicts between a subordinate group in this kind of social location and a dominant group. These are described in the next three propositions.

---

[19]Robert Coles has documented the psychological effects of perpetual mobility upon the children of migrant workers in his brief but moving book *Uprooted Children* (1970).

Proposition 13: The greater the degree of reward disparity and social segregation between a dominant and a subordinate group, the greater the likelihood that conflicts between them will be relatively infrequent.

It should be remembered that all of the theoretical propositions presented here deal with the general categories of dominant and subordinate groups. They therefore apply not only to instances of majority-minority conflict but also to some instances of minority-minority conflict (provided the conditions of the propositions are present), as well as to elite-mass relationships. But particular concern in this study is with their application to majority-minority conflicts.

Both the space arrangement and the distribution of resources contribute to the infrequency of social conflicts between a dominant group and a minority that is extremely deprived of rewards and forcibly segregated. First, as both Simmel (1908a) and Coser (1956) contend, social segregation limits the number of contacts between group members and thereby limits the occasions for social conflict. Second, the wide disparity (degree of inequality) of the resource positions of the two groups also contributes to a low frequency of conflict. From the standpoint of the minority group, social conflict is itself an expensive way of deploying the resources it possesses. Conflict requires organization, and organization requires time, money, and human effort. Moreover, the extreme resource deprivation and social segregation of the minority group serve as grim reminders of the superior advantage of the majority group. Both of these structural dimensions of the relationship between the two groups may function to intimidate the minority and restrain its members from initiating conflict. From the majority group standpoint, both segregation and economic deprivation have been employed to neutralize the efforts of minority group members and to restrict the collective role of the group in society. To the extent that both techniques precipitate relatively infrequent conflict, they do effectively satisfy the majority's goals. Yet it must be remembered that infrequent conflict is far from an indication of a stable relationship between groups. In a humanistic framework, one which assesses social phenomena in terms of the minimization of human pain and suffering, this kind of majority-minority relationship is not only dysfunctional for minority group members but for the majority group and the entire social system as well. For while conflicts may be relatively infrequent, they also tend to be both intense and violent. They tend to be the kinds of conflicts in which people suffer injuries to more than just their identities or egos.

Proposition 14: The greater the degree of reward disparity and social segregation between a dominant and a subordinate group, the greater the likelihood that conflicts between them will be relatively intense.

The term "intensity" refers to the amount of human energy or effort that is invested in a given action. If it is granted that the importance of any human activity may be measured in terms of the effort that people put into that activity, the intensity of social conflict is an appropriate way of measuring the importance of a given instance of social conflict for group members. It should be cautioned that intensity and emotionality are not the same thing. One may have a high degree of emotional commitment to the idea of equal rights and opportunities for all people but may never lift a hand to make it happen. The important question is: How much human effort or energy is expended? How important or intense is the conflict?

There are several reasons why social conflicts between a majority group and a minority group that is both deprived of resources and socially segregated will be relatively intense. First, it will be recalled that, as the degree of reward deprivation of a social group becomes greater, there is a tendency for each and every conflict to assume an all-or-nothing quality. The fate of the lives of group members seems to rise or fall with every victory or failure. Moreover, when the resource positions of two groups are extremely different, there is a tendency for the phenomenon that Dahrendorf calls superimposition (1959) to occur. That is, each social conflict situation produces the exact same pattern of dominance and subordination. The minority encounters the same majority in a position of wealth, power, authority, and privilege above it. From the minority's point of view, both total deprivation of resources and superimposition of conflicts increase the intensity of majority-minority conflicts.

On the other hand, the combination of resource deprivation and forced segregation is already an indication of the degree to which the majority views the minority group as either an extreme threat to its resources or as a serious contracultural threat to its life-style, its social values, and the social order generally. The majority has already indicated its willingness to expend significant efforts to restrain the minority. It is likely to do so again. This applies not only to the majority's reaction to minority-group-initiated conflicts but to majority-group-initiated conflicts as well. It is important to note that the relative positions of groups in the social structure are not simply indications of the way in which one group views the other but an indication of the reciprocal ways in which the two groups have come to view each other. The intensity of intergroup conflict stems from the views of both groups.

> *Proposition 15: The greater the degree of reward disparity and social segregation between a dominant and a subordinate group, the greater the likelihood that conflicts between them will be violent.*

In most societies, including the United States, dominant groups are the more frequent users of force and violence. The reasons for this are really quite simple. The dominant group usually has a relative, if not complete, monopoly over the instruments of violence. It has played the largest role in establishing both the laws and norms of the society as well as the police power of the state through which those norms and laws are enforced. Its possession of the instruments of violence and the fact that its use of violence is either institutionally legitimate or can be made to appear legitimate minimizes the risks involved for the dominant group in using violence.

But majority groups cannot employ violent means of conflict with equal ease against all minority groups. The situation in which a minority is both deprived of social rewards and socially segregated provides added impetus for majority group violence, regardless of whether that violence is perpetrated in the name of the legitimate order by the police or by some self-appointed vigilante group. The minority's lack of social resources gives it relatively little access to the institutional structures of the society, especially those institutions that distribute justice. In other words, the minority group has few ways of obtaining either compensation or redress for violence directed against it. The deprivation of resources makes a minority group a relatively vulnerable target. The segregation of social space further makes the minority group an easily distinguishable target. In fact, as race riots in the United States have shown both in the 1940s and 1960s, regardless of who initiates the violence, social segregation increases the probability that violent conflict and destruction of both life and property will be greatest upon minority group turf.

This is not to suggest that all violence is initiated by the majority group. This is clearly not the case. Minority groups that are both socially segregated and deprived of social rewards may, at times, view violence as the only meaningful avenue of action left to them. And it again must be remembered that social segregation is a two-way street. The minority holds the same kind of perception of enemy territory as does the majority.

Finally, while the first task in any theoretical exercise is to understand each proposition on its own grounds, this should not prevent considering the relationships between the different propositions. It will be recalled from Proposition 6 that, as the resource position of a group becomes lower in the stratification system, the probability of its initiating consensus-projecting conflicts increases. In other words, a minority group at the bottom of the system is more likely than a minority group possessing parity to initiate conflicts that the majority views as nonnormative or deviant, even if they are not illegal. It follows that the more a group initiates this kind of conflict, the greater the likelihood that the majority will react violently to quell actions that it sees as a threat to the very life of the social order. In summary, social conflicts between a majority group and a minority deprived of social resources and socially segregated are likely to be relatively infrequent but relatively intense and more often violent.

As has already been shown in Propositions 7 and 9, the initiation of either rigid-means or variable-means conflicts by minority groups that are deprived of social rewards must be understood in the context of the position of those groups in the stratification system. Rigid-means conflicts most frequently are predicated upon past failures, the lack of alternative means, and the level of frustration among group members. Variable-means conflict most often indicates the inability of the group to have one single means of conflict to which it can commit its resources with any degree of assurance that the effort will have an impact upon the social structure.

The situation of reward deprivation and segregation is the most extreme instance of minority group disadvantage. The case of parity with integration represents just the opposite extreme. This kind of majority-minority relationship is examined next.

Reward parity with integration. The situation in which a minority group possesses a significant stock of social resources and rewards and in which it chooses, and is able, to share social, especially residential, space with the majority and other minorities is most closely approximated in the United States by the major European ethnic and religious immigrant groups. It must be remembered that the four structural situations under discussion here are ideal types. They are analytical models to which various empirical cases may be compared. It was noted in Chapter 3 that ethnic and religious enclaves may still be found in the American cities and suburbs.[20] Yet it has also been shown that there are many American suburbs that are ethnically and religiously heterogeneous within social class boundaries. For the moment, it is being assumed that the heterogeneous suburb represents the more significant trend for analysis. Unfortunately, there has not yet been enough empirical research to either reject or verify this assumption. But if it is granted that the heterogeneous suburb is the trend for the future, the fact that this heterogeneity is typically found within social class boundaries does not contradict the foregoing theoretical propositions. For it has already been stipulated that the distribution of rewards between groups is a determinant factor in the ability of groups to implement their goals and desires. Residential segregation (discrimination) according to social class provides empirical confirmation of this theory.

Since it is frequently argued that the major European immigrant groups are the most assimilated American minorities, it will be useful here to reexamine Milton Gordon's seven assimilation variables as well as his theory of structural assimilation (1964). It may be granted at the outset that groups such as Italian Catholics, Jews, and various ethnic Protestants evidence high degrees of both (1) cultural and (2) structural assimilation. Large numbers of members of these groups appear to participate in the mainstream of American cultural life and values and have a significant share in the society's major institutions, often on the level of primary group associations. They must also be rated high on Gordon's next variable, (3) identificational assimilation.

[20]See the discussion on pp. 76–77.

To a large extent, members of these groups view themselves as Americans. It will be recalled from Proposition 5 that the greater the degree to which the members of a group share in the rewards and resources of a society, the greater the likelihood that conflicts that they initiate will be of the consensus-bounded type. This is because members of such groups view themselves as part of the social structure and have a high cognitive or psychological investment in the existing institutions and norms. In other words, identificational assimilation may be viewed, not as a consequence of structural assimilation, but as a result of two other factors: a high degree of reward parity and the absence of any ideological reasons on the part of group members for seeing themselves as separated from the host society. Obviously, where reward parity and the ideology of cultural separatism are found, the minority chooses segregation. But where there is resource parity and the absence of a strong separatist ideology, one would expect to find a high degree of identificational assimilation and, as previously noted, a tendency for consensus-bounded conflicts. In this context, Gordon's next assimilation variable, group intermarriage, must be examined carefully.

In Gordon's theory, minority group assimilation through intermarriage is one of the most significant indications of the total assimilation that follows from structural assimilation. In contrast, the theory being offered here contends that cultural, structural, and identificational assimilation result from the group's possession of significant rewards and resources gleaned from the existing institutions, and from the desire of the group to share social space and intermix as opposed to choosing segregation. In this framework, intermarriages represent nothing more than trade-offs resulting from increased social contact and shared social space. Contrary to Gordon's theory, intermarriages do not represent increased total assimilation. Just as segregation limits contact and thereby reduces the frequency of conflict, so integration increases group contact and increases the frequency of both conflict and coalition between group members. Members of groups that share social space are likely to produce increased intermarriage rates. The modern university campus that has emerged since World War II represents shared institutional space in which the offspring of minority groups that already possess significant stocks of social resources further compete for access to more social rewards and resources. The modern university campus has become a spawning ground for mixed marriages. Moreover, the degree to which groups occupy similar economic positions in society is not just a reward variable but also a life-style variable. Elements of commonality in life-style resulting from common class position serve to counteract old ethnic and religious differences. Intermarriages may not become more desirable, but they do become more workable, more tolerated—and more frequent.

Of course, both Gordon's theory and the one offered here would predict increased intermarriage rates between such groups, though for different reasons. Yet if the theory of structural assimilation is correct, one would predict not only increased intermarriage rates but also reductions in the size of minority religious groups through religious conversions resulting from intermarriages. The theory of assimilation assumes that minority group members will marry *into* the majority religious groups. The existing research on religious conversions that result from intermarriages does not support this contention. Rather, these studies support the trade-off theory of intermarriage offered here.

A number of studies conducted in selected American communities since 1957, when the last comprehensive United States Census data on intermarriage was collected, show that intermarriage rates for all three major religious groups, Protestants, Catholics, and Jews, have increased (Lazerwitz 1971). Studies of American Jews by Goldstein (1968) and by Goldstein and Goldscheider (1968) show increasing intermarriage with each successive generation. Andrew Greeley reports a similarly high rate of intermarriage for American Catholics (1964). Moreover, Catholics seem to intermarry more frequently when Catholics represent a relatively small part of the community. Jews seem to intermarry more frequently when their relative size in the community is either very small or very large (Lazerwitz 1971). This suggests the need for studying not only regional variations in group densities but also more discrete patterns of group size and residential integration from one kind of city to the next. In any case, the research discussed thus far shows increasing intermarriage rates. These rates may be viewed in one of two theoretical perspectives. They might be viewed as evidence for Milton Gordon's theory that structural assimilation will produce all other forms of assimilation, including intermarriage, and eventually total assimilation. On the other hand, they may be viewed as support for the theory that shared social space increases contacts and coalitions between group members, but not necessarily assimilation. In order to answer this question, one must turn to the research on religious conversions that result from these intermarriages. If Gordon's theory is correct, one would expect to see most intermarriages resulting in conversions to Christianity, and especially Protestantism. If the theory offered here is correct, one would look for a pattern of balancing trade-offs in religious conversions.

Based upon an examination of several major studies, Salisbury reports that the majority of all religious conversions result from intermarriages and that the conversion rates for Catholicism and Protestantism are about equal (1964). In other words, he does not find consistent assimilation by Jews and Catholics into Protestant religious groups. In fact, one minority religious group, Jews, has reaped a gross increase in members who convert as a result of intermarriages. A more recent study by Lazerwitz confirms these findings (1971). It may be concluded, then, that structural assimilation does not lead to total assimilation and that intermarriage is not necessarily a measure of assimilation. Given these findings, what kinds of measures would indicate actual assimilation or cultural amalgamation between a minority group and a majority group with which it shares resources and social space? Gordon's remaining three assimilation variables must be examined.

Obviously, the absence of discrimination is not a meaningful measure where reward parity and integration exist. By definition, this situation indicates that majority group discrimination has been largely overcome or neutralized by the minority. On the other hand, Gordon's remaining two assimilation variables, the absence of prejudice and the absence of value or power conflicts, are extremely important. As was noted earlier, as groups obtain a high degree of economic parity, social conflicts tend to center upon value and status disagreements. Moreover, in the absence of discrimination, value and status conflict may be accompanied by enduring levels of prejudice.[21] The existence of high levels of value, status, and power conflict, as well as prejudice, may be viewed as indications of the fact that assimilation in the total sense of the word

---

[21]The relationships between prejudice, discrimination, and conflict are discussed in Chapter 5.

is not occurring. Conversely, the absence of intergroup prejudice, value, power, and status conflicts indicates that the social stage has at least been set for the possible occurrence of assimilation or amalgamation. The existing information concerning America's various immigrant religious and ethnic groups, especially those that are situated above the lower-middle-class line and share social space with one another, does not present a picture of either assimilation or amalgamation in the total sense.

An important related question is whether or not there is any typical social process through which minority groups attain resource parity and/or social integration with a majority group? Milton Gordon, of course, stresses the importance of structural assimilation (1964). In essence, he argues that any pattern of convergence between majority and minority groups occurs through the infiltration, so to speak, of minority group members into majority group controlled institutions. Yet, as was suggested earlier, the participation of minority group members in dominant-group-controlled institutions hardly fosters assimilation if those members remain at the very bottom of those institutions.

In contrast to a pattern of structural assimilation, the major European religious and ethnic groups in the United States appear to have attained reward parity by either capturing some segment of the existing economic institutions or by creating their own in-group controlled segment of the economy. As was noted earlier, Italian dominance in the construction trades, Jewish preeminence in various manufacturing and retailing sectors, Irish domination in union leadership and some segments of the civil service, and Greek success in the retail food industry are merely a few examples. The prevailing pattern is one of a division of labor between groups in the economy. It may indeed be the case that groups attain resource parity and a common investment in the social system, not through sharing the same institutional structures (structural assimilation), but through a rather complex pattern of interrelated and interdependent structural differentiation.

In the case of the economy, the differentiation between groups is of the type that may be called "functional differentiation." This is not a case of simply parallel institutional structures. Rather, these structures are differentiated according to various service functions for the economy. Large numbers of members of different groups have been able to specialize in a given skill, trade, or service that is different from that of other groups. *to achieve same results*

The realm of political conflict and differentiation between groups presents a slightly different picture. Here again, different groups appear to compete with one another through the creation of parallel structures. This is most clearly evident in those Western European countries in which governments either rise or fall on the basis of coalitions between the various political parties, each of which represents a different political philosophy or group interest. In the United States, these kinds of political power coalitions also occur, but within the context of a unique two-party system. The two major American political parties represent, not monolithic social organizations, but internally diverse organizations exhibiting both internal conflict and internal coalition. Each party must produce both a ticket and a platform capable of delivering voting blocks along racial, ethnic, religious, and social class lines. In this sense, there is a high degree of structural differentiation between groups within the political system. But this kind of differentiation is not the same sort of functional differentiation or division of labor that is found in the economy. In the economy, groups form coalitions because each group has a unique resource or service to contribute to the whole. In the political sphere, coalitions are formed because different groups possess exactly the same kinds of resources, political power, votes, and political influence. In either case, it seems fair to conclude that interdependence results, not from the sharing of structures and institutional convergence, but from parallel structures.

These differences in the kinds of social differentiation between groups, depending upon whether one examines economic or political relationships, point to the difficulties in formulating general social theories. As Clinton Fink has observed (1968), differences in both the kinds of conflict being studied (economic, political, religious, etc.) and the units of analysis studied (individuals, groups, societies) complicate the task of integrating various sets of theoretical propositions into a well-articulated theoretical whole.

For instance, George Homans, in his fine study of social relationships in small group situations, argues that the more two individuals compete with one another, the more likely they are to exhibit the exact same kinds of behaviors. Homans concludes that conflict and competition between individuals will not usually produce a division of labor (1961:135). For example, two men competing in a game of tennis or a chess match are attempting to outdo each other at the very same task. They exhibit, not a division of labor, but the same kinds of efforts and activities. Can Homans' theoretical proposition about conflicts and competition between individuals be applied to the study of group competition and conflict? Interestingly, the answer is both yes and no. It depends upon the kinds of intergroup conflicts being studied. As was just noted, in the realm of economic conflict there is a pronounced tendency for groups to compete through a division of labor, through specialized activities within each group. In this case, Homans' proposition about conflict between individuals is quite wrong when applied to the study of intergroup conflicts. But if one examines political rather than economic conflict between groups, Homans' proposition about individual conflict rings true. A functional division of labor does not result. Groups that compete and conflict politically are more likely to exhibit similar kinds of behavior, each group attempting to wield power and votes, to employ and attain the same kind of resource. This, of course, assumes that both groups view the ground rules of the political system in which they are conflicting as legitimate.

Finally, it should be noted that social conflicts vary not only in terms of the kinds of social units and the kinds of rewards involved but also, most importantly, in terms of the kinds of social contexts in which they occur. Homans, for instance, is interested not just in social relationships between individual human beings but also in those social relationships that, by and large, are free from any prior patterns of domination and subordination. For this reason, much of the research he examines in order to generate his propositions about the "elementary forms" of social conduct involves experimentally created groups in laboratory situations. These are situations in which the individuals participating have had no prior relationship with one another. In contrast, this study focuses upon individuals primarily in terms of their interactions as members of collectivities and, especially, as preexisting patterns of dominance and subordination influence those interactions. The emphasis here is, not upon context-free interaction produced in a laboratory, but precisely upon the way in which contextual, structural variables such as types of societies, the distribution of rewards between groups, and the arrangement of social space between groups influence social conflicts between group members. It is important, then, to recognize both the potential applications and limitations of any set of theoretical propositions. For the moment it seems clear that dominant and subordinate groups that evidence both reward parity and shared social space engage in both conflicts and coalitions, not through one set of social structures into which the minority assimilates, but through differentiated social structures, regardless of whether that differentiation represents a division of labor or mere parallel structures. What kinds of general propositions may be formulated about the nature of conflicts between such groups?

Proposition 16: The greater the degree of reward parity and social integration between a dominant and a subordinate group, the greater the likelihood that conflicts between them will be relatively frequent.

Both the distribution of resources and the social-space arrangements between the groups contribute to the frequency of social conflict. First, shared social space increases the frequency of contact between group members and thereby increases the frequency of social conflict. Moreover, the fact that the two groups are at relatively similar levels in terms of resource position increases the probability that they will compete for the same kinds of resources within the same kinds of institutional spheres, especially where status and power conflicts are involved. Such groups are likely to play significant roles in the political process and be frequent combatants in that process. This applies at the national, state, and municipal levels of the political system. Moreover, shared space carries those kinds of conflicts to the local level, such as school board elections, local political party organizations, and the like.

Proposition 17: The greater the degree of reward parity and social integration between a dominant and a subordinate group, the greater the likelihood that conflicts between them will not be intense.

As Coser suggests (1956), the frequency of conflict itself creates a kind of built-in toleration for conflict. But in addition to this fact, the resource positions of the groups is another important factor that reduces the intensity of conflicts. As any social group attains a position of parity in the stratification system, there is a tendency for different kinds of conflicts to become disassociated from one another. The pattern that Dahrendorf calls superimposition (1959) does not occur. No single conflict is an all-or-nothing contest. Finally, just as shared space and resource positions create frequent conflict, they also create frequent coalitions between groups. Surely, in-group members still view out-group members as "one of them." But the interrelated patterns of conflict and coalition between groups means that, in any given instance, groups have as much in common as they have differences. They share both geographical space and life-style (social class), in spite of the fact that they are competitors.

> *Proposition 18: The greater the degree of reward parity and social integration between a dominant and subordinate group, the greater the likelihood that conflicts between them will not be violent.*

The very same factors that contribute to the relatively nonintense quality of conflict also contribute to the absence of violence. Such groups have come to tolerate not only the occurrence of frequent conflict but also, in a larger sense, have come to tolerate each other's differences. Where toleration exists, violence is improbable. Mutual toleration between America's middle-class groups, especially in the realm of their religious differences, has been a subject of great interest to sociologists. Several writers have argued that the unique toleration between white Protestants, Catholics, and Jews is possible because they all, majority and minority alike, participate in a common "civil religion." This common-core American faith unites members of America's three-religion pluralism regardless of the theological differences between the different religious groups (Herberg 1955, Bellah 1967). Thus the ability of different majority and minority groups to share social resources and social space does not mean that all their differences will disappear or that assimilation or amalgamation is taking place. It only means that, like it or not, they have learned to tolerate their differences, and those differences, be they religious, ethnic, philosophical, political, or even racial, are somewhat transcended by other things the groups have in common. This does not mean that assimilation or amalgamation cannot happen between such groups either by design or as an unintended consequence of the social situation. But at the moment the existing data on intermarriage and religious conversion do not support such an interpretation of the American scene. As long as such groups continue to view each other as resource competitors or value threats, conflicts between them, on the basis of the factors just discussed, are likely to be frequent, though neither intense nor violent.

Finally, as was suggested in Propositions 8 and 10, these kinds of groups, which have a high share of the resources of the society, are likely to initiate either rigid-means or variable-means conflicts precisely because of their superior resources and positions in the social structure.

Reward parity with segregation. As is stipulated in Proposition 11, the greater the degree of resource parity between two groups, the greater the likelihood that either social integration or segregation between them will represent the desires of the subordinate (minority), rather than the dominant (majority), group. Contrary to the theory of assimilation, and even some versions of the theory of cultural pluralism, not all minority groups have the same social goals. Some minority groups prefer segregation. Parity of social resources coupled with social segregation is evidence of the ability of the minority group to impose its own self-definition of its distinctiveness as strongly subcultural or contracultural. If one follows either Hansen's law (1938) or the Glazer-Moynihan hypothesis (1963), it is already clear that social groups may change their goals at different points in time.[22] Hansen's law contends that changes in the social policies desired by groups correspond to generational changes. While the second generation typically attempts to assimilate, the third generation typically chooses cultural pluralism. In the first instance, then, reward parity with segregation may be understood as a generational phenomenon that, at least for the major European ethnic and religious immigrants, has followed a fairly stable pattern for the first three generations.

Yet there are two other important instances of reward parity with segregation in American society that are not simply generational or temporary social arrangements. The first of these is the situation of Asian-Americans, Chinese, Japanese, and even Korean self-segregated communities. In most cases Asian-Americans, like most other first-generation immigrant groups, experienced reward deprivation and forced social segregation. But with the attainment of reward parity, most Asian-American groups, especially where they constitute a sizable part of the community, have chosen to remain segregated. They have to a

---

[22]Hansen's law is discussed in Chapter 3, pp. 75–76.

large extent built their own economic structures and have also been able to maintain political control of their communities. It is for this reason that public school desegregation cases in the early 1970s, especially in the state of California where there exists the strongest self-contained Asian-American community, have met with strong opposition from Asian-Americans. They do not want to lose the cultural distinctiveness of their community and suspect that if the schools, an important instrument of socialization, are desegregated, this loss will occur. Asian-Americans represent one of the most outstanding instances of successful self-segregation in the United States. They have preserved a distinct set of cultural values and traditions within the larger society.

The second type of nongenerational voluntary self-segregation in the United States is found in the large number of religious and social communal groups. Such groups as Hasidic Jews, the Amish, Mennonites, Quakers, the Society of Brothers, and hippie communes have received a great deal of attention from sociologists of religion, students of social organization, and students of social movements. These groups, because they contain cognitive norms that differ greatly from the host society and because of the unique form of communal organization that they create, are intrinsically interesting from a sociological perspective. But it is less frequently recognized that they are also cognitive and behavioral minorities. They are typically small (certainly less than one-half the total population of a society); they clearly represent norms, whether based upon either social or religious philosophy, that vary from and often conflict with those of the larger society; and they are subordinate with regard to the distribution of power. It is hard to avoid the conclusion that students of minority groups have overlooked these groups because, except for relatively brief periods of time, they are not the objects of extreme forms of social discrimination. As was noted in Chapter 2, the extreme instances of prejudice and discrimination have been an important definitional lens for sociologists interested in minority groups. Yet these kinds of self-segregated groups represent but another facet of social-structural and cultural pluralism in American society. They typically choose self-segregation in order to preserve a life-style or values that they view as better than those of the larger society.

Before turning to the theoretical propositions about conflicts between minority groups possessing reward parity with voluntary segregation and majority groups, one further case of this type that is not found in the United States should be considered. It will be recalled that one of the most unique instances of reward deprivation with segregation is that of the migrant worker. Perpetual mobility is only a variation on the theme of social segregation. In the case of the migrant worker, forced mobility has the same, if not worse, effects as ghettoization. But mobility as a form of segregation may also be both forced or chosen. The most interesting example in nonindustrialized societies is that of the nomad. Both the ancient Hebrews and various modern Arab tribes are examples. The prime example in more modern, pluralistic societies is that of the gypsy. In several modern European countries, gypsies maintain their cultural distinctiveness and avoid "contamination" by the foreign traditions of their host societies through perpetual mobility. Simply because this kind of self-segregation is not prevalent in the United States does not mean that it does not happen or that it is not an important case for comparative study and theory building.

Proposition 19: The greater the degree of reward parity and social segregation between a dominant and a subordinate group, the greater the likelihood that conflicts between them will be relatively infrequent.

The relative infrequency of majority-minority conflict in this type of relationship stems from two factors. First, as previously noted, the segregation of social space limits the frequency of contact between group members and thereby limits the frequency of social conflicts between them. Second, as noted in Proposition 11, where resource parity is accompanied by segregation, it is typically the case that segregation prevails at the desire of the minority group. In other words, these kinds of minority groups withdraw rather than fight, or fight only on their own terms or only when necessary. The fact that the minority has created a self-contained community is a symbolic representation of its desire for disengagement and its rejection of some segment of the values and norms of the host society. It is therefore highly probable that most conflicts, especially those other than economic conflicts, will be initiated by the majority group. Typically, such conflicts result because the majority views the minority as an extremely threatening contracultural departure. These considerations suggest yet two more general propositions.

Proposition 20: The greater the degree of reward parity and social segregation between a dominant and a subordinate group, the greater the likelihood that conflicts between them will be initiated by the dominant group.

Proposition 21: The greater the degree of reward parity and social segregation between a dominant and a subordinate group, the greater the likelihood that the conflicts between them will be relatively intense.

Since the minority group, wherever possible, has avoided interaction with majority group members, contacts and conflicts between members of the two groups will result, not from the regular course of events, but through a concerted effort on the part of one group to seek out the other. The majority must have strong reasons and must exert concerted energies to interact with the segregated minority, and both of these factors create a more intense form of group interaction. Similarly, such a minority group is likely to react intensely when it finds that it is the object of an unprovoked attack.

Proposition 22: The greater the degree of reward parity and social segregation between a dominant and a subordinate group, the greater the likelihood that conflicts between them will be violent.

The likelihood that these conflicts will be violent follows from what has already been said about the probable conditions under which these conflicts occur. Both violence and intensity of conflict are predicated on the fact that the majority aggresses against the self-segregated minority because it views such minority groups as serious contracultural threats, threats that endanger the morale of the larger community. For instance, in the early nineteenth century, Mormon communities were driven from New York State at gun point. Both their "deviant" religious beliefs and, probably more importantly, their practice of polygamy were viewed as highly threatening to the larger society. As they crossed North America westward, they encountered intense and violent conflict almost everywhere, until they were able to settle in the still uncivilized parts of the West, now the states of Nevada, Utah, and California (O'Dea 1957).

While conflicts between this type of minority group and the majority are infrequent, one need not look as far back as even the nineteenth century to find examples of it. In the early 1970s a group of Black Muslims attempted to establish a self-supporting farming community in one of the southern states. The surrounding white community repeatedly poisoned their livestock and the Black Muslims were forced to move elsewhere. Of course, the internment of Japanese-Americans during World War II is yet another example of majority group aggression against a self-segregated minority. It is a rather unique example because of the obvious fact that the majority's definition of the minority was based upon events outside the social system, war with Japan. Yet all three cases, those of the Mormons, the Black Muslims, and Japanese-Americans, follow the same pattern. Conflict is infrequent, though intense and violent. Conflict is typically instigated by the majority group because it sees the minority as a strong contracultural or value threat.

Reward deprivation with integration. The last situation to be considered here is that in which a minority group is deprived of social resources but remains integrated with the majority group and other minority groups. The wide diversity of kinds of minority groups that fit this description makes the formulation of theoretical generalizations a bit tenuous. Nevertheless, four propositions will be offered. Before presenting these propositions, it will be useful to first examine some examples of these kinds of groups.

A first type of group in this category is the physically handicapped. While they are physically distinct, it is important to note that they do not possess the kinds of physical traits that generate a racial label. The blind, the crippled, and the dwarf all possess relatively low social status and are typically relegated to marginal economic roles in society. Just as blacks experience institutional racism, so the handicapped experience institutional discrimination. Both kinds of physically distinct groups, racial groups and the handicapped, are "stigmatized" because of their physical variance from the social norms.[23] But there is, of course, an important difference in the kind of social treatment of these two types of groups. While one is forcibly segregated, the other remains residentially integrated.

Groups that are deprived of social rewards and socially segregated

[23]Erving Goffman's concept of "stigma" is discussed in Chapter 5, pp. 216–217.

are often viewed by the majority as a severe and serious threat to either majority group norms and values or resources. It is for this reason that conflict is often intense. In this situation, dominant groups typically create powerful ideologies about the minority, like racism. Obviously, there is no such corresponding ideology of this type where the handicapped are concerned. Rather, the dominant group ideology denies the ability of the minority group to compete at all. Institutionalized discrimination results from the unwillingness of the majority to recognize the minority as a competitor. Social space may be shared precisely because the majority does not see the minority as a competitor, nor does the majority fear that social relationships with such a group will be "dangerous." Rather, the prevailing mythology about the handicapped as well as existing patterns of discrimination guarantee that social interaction will be casual and inconsequential in spite of shared social space.

A second type of group that experiences reward deprivation but remains socially integrated is a group that exhibits some form of either behavioral or cognitive variance that conflicts with the values of the dominant group. These are groups that sociologists have traditionally viewed as "social movements." For instance, early in the twentieth century a relatively new and growing religious group, the Seventh Day Adventists, experienced intense conflict with the larger society. Large numbers of Seventh Day Adventists were deported during the Palmer Raids in 1919 and 1920. Their ideas were viewed as foreign and threatening to the social order. Both the Communist party (a cognitive minority) and homosexuals (a behavioral minority) have been given deviant status (i.e. illegal status) precisely because the larger society was not able to tolerate their particular forms of variance and viewed these forms of variance as threatening to the social order.

A final example of a social movement possessing a cognitive trait (ideology) at variance with the social norms is the Women's Liberation Movement. The question immediately arises: Why not view all women and not just the Women's Liberation Movement as a minority group (a physical minority)? It was argued in Chapter 2 that a minority group is any group that is relatively subordinate with regard to the distribution of power, possesses some trait that is at variance from the social norms and archetypes, and rarely constitutes more than one-half of the total population of a society. Women, of course, constitute the numerical majority in American society, but this fact alone is not sufficient to rule them out as a minority group. It is more important to note that there are highly desirable normative social roles for both men and women in society. In other words, being female is not a form of variance from society's sexual norms. On the other hand, in most, if not all, societies, sex differentiation is a factor in the stratification system: and there is discrimination, especially in economic terms, against women in American society. It is essential, then, to distinguish between subordinate social status and minority social status, which is but one kind of subordinate group status.

Dominance and subordination are all but universal phenomena in societies. For instance, industrial workers represent a relatively subordinate social stratum, but they are not a minority group in the sense that the term has been used in this book. As was noted earlier, criminal groups are yet another type of subordinate group, but they are still different from minority groups. Minority groups, then, are merely one important type of subordinate group in societies. Simply because women experience discrimination in economic institutions and occupy a relatively subordinate social status to men does not mean that the term "minority group" applies.

On the other hand, those women who participate in and strongly identify with the Women's Liberation Movement may be viewed as a minority group. Like any number of other minority group social movements, they possess a distinctive trait (in this case, cognitive or ideological) that becomes the focal point for both collective group consciousness and for intergroup relationships. This particular minority movement has been on the American scene for well over a century. While in a contemporary perspective, Women's Liberation sounds quite "radical," Women's Liberation in the 1970s still has not experienced the kind of intense and violent conflict with the larger society that preceded the passage of the Nineteenth Amendment to the Constitution of the United States. Women's Liberation is a significant cognitive minority that has already experienced a history of infrequent, although turbulent, conflict with the larger society.

In spite of the wide diversity of groups that are deprived of social resources but are still integrated with the larger society, there are at least four theoretical generalizations that may be offered concerning conflict between this type of subordinate group and a dominant group.

Proposition 23: The greater the degree of reward disparity and social integration between a dominant and a subordinate group, the greater the likelihood that social conflicts between them will be initiated by the subordinate group.

This is one of the key differences between reward parity with segregation and reward deprivation with integration. In the former case, conflicts are likely to be initiated by the dominant group because the minority group has voluntarily withdrawn. But where reward deprivation and integration prevail, the minority is of the type that emerges out of the existing society and aggresses against it. As long as these groups do not aggress or proselytize their views in a way that threatens the dominant group, integration between them is permitted by the dominant group. It is the act of protest or aggression by the minority that generates social conflict.

It will be recalled from Chapter 2 that Milton Yinger's concept of contracultural groups was employed to describe those minorities that were neither simply variations from the norm nor actually deviant. Contracultural norms are those that strongly oppose the dominant group's norms but do not actually break the law. Yinger employs the term "contraculturalism" in an even more specific sense that is relevant to some of the kinds of minority groups being discussed here. Yinger contends (1960) that contracultural groups possess norms that are, in fact, specific reactions against the dominant culture. In other words, these groups grow out of the existing culture in reaction to it. Women's Liberation is not a group that simply happens to possess a distinctive trait and happens to find that trait in opposition to the host society. In this context, while for most of the groups discussed here economic parity and disparity has been the central aspect of stratification being examined, the kind of group to which Yinger points exhibits extreme status deprivation. This is somewhat of a departure from most of the other kinds of groups discussed here.

Proposition 24: The greater the degree of reward disparity and social integration between a dominant and a subordinate group, the greater the likelihood that conflicts between them will be relatively infrequent.

This proposition follows from the fact that the dominant group has permitted social integration. All other things being equal, the majority is able to tolerate the minority group's particular form of social variance. It is only when the minority group aggresses that the variance becomes threatening. Moreover, a high degree of integration between the two groups creates an organizational hurdle for the minority. Minority group members must be drawn out of the social structures that they share with the dominant group for the purpose of changing those very structures. Groups that have both parity and integration have a strong historical consciousness about the traits that brought them minority status and probably have strong in-group organizations that were formed for the purpose of group advancement. But the minority that emerges from the existing society as a social movement has a unique problem of social organization. Such a group must, in effect, persuade its members to become an "enemy from within." It is indeed difficult for such a group to sustain frequent and continuing conflict, nor is it likely that a dominant group will tolerate continual aggression from a group within its midst. This also contributes to the intensity of such conflicts.

Proposition 25: The greater the degree of reward disparity and social integration between a dominant and a subordinate group, the greater the likelihood that conflicts between them will be intense.

Both Coser (1956) and Simmel (1908a) have observed that conflict is extremely intense when the enemy turns out to be "one of us." And this is just the case when a minority group is well integrated with the rest of the society.

Proposition 26: The greater the degree of reward disparity and social integration between a dominant and a subordinate group, the greater the likelihood the conflicts between them will be violent.

It has been seen throughout this chapter that the intensity and violence of conflict tend to vary together. And this is again the case where there is infrequent conflict between a subordinate group that occupies a position of reward deprivation and social integration, and a dominant group. The substance of Propositions 11 through 26 are summarized in Table 11.

In summary, the foregoing discussion has centered upon a large

TABLE 11. Groups, Structures, and Social Conflicts: Part 2

Group goals and interaction	Vertical and horizontal social structures— subordinate group position	Conflict frequency	Conflict intensity	Conflict violence	Conflict initiation
	(result in)	(accompanied by)			
Mutual recognition of group competition and differences, but also of complementary social goals and interests	→ Reward parity with social integration	+	−	−	Either group
Mutual recognition of subordinate group enforced segregation and cultural distinctiveness	→ Reward parity with social segregation	−	+	+	Dominant group
Either dominant-group-enforced integration or emergence of subordinate group contracultural social movements	→ Reward deprivation with social integration	−	+	+	Subordinate group
Dominant-group-enforced segregation and definition of subordinate group as contra-cultural or a competitive threat	→ Reward deprivation with social segregation	−	+	+	Either group
Propositions 11 and 12		Propositions 13, 16, 19, 24	14, 17, 21, 25	15, 18, 22, 26	20, 23

number of theoretical propositions about dominant-subordinate or majority-minority group social conflict. There are certain regularities in the kinds of social conflicts that occur between social groups, and those regularities are best understood in terms of how the goals of those groups have precipitated different structural arrangements and how those structural arrangements in turn are convenient measuring devices for predicting the nature of social conflicts between groups.

What in the final analysis can be said about the social processes that characterize pluralistic societies? What are the central tendencies of group relationships? The answers to these questions can best be summarized by reviewing the major themes of Chapters 3 and 4.

Assimilation and Pluralism Reexamined

Part II of this book constitutes an attempt to do three things: to review the major sociological theories of majority-minority relationships in the United States, to assess the utility of those theories, and to offer an alternative theory.

The earliest attempts by sociologists to understand the nature of majority-minority relationships in the United States relied upon the three theories of assimilation, amalgamation, and cultural pluralism. While each theory depicts a somewhat different pattern of group interaction, each of these theories argues that eventually social order and group consensus will be achieved. Whether it be through the absorption of minority groups into the dominant group (assimilation), a mutual blending of dominant and subordinate groups (amalgamation), or a peaceful coexistence between groups (cultural pluralism), the theme of social consensus provides the overriding motif in all three theories.

While interest in the study of minority groups increased greatly after World War II, it was not until the early 1960s that new theoretical insights were provided. The Glazer-Moynihan hypothesis (1963) contributed a new understanding of how both assimilation and pluralism prevailed for the larger religious, ethnic, and racial minority groups. Drawing heavily upon the experience of the European immigrant groups, Glazer and Moynihan argued that minority groups assimilate by attaining new Americanized meanings of their distinctiveness. Moreover, instead of predicting an eventual static outcome of group relationships, Glazer and Moynihan recognized that group conflict was an essential technique through which groups would find their place in the social system. Even though *Beyond the Melting Pot* predicted intergroup conflicts, it retained a consensus framework. For the authors of this comparative study maintained that all minority groups enter the same ordered social process. The only real difference between different minority groups was the rate at which they would enter and progress in that process.

A second study of theoretical importance that emerged in the early 1960s was Milton Gordon's *Assimilation in American Life* (1964). As the title indicates, Gordon's study was based upon the assumption that social order and consensus between groups is the paramount problem that must be understood. While Gordon provides some useful concepts for illustrating the diverse kinds of assimilation processes that may occur between groups, his theory retains a strictly linear view of majority-minority relationships and a monolithic understanding of the goals of minority groups. Unlike Glazer and Moynihan, who at least predict social conflict as a probable occurrence between majority and minority, conflict enters Gordon's theory only as an explanation for why the expectable (assimilation) does not occur. As has been shown in the foregoing analysis, all groups do not assimilate culturally, and there are strong reasons for questioning the use of structural assimilation and intermarriage as indications of assimilation in the traditional sense of the word.

In the context of these previous theories, this study has attempted to provide an alternative perspective for understanding majority-minority relationships. On the one hand, it has been argued that the term "minority group" must be understood to include many more groups than just the traditionally studied racial, religious, and ethnic groups. The aged poor, the handicapped, the residents of Appalachia, and any number of religious and social sects are also minority groups according to the definition offered in Chapter 2. Most importantly, it has been shown that different kinds of social groups have different kinds of social goals and objectives and that majority-minority relationships cannot be understood without considering the goals of different groups as well as the different kinds of social structures in which they interact. Specifically, a fourfold model of minority group social location has been offered as a framework for focusing upon these differences.

While it has been argued that both intergroup conflict and intergroup consensus are equally important aspects of all societies, it has also been shown that there are important empirical and theoretical justifications for viewing social conflict, that otherwise-overlooked aspect of group relationships, as the focal point for a theory of majority-minority interaction.

In the final analysis, what may be said of the concepts of assimilation and pluralism? Do they remain useful theoretical constructs or have they become useless intellectual products? Both terms remain useful if sociologists are willing to refrain from predicting the ultimate outcome of group relationships and the larger social process that those relationships constitute. Milton Gordon's identification of the subprocesses of assimilation and group coalitions remains useful as long as it is remembered that not all groups become "American" in the same way. Some groups become less culturally assimilated than others. Different groups will express these choices in terms of very different kinds of structural arrangements. In principle, there is nothing to prevent the eventual disappearance in the future of those racial, religious, and ethnic differences that have been sources of division among America's social groups in the past. While it seems more likely that these kinds of differences will not disappear, they may become less important for the social fabric of a society that revolves around new kinds of differences —differences in social class, occupational status, and social ideology. In other words, it is no more theoretically defensible to rule out the reemergence of old pluralisms than to rule out the emergence of new ones.

Pluralism and assimilation remain useful concepts if they are viewed, not as absolutes, but as reciprocal aspects of group relationships. Like social change and social order, group conflict and group consensus, pluralism and assimilation may be viewed as twin aspects of the social structure. For just as any given instance of social conflict may split two groups farther apart, it may at the very same time drive other groups closer together. Even as groups attempt to assimilate into the social, political, and economic mainstream of a society, they must organize and develop a sense of their group distinctiveness in order to enter the social process.

As Simmel suggests (1908a), those societies that, for lack of a better label have here been called pluralistic, evidence a never-ending "web of group affiliations'' and conflicts. Groups that at one point in time may be allies, may later be antagonists. Every public issue, every new occasion for conflict, stimulates a rearrangement of group relationships. It is indeed rare that any one issue or conflict will completely bisect such a society. In this sense, pluralistic societies evidence a special kind of social order in which the multiple allegiances and conflicts between groups produce a kind of creative tension, a tension that is at once ordered and yet conflict ridden. Lewis Coser has restated this important theme of Simmel's in the following manner:

> Thus, multiple conflicts, although varying in intensity, are likely to crisscross one another and thereby prevent cleavages along one axis. The pluralism of associations in such types of societies leads to a plurality of fronts of conflict. . . . Segmental participation in a multiplicity of conflicts constitutes a balancing mechanism within the structure. In this way, conflicts may be said to sew pluralistic societies together (Coser 1968:234).

In this context, it becomes indeed simplistic to attempt to understand such a society in terms of a single conceptual metaphor. Such a society is a complex phenomenon and there is little reason to expect that social theories that describe the central tendencies of such a society will be simple. The purpose here has been to break into the diverse processes of pluralistic society at one outstanding point—the occurrence of intergroup conflict—and to use that point of entré to provide some basic understandings of some of the ways in which social change and social order, group alliance and group divergence, are brought about. Conflict has been chosen as an organizing concept here both because it has been one of the most overlooked aspects of majority-minority relationships in previous theories and because it appears to be a central phenomenon in this kind of society. To this extent, the theoretical propositions offered here are intended to explain some, but surely not all, aspects of American society and the group relationships within it.

FOR FURTHER READING

ARON, RAYMOND
    1965 *Main Currents in Sociological Thought*. 2 volumes. New York: Basic Books. (Paperback ed. 1968, Garden City, N.Y.: Doubleday.) This is a

translation of Aron's excellent lectures on Montesquieu, Comte, Marx, Tocqueville, Durkheim, Pareto, and Weber.

BELLAH, ROBERT

1967   "Civil religion in America," in *Daedalus,* Volume 96, pp. 1–21. Bellah's "civil religion" thesis is an attempt to explain the meaning of American religious pluralism.

BURKE, KENNETH

1935   *Permanence and Change*. Palo Alto, Calif.: Hermes Press. (Rev. ed., paperback, 1965. Indianapolis, Ind.: Bobbs-Merrill.) Burke is a literary critic whose writings on society have had a significant impact on the "symbolic interactionist" school of sociological thought. His central focus is upon human motivation as it is variously situated in social settings.

COLES, ROBERT

1970   *Uprooted Children, The Early Life of Migrant Farm Workers*. Pittsburgh: University of Pittsburgh Press. (Paperback ed., 1970. New York: Harper & Row.) Coles describes, from a psychological point of view, the devastating effect of economic deprivation and perpetual mobility upon young children.

COSER, LEWIS

1956   *The Functions of Social Conflict*. Paperback ed., 1965. New York: Free Press. Coser's study in social theory bridges the gap between the conflict and consensus theories of society by arguing that conflict is functional. His study is based upon Simmel's *Soziologie* (1908). While the present study has benefited from Coser's insights, it has not endorsed his functionalist framework.

1957   "Social conflict and social change," in *British Journal of Sociology,* Volume 8, pp. 197–207. This essay continues the investigation of certain aspects of social conflict discussed in Coser's book (1956).

1968   "Sociological aspects of conflict," in *International Encyclopedia of the Social Sciences,* pp. 232–236. Edited by David L. Sills. New York: Crowell Collier Macmillan. A brief summary of the theoretical literature on the subject.

1971   *The Masters of Sociological Thought*. New York: Harcourt Brace Jovanovich. Appropriately subtitled *Ideas in Historical and Social Context,* Coser's work is an analysis of the classical tradition. Much of what is worth knowing about the classical writers may be gleaned from this book and Zeitlin's work (1968).

DAHRENDORF, RALF

1959   *Class and Class Conflict in Industrial Society*. Stanford, Calif.: Stanford University Press. This volume was translated and revised by

Dahrendorf from an earlier German edition (1957). Along with Coser's book (1956), this one marked a return to the study of social conflict in the mid-1950s. While Coser stresses the consensus elements in conflict, Dahrendorf argues for a balanced view of the two phenomena.

DURKHEIM, EMILE

1893 *The Division of Labor in Society*. Translated by George Simpson, 1933. New York: Free Press. Durkheim depicted societies as ordered, consensual systems in this first of his major works.

1895 *The Rules of Sociological Method*. Translated by Sarah A. Solovoy and John H. Muller, and edited by George E. G. Catlin, 1953. New York: Free Press. (This edition was preceded by the earlier University of Chicago edition of 1938.) Durkheim was one of the few classical writers to present a rounded methodological treatise. As in his substantive works, he argues here for the externality and historicity of "social facts."

ERICKSON, KAI T.

1966 *Wayward Puritans*. New York: Wiley. Erickson uses seventeenth century Puritan life as a case study for theory-building in the area of social deviance. His introductory remarks concerning the nature of territory and social space between groups are particularly relevant to the study of minority groups, as well as to the study of deviant groups.

FINK, CLINTON F.

1968 "Some conceptual difficulties in the theory of social conflict," in *Journal of Conflict Resolution,* Volume 12, pp. 413–460. This is an excellent discussion of the problems involved in integrating the different kinds and levels of theories about social conflict.

FRAZIER, E. FRANKLIN

1963 *The Negro Church in America*. Liverpool: The University of Liverpool. (American ed., 1964. Paperback ed., 1966. New York: Schocken Books.) Frazier's book has become the standard work on the subject.

GLAZER, NATHAN, AND DANIEL PATRICK MOYNIHAN

1963 *Beyond the Melting Pot*. Rev. ed., 1970. Cambridge, Mass.: MIT Press. As has already been noted, this was the first major comparative study of American minority groups and is based on the idea that both assimilation and cultural pluralism are occurring.

GOLDSTEIN, SIDNEY

1968 *A Population Survey of the Greater Springfield Jewish Community*. Springfield, Mass.: The Greater Springfield Jewish Community Council. A community study containing intermarriage data on American Jews.

GOLDSTEIN, SIDNEY, AND CALVIN GOLDSCHNEIDER

1968   *Jewish Americans*. Englewood Cliffs, N.J.: Prentice-Hall. This is a three-generational study depicting increasing intermarriage rates. The book is one in a series on major American minority groups.

GORDON, MILTON

1964   *Assimilation in American Life*. New York: Oxford University Press. This work is considered equally as important as the Glazer-Moynihan volume (1963). Gordon argues that assimilation is a multidimensional phenomenon.

GREELEY, ANDREW

1964   "Mixed Marriages in the United States" (mimeograph). Chicago: National Opinion Research Center. Greeley's findings are based upon a national sample.

GROVER, ROBERT

1961   *One Hundred Dollar Misunderstanding*. New York: Ballantine. This novel is the first in a trilogy that delightfully illustrates the problem of reciprocal misunderstanding.

HANDLIN, OSCAR

1951   *The Uprooted*. New York: Grosset & Dunlap. This book, which won a Pulitzer Prize, is a dramatic historical interpretation of the plight of the European immigrants. Handlin has contributed a number of other important works on minority groups.

HERBERG, WILL

1955   *Protestant-Catholic-Jew*. Garden City, N.Y.: Doubleday. Herberg's study of America's three-religion pluralism has become a classic on the subject.

HOMANS, GEORGE C.

1961   *Social Behavior: Its Elementary Forms*. New York: Harcourt Brace Jovanovich. Homans is probably the best-known representative of exchange theory in sociology. His basic assumption is that most, if not all, social interaction revolves around the exchange of services and rewards between individuals.

HORTON, JOHN

1966   "Order and conflict theories of social problems as competing ideologies," in *American Journal of Sociology*, Volume 71, pp. 701–713. Horton shows the way in which different kinds of theories contain biases toward the conflict and consensus views of society. Moreover, he warns that when applied to the realm of social problems, these two forms of theory may have serious ideological implications (i.e. the argument that segregation is functional because it maintains order).

ICHHEISER, GUSTAV

1970   *Appearances and Realities: Misunderstanding in Human Relations.*
San Francisco: Jossey-Bass Publishers. Ichheiser has remained an
obscure and little-known figure in American sociology. In this posthumously published work, he writes in a vien clearly similar to the
phenomenological approach of Alfred Schutz. Yet while Schutz
emphasized the way in which a common meaning structure sustains
the social world, Ichheiser examines the opposite side of the coin,
the role of reciprocal misunderstanding. In spite of the sometimes-
naive psychologism of his perspective, Ichheiser's work is very
stimulating.

LUAE, JAMES HOWARD

1965   "Direct Action and Desegregation: Toward a Theory of the Rationalization of Protest" (unpublished dissertation, Harvard University).
Laue's work contains the quote cited in Matusow (1969).

LAZERWITZ, BERNARD

1971   "Intermarriage and conversion: A guide for future research," in *The
Jewish Journal of Sociology,* Volume 13, pp. 41–63. Lazerwitz presents a concise summary of the previous studies in this field for
the purpose of examining some new data. His emphasis is upon religious identity within Judaism.

LORENZ, KONRAD

1966   *On Aggression.* New York: Harcourt Brace Jovanovich. (Paperback
ed., 1966. New York: Bantam.) This interesting volume, which first
appeared in German (1963), examines many aspects of the behavior
of lower animals that may be equally evident in human behavior.

MARX, KARL, AND FREDERICK ENGELS

1845–1846 *The German Ideology.* Translated by C. J. Arthur, 1970. New
York: International Publishers. This is the most recent and complete
edition of these early writings in which Marx examined some basic
questions about the nature of social reality.

1848   *The Communist Manifesto.* There are many American editions. This
well-known political treatise begins with the authors' claim that all
history is the history of conflict and group struggles.

MATUSOW, ALLEN J.

1969   "From civil rights to Black Power: The case of SNCC 1960–1966,"
in *Twentieth Century America: Recent Interpretations,* pp. 531–536.
Edited by Barton J. Bernstein and Alan J. Matusow. New York:
Harcourt Brace Jovanovich. Matusow's case study contains the quote
cited from Laue (1965). Matusow's essay is also reprinted in John

Bracey, August Meier, and Elliott Rudwick (eds.), *Conflict and Competition: Studies in the Recent Black Protest Movement* (Belmont, Calif.: Wadsworth Publishing Co., 1971).

MERTON, ROBERT

1938   "Social structure and anomie," in *American Sociological Review*, Volume 3, pp. 677–682. Merton's essay focuses upon the probable results when either social goals or the means to those goals, or both, are not available to individuals. This essay is reprinted in Merton (1949/1957).

1949   *Social Theory and Social Structure*. Rev. ed., 1957. New York: Free Press. Merton is one of the best-known representatives of the functionalist position in American sociology. This collection of his essays contains his discussion of manifest and latent functions. This essay also appears in a more recent paperback edition of his essays entitled *On Theoretical Sociology* (New York: Macmillan, 1967).

MILLS, C. WRIGHT (ED.)

1960   *Images of Man*. New York: Braziller. A collection of writings by sociology's classic figures. Mills, of course, is well known for his plea for a more holistic sociological approach, focusing upon the "main drift" of societies. This, he felt, was the major contribution of the classic European theorists.

MYRDAL, GUNNAR, ET AL.

1944   *An American Dilemma*. New York: Harper & Row. This was the first major study of the effects of racism and discrimination in the United States. A shorter presentation of the findings was later published by Myrdal's co-worker, the late Arnold Rose, as *The Negro in America* (Boston: Beacon, 1959).

NISBET, ROBERT

1966   *The Sociological Tradition*. New York: Basic Books. Unlike several other treatments of the classic writers that offer capsule views of each author's works, Nisbet's book is organized around five "unit ideas" that connect the various classical theorists.

O'DEA, THOMAS

1957   *The Mormons*. Chicago: University of Chicago Press. This is a sociohistorical analysis of the topic.

PARK, ROBERT, AND E. W. BURGESS

1921   *Introduction to the Science of Sociology*. Rev. ed., 1924. Chicago: University of Chicago Press. This is an early text by two prominent figures in the Chicago school tradition in American sociology. Park and Burgess' distinction between conflict and competition has been widely employed.

PARSONS, TALCOTT

1937 *The Structure of Social Action*. New York: McGraw-Hill. (Paperback ed., 1968. 2 volumes. New York: Free Press.) Although the functionalist approach in social theory, as well as consensus theory, has diminished in popularity in sociology today, this volume had a tremendous impact upon American sociology by showing how the classical writers could be interpreted in such a framework. It has become part of the standard sociological literature.

1951 *The Social System*. New York: Free Press. This volume is Parsons' theoretical characterization of societies as functionally integrated systems. It is the mature, though difficult to read, exposition of the structural-functional approach to which Parsons' earlier work (1937) pointed.

SALISBURY, W. SEWARD

1969 "Religious identification: Mixed marriages and conversion," in *Journal for the Scientific Study of Religion*, Volume 8, pp. 125–129. Salisbury's discussion shows a pattern of trade-offs between groups.

SCHERMERHORN, RICHARD

1970 *Comparative Ethnic Relations*. New York: Random House. This text addresses theoretical issues and proposed avenues for comparative research.

SHIBUTANI, TAMATSO, AND KIAN KWAN

1965 *Ethnic Stratification*. New York: Macmillan. This was the first major text on the subject to be built around stratification theory.

SIMMEL, GEORG

1908a "Conflict," in *Conflict and the Web of Group Affiliations*. Translated and edited by Kurt H. Wolff and Reinhard Bendix, 1955. New York: Free Press. Simmel's essay on conflict first appeared as Chapter 4 of his work *Soziologie*.

1908b "The web of group-affiliations," in *Conflict and the Web of Group Affiliations*. Translated and edited by Kurt H. Wolff and Reinhard Bendix, 1955. New York: Free Press. This essay originally appeared as Chapter 6 of Simmel's *Soziologie*.

VAN DEN BERGHE, PIERRE

1967 *Race and Racism*. New York: Wiley. This is a comparative study of racism in four societies. As opposed to focusing upon assimilation, van den Berghe's study is couched in the analysis of pluralism.

WEBER, MAX

1904–1905 *The Protestant Ethic and the Spirit of Capitalism*. Translated by Talcott Parsons, 1958. New York: Scribner. Weber's particular focus is upon the way in which Protestantism provided the ethos for capitalism and an achievement-oriented stratification system in the West.

1917   "The meaning of ethical neutrality," in *The Methodology of the Social Sciences*. Translated and edited by Edward A. Shils and Henry A. Finch, 1949. New York: Free Press. This essay contains Weber's strong statement about the ubiquity of social conflict.

1922   "Class, status, party," in *From Max Weber*. Translated and edited by Hans Gerth and C. Wright Mills, 1946. New York: Oxford University Press. This important essay first appeared posthumously in the German edition of Weber's opus *Wirtschaft und Gesellschaft*.

WIRTH, LOUIS

1945   "The problem of minority groups," in *The Science of Man in the World of Crisis*. Edited by Ralph Linton. New York: Columbia University Press. Wirth's essay contains his typology of minority groups.

YINGER, J. MILTON

1960   "Contraculture and subculture," in *American Sociological Review*, Volume 25, pp. 625–635. Yinger's stimulating essay attempts to show that there can be important differences between the types of groups in a society that vary from the norms.

ZEITLIN, IRVING M.

1968   *Ideology and the Development of Sociological Theory*. Englewood Cliffs, N.J.: Prentice-Hall. This analysis of the classical thinkers in sociological thought argues that the history of sociology cannot be understood without reference to the philosophical debates in the eighteenth century and to the works of Karl Marx.

PART III
THE CONSEQUENCES
OF INTERGROUP CONFLICTS

CHAPTER 5
Prejudice and Discrimination

An Overview

It was noted in Chapter 1 that sociological problems and social problems do not always coincide.[1] Sociological problems involve the structures, processes, and conditions under which events occur in the social world. The sociologist is generally interested in the patterns of relationship between different social phenomena. On the other hand, social problems entail pain and suffering for individuals and groups or dislocations in society. Prejudice and discrimination represent both social and sociological problems. They are the source of immense human pain and suffering. They have also been the focus of much social scientific research, theorizing, controversy, and puzzlement. Unfortunately, the social sciences do not yet possess any concise recipes for eliminating these damaging and undesirable social patterns. In spite of the fact that scientific knowledge about prejudice and discrimination remains far from complete, the sociological perspective does provide some basic insights about these two phenomena.

The following discussion addresses four related aspects of prejudice and discrimination. First, the problems of defining these two phenomena as well as clarifying the empirical relationships between them must

[1] See the discussion on pp. 4–6.

be examined. Most importantly, it will be shown that prejudice does not necessarily cause nor accompany discrimination. The two phenomena may vary independently of each other. They are conceptually and empirically distinct from one another.

One of the major aims of this chapter is to consider the relationships between prejudice, discrimination, and social conflict. The central argument of the chapter is that prejudice and discrimination are weapons used by groups in social conflict and that prejudice and discrimination may be viewed as measures of social conflict. Just as it was shown in Chapter 4 that intergroup conflicts vary according to the locations of minority groups in the social structure, so it will be shown here that prejudice and discrimination, viewed as weapons employed in conflict, vary according to the same structural conditions. Before illustrating these themes, it is necessary to review some of the major research findings about, and theoretical interpretations of, prejudice and discrimination. One can then assess the degree to which the model employed here is capable of integrating previous research findings and theories.

Finally, while all social phenomena are in a continual process of change, one of the perplexing things about patterns of prejudice and discrimination is that they change slowly. They are the very kinds of social phenomena that, as Durkheim suggested, have "historicity" (1895). They connect rather than change with successive generations. This chapter concludes with an examination of some of the social-psychological mechanisms that allow the maintenance of these patterns. In summary, four issues are addressed: What are the basic properties or elements of prejudice and discrimination, and what are the empirical relationships between them? What are the central avenues of empirical research and theory about these two phenomena? To what extent can the theory of social conflict discussed in Chapter 4 be employed to further our understanding of prejudice and discrimination? Finally, what are some of the social-psychological mechanisms through which these patterns are maintained?

Problems of Definition

Several general limitations of scientific concepts have already been discussed in Chapter 1.[2] It will be recalled that all language is essentially

---

[2]See the discussion on pp. 7–9.

an arbitrary system of symbols. No single word or concept will ever encompass all aspects of the phenomenon to which it refers. Yet the task of defining prejudice and discrimination underscores a definitional complexity that is unique to the social sciences. The lexicon used in everyday conversation to discuss and describe society is the same as that used in social science. Differences between the everyday and sociological meanings of the same words may create confusions, especially for those who are first beginning to view social life from a sociological perspective. For instance, in everyday discourse one may speak of "high society" or "The Society for the Prevention of Cruelty to Animals." Neither of these uses of the word "society" conveys the sociological meaning of the concept "society." Differences between everyday and more technical scientific meanings of words become all the more problematic when such complex and emotionally charged subjects as prejudice and discrimination are being studied. One often hears the claim that a person's conduct was "prejudiced" or that something that someone said was "discriminatory." Yet, as will be seen, neither of these uses of the words "prejudice" and "discrimination" conforms to their sociological meanings.

Before offering specific definitions of these two terms, it is useful to examine their place within the general categories of phenomena that are studied by social scientists. As Glock and Stark have observed, the datum of human experience may be divided into three distinct categories: action, cognition, and emotion (1966/1969:103). One may distinguish between what men do, what men think, and what men feel. Further, within the cognitive realm there is a difference between what men know and what men believe. One knows that a bus will stop at a given street corner at a specific time each day, but one believes that there is a God or that there is an afterlife. Beliefs may be viewed as more emotional in quality than the "known facts" of everyday life. The term "belief" often implies an element of commitment to something that may be beyond empirical demonstration or proof. Regrettably, social scientists frequently employ terms like "opinions," "attitudes," "action-orientations" and "predispositions to action" without specifying to which category of phenomena these concepts refer. For the following discussion, it is important to note that prejudice is not an act. Prejudice is cognitive. Discrimination is an act. Both of these phenomena involve emotion, especially when they are consciously and intentionally directed toward other persons or groups of persons. But prejudice is more than just an emotion or feeling. The statement "That's the way I feel about them" can almost always be shown to involve beliefs and ideas about "them." These basic considerations are summarized in Figure 5.

Prejudice may be defined as any set of ideas and beliefs that negatively prejudge groups or individuals on the basis of real or alleged group traits or characteristics. There are four major components of this definition. First, as has already been noted, prejudice is cognition, not action. Second, prejudice is a group-based or collective phenomenon and, therefore, a social phenomenon. There are, of course, important psychological aspects of prejudice, and any comprehensive study of prejudice must recognize psychological, psychoanalytic, and social-psychological aspects of the subject. But it would be erroneous to view prejudice as primarily a manifestation of certain mental disorders, types of personalities, or inner psychic states of mind. There have, of course, been numerous attempts to apply a personality-types approach to the study of prejudice and discrimination. The most well-known research of this kind is T. W. Adorno et al.'s *The Authoritarian Personality* (1950). While this study depicts six different types of "prejudiced personalities," it has been criticized on a variety of both substantive and methodological grounds (Christie and Jahoda 1954). As Simpson and Yinger observe (1953/1965:62–79) more recent research has stressed the importance of social and situational, rather than personality, factors in prejudice and discrimination.

Prejudice occurs in a social context and consists of ideas, not about individuals, but about groups. As Gordon Allport observes in his study *The Nature of Prejudice,* a certain degree of "ethnocentrism"

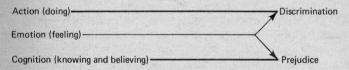

FIGURE 5. Prejudice and discrimination viewed in terms of action, emotion, and cognition.

(preference for one's own group) is always involved in prejudice. "An in-group always implies the existence of an out-group" (Allport 1954:41). In other words, prejudice typically involves the evaluation of one group and its traits (real or alleged) as compared to another. Herbert Blumer stresses this aspect of prejudice by suggesting that prejudice always involves a sense of group position in society. Prejudice typically conveys the notion that one group is *below* the next and that one group *belongs* in a given position in society, while the other does not (Blumer 1958). Moreover, there is general agreement among social scientists that prejudice, like all culture, is learned, taught, and transmitted through the process of socialization into one's group and society. Group stereotypes are the socially approved images that the members of one group have of the next.

The importance of understanding prejudice as a group-based or collective phenomenon may be stressed here by viewing prejudice in the framework of the sociology of knowledge. The sociology of knowledge is that branch of sociology that studies the relationships between human thought and social structures. As Peter Berger and Thomas Luckmann suggest, the term *knowledge* refers not just to specialized bodies of information like philosophy, medicine, electronics, or sociology but to all that is *known* in societies.

> The need for a "sociology of knowledge" is thus already given with the observable differences between societies in terms of what is taken for granted as "knowledge" in them. . . [the] "sociology of knowledge" will have to deal not only with the empirical variety of "knowledge" in human societies, but also with the process by which *any* body of "knowledge" comes to be socially established *as* reality[3] (1966/1967:3).

In this framework, group stereotypes and prejudice may be viewed as part of the taken-for-granted, socially approved stock of knowledge that the individual acquires through the process of socialization. This does not mean that socialization causes prejudice. But socialization is an important factor in sustaining and transmitting prejudice from one generation to the next. For through socialization, one acquires

[3]Italics in original.

not only such social knowledge as what clothing to wear, how to speak the language, where to get a bus, and how to find a job but also knowledge of the structures of society as well as the ''place'' of different groups within those structures. Prejudice is part of that larger picture of social reality that the group imparts to individuals. Prejudice may be viewed as socially transmitted knowledge about the place of different groups in the social structure, as well as about the alleged stereotypical traits of different groups.

The collective dimension of prejudice and discrimination is, of course, one of the most frustrating aspects of these phenomena for groups and individuals against whom they are directed. The individual is socially defined and treated, not on the basis of his or her individual qualities, but on the basis of his or her membership in a social group. Prejudice is a social phenomenon consisting of ideas about groups, not individuals. It is learned and taught.

This brings to light the third component of prejudice, that it is prejudgment. Prejudice is judgmental because it consists of evaluations of one group by another, beliefs held by the members of one group about the members of another group. It may be viewed as prejudgment because of the fact just noted, that individual qualities are disregarded in favor of defining the individual through a prior social category: membership in a group. The statements ''He's just like the rest of them,'' or ''What do you expect from one of them?'' illustrate the phenomenon referred to here. While surely prejudice is shaped by social interaction, it is also shaped by something prior to interaction, the identification of an individual as a member of a group. It is this overriding criterion of judgment or assessment that makes prejudice a prejudgmental phenomenon. The individual is judged prior to his social performance on the basis of his group membership.

Finally, while prejudice is a negative view of another group, this does not mean that all of the specific unit ideas involved in stereotypes and prejudice are of an entirely negative quality. Georg Simmel provides an illustration of this point in his distinction between jealousy, envy, and begrudging. According to Simmel, jealousy always involves the notion of legitimacy. One who is jealous of the possessions or social position of another group or person always believes that he or his group is more worthy, has a right to, or is legitimately entitled to that which the other possesses. Envy entails a desire for an object or social position without a claim to legitimacy. Finally, Simmel contends that a grudge arises simply because the other party possesses something. A grudge rarely involves a claim to legitimacy and may not even involve an actual desire for the object (Simmel 1908a/1955:50–55). Of these three types of antagonistic views, jealousy and envy are particularly relevant to the concept of prejudice and to the role of positive, rather than negative, group stereotypes involved in prejudice. An anti-Semite may be jealous or envious of the alleged wealth of Jews. In either case, his prejudice or negative view of Jews is based upon the perception of a positive and desirable alleged group trait, wealth or the ability to attain wealth.

In this context, all stereotypes and prejudices may be viewed as sets of ideas consisting of both a descriptive and an evaluative component. The descriptive component may be either negative (they're stupid, lazy, dirty) or positive (they're rich, successful, have beautiful women). The evaluative component is always negative. In most instances, the descriptive and evaluative components of group stereotypes stand in a cause-and-effect relationship. For instance, many Jews are successful and wealthy (a positive, descriptive, alleged trait), which is because they are crafty and cheat a lot (an evaluative and causal alleged trait). Many blacks are poor (a negative, descriptive, alleged trait), which is because they are stupid and not equal to other people (an evaluative and causal alleged trait). Examples of such stereotypes could be listed endlessly. The important point for the moment is that not all of the unit ideas in prejudice and group stereotypes are of a purely negative quality. The out-group may possess a highly desirable trait that is the object of jealousy or envy. But there is also always some negative evaluation or disvaluation of the out-group.

In summary, prejudice involves four central characteristics. It is cognitive, collective or group-based, prejudgmental, and always consists of a negative evaluation of an out-group even if positive and desirable group traits are involved.

Discrimination may be defined as any act of differential treatment toward a group or an individual perceived as a member of a group. Moreover, the intent and/or effect of differential treatment is to create a disadvantage of some sort. While the phrase "differential treatment'' may be somewhat useful for conceptualizing the idea of discrimination, it also is fraught with difficulties. Just as all social relationships exhibit varying degrees of inequality between social actors, so all social relationships involve varying degrees of differential or preferential treatment of one actor by the other. As Alfred Schutz has observed, most, if not all, social interaction is possible because of ''typified'' perception (1953). One knows the appropriate or required roles and social responses in a situation by locating other actors cognitively in a socially stratified map of typical human, social characteristics. One acts differently toward other people on the basis of their age, race, sex, social class, occupation, and any number of other typified attributes. The importance of these taken-for-granted typifications becomes obvious when one commits a social *faux pas* because of faulty perception or because of incomplete knowledge about another person's social attributes. For instance, an individual may make an indiscreet remark about Catholics only to find later that the person who was standing next to him is Catholic. In other words, all social actors are in a continual process of perceptually distinguishing the typical social categories into which other social actors may be placed and designing strategies of action on this basis. All social action entails varying degrees of preferential and differential treatment based upon the perception of typifications. In this framework, the term ''differential treatment'' becomes a rather weak distinction for defining discrimination. It must be concluded that what is meant by ''discrimination'' is an extremely high degree of differential treatment.

Even if it is granted that the definition offered here is at least meaningfully adequate, if not conceptually precise, the interesting thing is that sociologists rarely, if ever, actually study or measure discrimination or differential treatment. As Hubert M. Blalock observes, while these two terms are conceptually useful, sociologists actually study either segregation or various forms of inequality (1967/1970:15–21). Thus, while the concept of discrimination holds a central place in the literature on minority groups, it is never really operationalized in empirical research.

In spite of these basic problems of definition, there are several additional aspects of discrimination that may be described with greater precision. Discrimination is an act. Unlike prejudice, it is not something that people think but something they do. Discrimination is not the acting-out of prejudice. While discrimination does require that the social actor perceive or recognize another individual as a member of a specific group, this does not mean that the discriminator justifies or explains his discrimination on the basis of prejudices about members of that group. This central point may best be explained by turning to Robert Merton's discussion of the four possible relationships between prejudice and discrimination. For, as Merton has shown, it is just as possible that a prejudiced individual will not discriminate as it is that a nonprejudiced individual will discriminate (1949).

Prejudice and Discrimination: Four Relationships

Robert Merton (1949) has shown that there are four alternative relationships between prejudice and discrimination. Viewed as unit occurrences on the part of individuals, Merton labels the four cases: the prejudiced discriminator, the prejudiced nondiscriminator, the nonprejudiced discriminator, and the nonprejudiced nondiscriminator. As Merton points out, there is a tendency in American society to view these four alternative occurrences in terms of personality types, usually labeled: the bigot, the timid bigot, the fair-weather liberal, and the all-weather liberal. These two alternative ways of viewing prejudice and discrimination, as relationships between two variables and as man-

TABLE 12. Prejudice and Discrimination Alternatively Viewed as Personality Types and as Social Variables

Four relationships between two social variables		Four personality types
Prejudice	*Discrimination*	
1. +	+	Bigot
2. +	−	Timid bigot
3. −	+	Fair-weather liberal
4. −	−	All-weather liberal

Source: Adapted from Robert Merton, "Discrimination and the American Creed," in Robert MacIver (ed.), *Discrimination and National Welfare* (New York: Harper & Row, 1949), p. 103. Copyright 1949 by the Institute for Social and Religious Studies. Used with permission of the author and publisher.

ifestations of personality types, are depicted in Table 12. As will be seen, these personality types or, as Merton calls them, "folk-labels," are misleading; for it is not always the case that a prejudiced individual practices discrimination or that a nonprejudiced person does not discriminate. Moreover, whether a single given individual fits one type or the other may change over time. The critical variables that explain such changes are social-situational.

The first situation to be considered is that in which an individual expresses prejudice (or in some way can be shown to be prejudiced) and in which he discriminates against a member of some other group. In terms of popularized folk-labels, such a person is usually referred to as a bigot. Regrettably, examples of this situation are all too easy to find. A white restaurant owner in the Deep South may refuse to serve a black customer on the explicit grounds that there are group characteristics of blacks that justify not extending service to a member of this group. There are few groups in American society that have not been the object of socially sanctioned discrimination. Signs reading "no Irish or dogs allowed" were not uncommon in the United States in the nineteenth century. Social norms in this country have also sanctioned similar treatment of Italians, Jews, Spanish-speaking Americans, and American Indians—even in the twentieth century. Yet it remains questionable whether the concept of the bigoted personality is a meaningful scientific ideal type or a quasi-scientific stereotype.

Due to biographical factors, which for the moment are unimportant, the bigot in the example above may sell his restaurant in the Deep South and open a new business in New York City. He now may become a timid bigot, or a prejudiced nondiscriminator. Perhaps he finds, unexpectedly, that his new restaurant in midtown Manhattan is frequented by a large number of black customers. Suddenly, discrimination is no longer consistent with his self-interest. It may ruin his business. Discrimination in this situation may be explicitly forbidden by the larger community and may, in fact, be punishable by law. A changed social environment can drastically affect the actions of even the most strongly prejudiced individual. Yet situational factors, which in this example induce a prejudiced individual not to discriminate, may also induce a nonprejudiced individual to discriminate.

This is the situation of the so-called fair-weather liberal. While he is not prejudiced, he does not practice what he preaches. The personnel manager of an exclusive store may not be prejudiced against either Jews or Catholics. But he may refuse to hire members of either group because both the employees and customers of his store have traditionally been white Anglo-Saxon Protestants. In this instance, a discrepancy between action and cognition is created by situational factors, the influence of so-called reference groups to which the individual turns for social approval or from which he fears some form of social punishment. The owner of a neighborhood tavern may not be prejudiced against homosexuals, but he may refuse to serve them on the rationale that he will lose his other, regular customers. A black real estate salesman may consistently avoid showing or selling to black customers homes in particular parts of town. His action is based upon the knowledge or presumption that if he does cross the color line, other, predominantly white, real estate salesmen will stop sending him customers and listings of homes for sale. While the black salesman is not prejudiced against his own people, he may discriminate against them.

The final case in Merton's typology is the all-weather liberal, or nonprejudiced nondiscriminator. This fourth case raises once again the problem of defining discrimination and prejudice and illustrates the point that both of these phenomena are matters of degree. Both sociological theory and social experience suggest that no individual is completely free from prejudice. All social perception involves typification and ranking. As was previously noted, ethnocentrism, the notion that one's own group is best or at least preferable, always involves some comparative knowledge and evaluation of other groups. This same point is conveyed in George Herbert Mead's theory of the social self. Mead contends that the concept of the self and the concept of the social structure arrive at the same moment for the young child. For it is only by recognizing the social structure and "others" that the young child, by comparison, knows that he has a distinct social indentity both as an individual and, later in life, as a member of some social group (Strauss 1934). There are numerous theoretical paths that lead to the conclusion that the nonprejudiced nondiscriminator is a meaningful concept or ideal type only in comparison to the other three possible cases. The nonprejudiced nondiscriminator is, at best, an individual who either exhibits a relatively low degree of prejudice toward other groups or who consciously is able to overcome his own minimal prejudices.

The four kinds of situations discussed here demonstrate that prejudice and discrimination, rather than being viewed as functions of personality types, are best understood in terms of social-situational variables. As was noted earlier, prejudice may be viewed as part of the socially approved knowledge transmitted to the individual through socialization. Whether or not an individual is prejudiced and the degree to which he is prejudiced depend upon the social values and sentiments taught to him through the process of socialization into his group. Prejudice that the young child acquires may, of course, be modified later in life through exposure to and participation in new groups. But whether the prejudiced individual actually discriminates depends again upon the norms and values of the social groups to which the individual turns for social approval or from which he fears some form of social punishment. Discrepancies between individuals' conduct and cognition, between what people do and what they think or believe, are best understood in terms of reference group theory. As Shibutani observes:

> Deliberately, intuitively, or unconsciously each person performs for some kind of audience; in the drama of life, as in the theater, conduct is oriented toward certain people whose judgment is deemed important (Shibutani 1962, in Rose 1962:129).

From the standpoint of reference group theory, the individual is likely to act in a manner consistent with the perceived values of the groups to which he plays out his social roles. In this way, social groups serve as agents of social control over the acts of individuals and can often induce an individual to act in a manner inconsistent with his own beliefs. Thus, while the prejudiced nondiscriminator and the nonprejudiced discriminator both exhibit somewhat perplexing discrepancies between their values and their actions, these two cases may be understood through the insights of reference group theory. More importantly, reference group theory clearly shows that prejudice and discrimination may vary independently of each other. Prejudice does not automatically produce discrimination. The two phenomena are conceptually and empirically different.

To the extent that reference group theory requires some general understanding of the human personality, it may be stipulated that most people most of the time act in a manner consistent with their ''self-esteem''

(Becker 1962). Yet what the individual views as right from the perspective of his self-esteem may not be the same as what he knows to be right in terms of his self-interest or his moral principles. The non-prejudiced individual may refrain from discriminating even though he knows that certain groups are likely to retaliate against him. Here, self-esteem is not consistent with immediate self-interest. Moreover, in terms of reference group theory, such an individual is playing to an audience other than the one that is capable of providing immediate punishment for his actions. Campbell and Pettigrew (1959) studied just such a situation in Little Rock, Arkansas in the late 1950s. They found that some clergymen expressed liberal views on racial integration even though they knew that this kind of conduct was likely to place them in a tenuous position with the prosegregationist members of their churches. While such clergymen were aware of the ability of their congregations to punish them for their actions (they could lose their jobs), these clergymen were obviously playing to some reference group other than their congregations. Thus, the reference group through which the individual obtains his self-esteem may not always be the same group that is capable of providing immediate reward or punishment. Yet, as Shibutani observes (1962), situations in which there are dramatic overt conflicts between the individual and his immediate reference groups are not terribly frequent or likely.

It is more often the case that the individual conforms to the norms of the immediate group. Both the prejudiced nondiscriminator and the nonprejudiced discriminator act in a manner that contradicts their moral principles. Both conform to the norms of the immediate reference group and rationalize their actions in terms of self-esteem. The nonprejudiced discriminator may argue that discrimination is justified because it protects his obligations to his family as a breadwinner. By not making himself vulnerable to economic retaliation and by conforming to group norms that he knows are morally wrong, he has acted "responsibly." The prejudiced nondiscriminator may offer exactly the same kind of explanation for not discriminating. Whether one labels such individuals as hypocrites is not a question for social science but for social philosophy. Social science can at best provide some understanding of the process through which individuals' actions may contradict their beliefs. The decision of the individual to discriminate or to refrain from discrimination is strongly influenced by the norms of his reference groups as well as his own ability to rationalize discrepancies as being consistent with his self-esteem, if not his moral principles or self-interest.

In summary, prejudice and discrimination are social phenomena. Prejudice refers to any set of ideas that negatively prejudge individuals or groups on the basis of real or alleged group characteristics. Even where positive or desirable group traits are involved, the evaluative aspect of prejudice is always negative. Discrimination refers to acts of differential treatment toward groups or individuals perceived as members of groups. Contrary to the popular labeling of individuals as personality types (bigots, timid bigots, etc.), there is no conclusive research that demonstrates that the appearance of prejudice or discrimination is a function of personality types. Rather, the closely related perspectives of the sociology of knowledge and reference group theory point to the social conditioning of both prejudice and discrimination. Prejudice may be viewed as part of the socially approved and transmitted stock of knowledge that individuals acquire through socialization. Prejudice consists of the images and evaluations that one group has of the next. Discrimination does not necessarily follow from prejudice. Rather, discrimination is a group norm for action. The individual, regardless of his prejudices, may or may not discriminate, depending upon how highly he values the approval of the group or fears the punishment of the group. In most instances, reference groups exert a considerable influence over the individual's conduct, even if the norms of the group conflict with the values of the individual. In such cases, individuals are capable of rationalizing their conduct by finding some element of consistency between their self-esteem and the prescriptions of the group. Having considered these basic conceptual issues, the diversity of research findings and theoretical trends in the field may now be examined.

Theory and Research: Examining Previous Trends

Prejudice and discrimination have been the focus of a highly diverse assortment of theoretical perspectives and research techniques. In spite of the complex mixture of research approaches and findings, as well as the sometimes contradictory theoretical avenues of analysis, there have been several major trends of theory and research to which one may point. As was noted earlier, one of the major purposes of this chapter is to consider the utility of the social conflict theory offered in Chapter 4 for understanding prejudice and discrimination. Before this can be done, it is first necessary to consider previous theory and research. It will then be possible to assess the degree to which social conflict theory is capable of incorporating previous research findings as well as the way in which conflict theory compares with other theoretical perspectives on the subject.

Unfortunately, there are a number of rather simplistic general theories of prejudice and discrimination that, in spite of the fact that they no longer have much credibility in the scientific community, remain popular among the lay public. Both psychology and sociology have contributed equally to this kind of theorizing. A few of the more popular theories of this type may be briefly examined. Turning first to sociology, it is frequently asserted that dislike of the unlike, group ethnocentrism, and socialization processes are major causes of prejudice and discrimination. Each of these three theories contains an ounce of truth, but all of them are too simplistic to be meaningful on their own grounds. For instance, it was argued earlier that from the standpoint of the sociology of knowledge, prejudice may be viewed as collectively held beliefs that are transmitted from one generation to the next through socialization. But before those beliefs and stereotypes may be transmitted, they must first be invented or produced. Socialization is an important mechanism through which prejudice is transmitted, but socialization does not explain how or why prejudice emerges in the first place. In other words, socialization *maintains* but does not *cause* prejudice.

In this context, it is often argued that group ethnocentrism or dislike of the unlike are the motor forces for those prejudices that are, in turn, transmitted through socialization. It was, in fact, suggested earlier that prejudice does involve a certain element of ethnocentrism. As Blumer maintains, all prejudice involves notions of relative group position in society (1958). Similarly, it may be granted that people often tend to be suspicious, curious about, or even fearful of other people who either act, appear, or express ideas that are strange or different from those of their own group. This, of course, is not always the case. The stranger may become an honored guest in the community,

a novelty that is highly valued and prized (Simmel 1908b, Schutz 1944).[4]
But if for the moment it is granted that social relations between members
of different groups do tend to exhibit minimal levels of ethnocentrism
and mutual suspicion, this does not explain why one group becomes
the object of extreme prejudice and discrimination while another does
not. For if ethnocentrism and dislike of the unlike are assumed to
be universal phenomena, neither of these factors alone is sufficient
to explain important variations in the relationships between groups.
It may be argued that ethnocentrism is an important contributing factor
to the assignment of minority group status in society. But again, as
was noted in Chapter 2, not all minority groups are the objects of
extreme prejudice and discrimination. These two theories tell part of
the story, but they do not possess the power to either explain or predict
the kinds of differences and variations in group relationships that interest
us here. They are simply much too general.

To consider a parallel illustration of this kind of generality, it was
argued in Chapter 4 that the mutual perception of a threat is an important
precondition for intergroup conflicts. But this proposition did not explain
why conflict is more prevalent in one society than the next; why different
types of conflicts emerge, or why there are significant variations in
the relative frequency, intensity, and violence of different intergroup
conflicts. To have carried the theory of social conflict no farther than
this basic proposition would have been of very little use. The theory
would not have possessed the power to explain or predict the kinds
of variations that were of interest in Chapter 4. It is not that the theory
would have been wrong, but it would have lacked sufficient specificity
to distinguish one conflict situation from the next. This is precisely
the problem with the theories of ethnocentrism and dislike of the unlike.
They may to some degree be accurate, but not to the degree that important
observed differences may be explained. Regrettably, there is always
the danger that these kinds of extremely simplistic generalizations will
obscure the need for more detailed empirical investigations and more
complex, though more powerful, theorizing.

The kinds of sociological generalizations just discussed have their
parallel in psychological theory as well. One of the most frequently

---

[4]A discussion of this point follows on pp. 217–219.

encountered psychological theories of prejudice and discrimination maintains that these phenomena result from displaced aggression. In brief, the theory stipulates that individuals are always building up reserves of psychic frustration that must be released in some way for the individual to remain in a state of mental or psychic health. These frustrations are released in the form of interpersonal aggressions that are typically displaced away from the object that caused the frustration and toward minority group members (Simpson and Yinger 1953/1965:49–62). Even if one accepts some of the basic components of the theory— for instance, it seems quite plausible that individuals do experience a great deal of frustration in highly industrialized, bureaucratized, complex societies—the theory is still sorely lacking in specificity. What are the specific psychological or sociocultural factors that determine if and when frustration will be released as aggression? Under what conditions is aggression self-directed as opposed to other-directed or displaced? Even if aggression is other-directed, under what conditions are aggressions directed toward one's friends and associates as opposed to strangers or minority group members? None of these conditions and variations is specified in the theory of frustration-aggression or aggression-displacement. Moreover, as Simmel suggests (1908a), more intimate social relationships seem to be characterized by, and are more capable of tolerating, frequent acts of aggression. In simple terms, after a bad day at the office or after a frustrating encounter with some run-of-the-mill bureaucrat, one is much more likely to provoke an argument with one's spouse than to take a swing at the first minority group member encountered on the way home. This is not to suggest that such fundamental psychological phenomena as frustration and aggression are not involved in prejudice and discrimination. But it seems more likely that these are consequential, rather than causal, factors in prejudice and discrimination. In either case, the psychological theory of frustration-aggression, like the sociological theories of dislike of the unlike and ethnocentrism, does not offer the kind of specificity and explanatory power to distinguish one situation from the next.

Having considered some of the more popular, though inadequate, theories of prejudice and discrimination, the realm of empirical research and interpretations of the research are examined next. Previous research may be divided into two general categories. The first and more static approach has been the attempt to identify the specific social traits or correlates of those individuals who either are prejudiced or who discriminate. The more prominent variables that have been studied in this framework are age, education, socioeconomic status, religion, and place of residence. The second and more dynamic approach has been the study of contextual and situational variables that appear to condition prejudice and discrimination. While the kinds of variables studied in this framework have also been varied, some of the more important ones are group sizes and proximities, social mobility, the degree of social visibility of minority groups, economic competition, and social change. Since most researchers readily admit that no single variable may be viewed as a completely independent cause or conditioning agent of either prejudice or discrimination, it is most useful to examine both static and dynamic variables in relationship to one another.

Bruno Bettelheim and Morris Janowitz's work *Social Change and Prejudice* (1964) contains one of the most concise summaries of research findings about the social correlates of prejudice. The book, which contains the full text of their earlier study *The Dynamics of Prejudice* (1950), attempts to assess the results of that study in the light of subsequent research. The authors describe the relationships between age, education, socioeconomic status, and prejudice in the following manner:

> First, younger persons are likely to be less prejudiced than older persons; second, better educated persons are less likely to be prejudiced than less well-educated persons; and third, higher socioeconomic status is likely to be associated with less prejudice than is lower status (1964:15).

Yet, as Bettelheim and Janowitz observe, while these are accurate generalizations, a more detailed analysis of the relationships between age, education, socioeconomic status, and prejudice reveals a number of subtle complexities. These generalizations are not quite as simple or useful as they might appear at first glance. It is frequently argued that younger persons are less prejudiced because they are less wedded to older social values and norms that are in a continual process of change. But Bettelheim and Janowitz observe that much of the research upon which this claim is based was conducted after World War II and therefore contains a built-in bias. Due to the educational explosion that followed the war, younger people in the United States are, by definition, much better educated than their elders. Accordingly, it is questionable whether these studies have really isolated the social variable, age (1964:17).

In spite of the difficulty in isolating the variables age and education, Charles H. Stember has provided some important, though complex, research findings about the relationship between education and people's views toward blacks and Jews. He found that highly educated persons are less likely to hold stereotypes about these two groups, less likely to endorse discriminatory social policies, and less likely to reject casual social relationships with minority group members. Yet he also observed that the better educated, when they are found to possess stereotypes, evidence more highly charged and derogatory views than less educated persons. Further, the better educated are more likely to endorse informal types of discrimination and reject intimate social relationships with minority group members (Stember 1961:168ff.). Stember's findings seem to imply that better educated persons are more prone to pay lip service to an egalitarian ideology and may also be less inclined to discriminate in all but the most intimate social relationships. But education does not eliminate prejudice nor does it always inhibit discrimination. Bettelheim and Janowitz warn that education should not be viewed as a panacea for reducing prejudice in society. Numerous studies have shown that the "liberalizing" effects of education decrease as socioeconomic status increases (1964:20). In other words, education is less likely to soften or reduce the prejudicial views of people in the higher socioeconomic strata.

Even the relationship between socioeconomic status and education is not a simple one. Bettelheim and Janowitz's analysis of data from the 1957 Detroit Area Study reveals that the upper-middle stratum (professional and managerial people) are less prejudiced than the lower-middle stratum (clerical and sales people). Yet the upper-lower stratum (craftsmen and foremen) evidence less prejudice than the lower-middle stratum. In other words, the upper-middle and upper-lower strata greatly resemble each other in the amount or degree of prejudice expressed. People in the lower-lower stratum are the most prejudiced and typically express the most "extremist" social views (1964:22). The generalization noted earlier, that people in the upper socioeconomic strata are less likely to be prejudiced than people in the lower socioeconomic strata, is indeed accurate. But this generalization hides some important complexities. The fact that the upper-middle and upper-lower strata resemble each other and that these two strata evidence less prejudice than the lower-middle stratum means that the relationship between prejudice and socioeconomic position is not linear. The generalization is accurate only if one looks at the extremes. Between the two extremes, one finds rather complex nonlinear relationships.

Most attempts to explain these patterns rely upon reference group theory. As was noted earlier, one thrust of reference group theory has been to understand the ideas and actions of individuals in terms of the groups or audiences to which individuals play out their social roles. Thus, it was shown that the individual may acquire prejudice through socialization into the group and that the group can be an important source of social control in coercing the individual to discriminate even if the individual is not prejudiced. A second theme of reference group theory stresses the way in which the relative positions of groups in the social structure condition group members' views of each other and their views of the world generally. For instance, it may be argued that individuals in the lower-lower stratum are the most prejudiced because, regardless of what other social group to which they compare themselves, they always perceive their own deprivation and disadvantage. In terms of our analysis in Chapter 4, members of such groups always experience total deprivation, not only in terms of social resources, but especially in terms of social-psychological sustenance. It is frequently the case that members of other groups possess the same kinds of social rewards that they desire and to which they feel they have some legitimate claim.

It must again be stressed that there are always problems in viewing one single social variable (in this case, socioeconomic status) as the sole explanation for prejudice or discrimination. For, while reference group theory does provide a plausible case for viewing socioeconomic position as a key factor in prejudice, education must also be viewed as a related variable in the case just discussed. As one moves down the social stratification scale, the level of educational attainment generally drops as well. Education and socioeconomic status must be viewed as interrelated variables that help explain the high degree of prejudice in the lower strata.

Bettelheim and Janowitz's discussion of anti-Semitism provides another illustration of situational analysis or the application of reference group theory. They suggest that the pronounced degree of anti-Semitism among the better educated and upper socioeconomic groups is predicated upon the high frequency of contact and competition between Jews and members of these strata. The larger number of American Jews are in the middle and upper strata, and the strongest expressions of anti-Semitism are found in the non-Jewish segments of these strata (Bettelheim and Janowitz 1964:23). Again, it can be seen that the analytical emphasis is not so much upon individual traits or upon the position of a given group but upon the relative positions and perceptions of groups in the social structure. Moreover, reference group theory can be a useful theoretical framework for integrating the diverse kinds of findings about different social variables.

A comparison of the findings in *The Dynamics of Prejudice* (1950) with the findings of seven other major studies of prejudice reveals that patterns of social mobility may be as significant an influence upon the emergence of prejudice as the more static variable of social strata or social location. In other words, the direction of a person's movement within the stratification system may be as important, if not more so, than one's particular location in the system at any given time. Specifically, these eight studies show that prejudice is highly correlated with downward social mobility. In contrast, prejudice is less correlated with upward social mobility. Persons whose social positions are stationary occupy an intermediate position in the expression of prejudice between the upwardly and downwardly mobile (Bettelheim and Janowitz 1950, 1964).

Two additional variables that have been interpreted in situational contexts are place of residence and religion. Most researchers agree that rural residents are more prejudiced than persons living in urban areas. There are several related factors that may produce this trend. First, as was the case with differences between age groups, urban dwellers have greater exposure than their rural counterparts to rapid changes in social norms and values. Small towns and rural areas are, in a sense, always catching up to changes in social norms and values that are generated in urban America. Second, it may be argued that rural areas are less heterogeneous in terms of group composition. While social contact does not always guarantee social consensus, cooperation, and mutual acceptance among groups, social isolation can serve to maintain myths and stereotypes that are rarely, if ever, challenged by everyday contact and experience.[5]

Most studies of the relationship between religion and prejudice have focused upon anti-Semitism. Melvin Tumin's work *An Inventory and Appraisal of Research on American Anti-Semitism* (1961) summarizes most of the major research conducted on this specific form of religious prejudice between 1930 and the late 1950s. In order to consider the more general question of the role of religion, two more recent studies may be examined. They are Lenski's *The Religious Factor* (1961) and Glock and Stark's *Christian Beliefs and Anti-Semitism* (1966). Both of these studies contain information about interreligious and racial prejudice in the United States. Lenski studied the social relationships among four major groups: white Protestants, black Protestants, white Jews, and white Catholics. He found that white Protestants are the most critical of other groups and that white Protestants are the least criticized by other groups (1961/1963:63–67). It appears, then, that majority groups (in this case, white Protestants) are fairly successful in establishing their definition of the situation and their stereotypical prejudices even where minority-minority relationships are concerned. This interpretation is supported by Simpson and Yinger who, in comparing a number of different studies, conclude that minority groups tend to share the majority-defined stereotypes of other minority groups in the society (Simpson and Yinger 1953/1965:115). Yet in spite of the general tendency for majority-defined stereotypes to be endorsed by all groups, both Lenski and Simpson and Yinger contend that there are subtle variations in the stereotypes that a number of groups may have of a specific other group. In other words, groups A and B may both express prejudice toward group C. But the specific emphasis or content of that prejudice may differ. This, again, makes sense in terms of reference group theory. For in spite of the powerful role of dominant group definitions of social reality, each group in the social structure stands in a different relationship to both the majority and to all other groups in the social structure.

[5]The complexity of patterns of contact has already been discussed in Chapter 4, pp. 153–155.

Glock and Stark's study shows that Catholics evidence a lower degree of anti-Semitism than Protestants. This supports Lenski's finding that white Protestants express a higher degree of criticism toward other groups than other groups show toward either white Protestants or toward each other. Glock and Stark offer the hypothesis that Catholics, as a minority group, are reluctant to express hostility toward other religious minorities because they have all shared a similar experience involving religious prejudice at the hands of the majority population (1966/1969:67). Whether one accepts this explanation or some variant of it, it appears that religion, like the other variables discussed here, is far from an independent variable. Clearly, religious influences upon prejudice must be analyzed in the context of the relative social positions of majority and minority religious groups in the society. Both the social positions of the respective groups as well as differences in their religious ideologies must be examined in order to understand the nature of the groups' relationships.

In addition to the findings and variables already discussed, Gordon Allport, in his work *The Nature of Prejudice* (1954), examines a wide range of additional factors. Allport observes that the greater the degree of social diversity in a society, the greater the latitude for various types and forms of prejudice and discrimination. In other words, pluralistic societies provide a large number of points of reference for the emergence of prejudice and discrimination. Allport further argues that prejudice and a specific form of discrimination known as *scapegoating*, the practice of blaming general social ills on specific minority groups, become prevalent in situations of rapid social change or social upheaval. Durkheim's concept of *anomie* is often used to describe situations in which individuals perceive a threat to, or a weakening of, social structures. Thus, scapegoating may be viewed as a result of situations in which majority groups experience anomie and in which they blame a minority group for the weakened or damaged social structure. Hitler, for example, blamed the Jews for the economic and social crises in Germany. Yet to explain the Nazi persecution of the Jews as simply an instance of scapegoating is far from adequate, for there existed a strong history of anti-Semitism and persecution of the Jews in Germany, and in Europe generally, long before Hitler's rise to power. Thus, if the Nazi persecution of the Jews represents an instance of scapegoating, it must be realized that there were prior historical conditions that paved the way for scapegoating in this, and most other, instances of scapegoating. Even Allport admits that a sweeping generalization predicting the rise of prejudice and discrimination or scapegoating in situations of rapid social change or upset is not completely accurate. Foreshadowing Lewis Coser's more recent study of social conflict (1956), Allport recognizes that social change and conflict can as easily create group solidarity and alliances as group antagonisms (1954:221–227).[6] At best, then, further studies of the relationships between social change, prejudice, and discrimination would be required in order to offer more precise generalizations about the ways in which these three phenomena are related.

Group sizes and proximities are also important variables. Yet it is difficult to specify exact quantitative measures of these variables that will reliably predict the emergence of either prejudice or discrimination. The distinction between segregated pluralism and integrated pluralism discussed in Chapter 3 involved changes in both group size and proximity. The American Nativist Movement during the nineteenth century was a reaction to increased numbers of Catholic immigrants as well as to increased contacts between Catholic and non-Catholic populations.[7] While group size and proximity were important variables in the emergence of the ideology of assimilation, it is equally accurate to say that the ideology was also a response to dramatic social change. In other words, there are a number of different ways to describe any specific situation. Whether one explains the rise of American Nativism in terms of the social variables of group size and proximity or through the larger metaphor of social change is simply a question of what level of generality seems meaningful.

The social visibility of minority groups is an important related variable. Visible social traits not only provide an easily recognizable reference point for prejudice and discrimination but can also have severe social consequences for members of groups that are physically distinct from the rest of the population. For instance, members of racial groups and the physically handicapped may both experience what Erving Goffman has called *stigma* (1963). One is not a lawyer who happens

[6]See the discussion on pp. 226–228.
[7]See the discussion on pp. 54–60.

to be crippled, but a crippled lawyer. One is not an athlete who happens to be black, but a black athlete. In both cases, physical stigma is socially defined in a way that all but completely overshadows the individual's personality and social experience. This phenomenon, as it relates to the black experience in the United States, has been described in numerous autobiographies, including those by Malcolm X (1964), Claude Brown (1965), and Eldridge Cleaver (1968). The degree to which blackness may be socially defined in a way that pervades all aspects of an individual's social experience is graphically illustrated in John Howard Griffin's work *Black Like Me* (1960). In this instance, a white author darkened his skin in order to experience firsthand what it means to live in the stigmatized world of black Americans. Yet the experiences described by these various authors are not unique to American blacks or to physically distinct minorities. Edward Sagarin has edited a collection of essays on the social experience of homosexuals, dwarfs, cripples, lepers, and others who possess either visible or otherwise socially distinct traits (1971). These studies provide many illustrations of the argument presented in Chapter 2, that limiting the study of minority groups to the usual racial, religious, and ethnic minority groups is theoretically constricting. The problem of devalued or *spoiled identity* may be as severe for the American Indian, the homosexual, the hunchback, and the blind as it is for American blacks. The process of "stigmatization" occurs for physical minorities as well as minority groups that are distinct because of both behavioral and cognitive traits. While there have been many studies of social discrimination and of the effects of differential treatment and stigma for minority groups, there is much sense in Robert Bierstedt's call for "a sociology of majorities" (1948). If social discrimination and the psychological stigma it produces for minority group members are to be understood and eliminated, those groups that create stigmatized social definitions and patterns of conduct must be studied. Simply focusing upon the minority side of majority-minority relationships may reveal a great deal about the social consequences of prejudice and discrimination, but it will never provide a full comprehension of their genesis.

While visible social traits may easily become focal points for prejudice and discrimination, focal points that can have stigmatizing effects on individual group members, this is not always the case. Group size and visibility are closely interrelated variables. A single Puerto Rican or Asian family in an otherwise racially homogeneous community of Caucasians is not likely to produce prejudice and discrimination. The token minority group member or family represents more of a novelty than a threat. As both Simmel (1908b/1950:402–408) and Schutz (1944/1964:91–105) have shown, the "stranger" may often enjoy a great degree of social freedom. The outsider may achieve greater social intimacy than the long-time "insider." In other words, group size and group visibility are closely interrelated variables. Visibility alone is not a sufficient cause of either prejudice or discrimination, nor of the social-psychological phenomenon of stigma, which often results from highly institutionalized prejudice and discrimination.

Similarly, while, by definition, variance from the social norms is an essential factor in determining minority status in society, variance from the norms alone does not create extreme instances of prejudice and discrimination. Rather, as Hubert M. Blalock has argued, extreme instances of aggression or discrimination typically result in two kinds of circumstances. The first is when the majority group views discrimination as an effective tool for reducing the ability of the minority to act as a social competitor. The second is when the majority defines the minority's variance from the social norms as a form of social deviance that threatens its sacred traditions (values or norms) (Blalock 1967/1970:38–50, 204–207). It will be recalled from Chapter 4 that these same two conditions, resource threats and value threats, are the major prerequisites for social conflict. If it is indeed the case that social conflict, discrimination, and even prejudice result from the same situations, those in which groups view each other as competitive threats, there would appear to be much value in examining more closely the relationships between these three phenomena. It was shown in Chapter 4 that the social-structural positions occupied by various minority groups are an important factor influencing the frequency, intensity, violence, and types of social conflicts that are likely to occur. If prejudice and discrimination result from the same general factors that produce conflict between groups, it is reasonable to expect that variations in prejudice and discrimination are also related to these same factors. The next section of this chapter attempts to demonstrate this hypothesis. Moreover, an analysis of the relationships between prejudice, discrimination, and social conflict may also provide a context for understanding some of the diverse research findings already discussed.

Prejudice, Discrimination, and the Theory of Social Conflict

From the variety of research findings and interpretations of those findings already discussed, it is clear that there does not yet exist a well-integrated sociological theory of prejudice and discrimination. It is essential here to distinguish between two different kinds of questions about these phenomena. First, how are they transmitted and sustained in society? It has already been shown that the related perspectives of the sociology of knowledge and reference group theory provide a powerful argument for the view that prejudice and discrimination are essentially social phenomena. They are collectively held views and norms for action that are transmitted from one generation to the next through socialization. The social group is able to induce an individual to either discriminate or refrain from discrimination even when the group norm contradicts the individual's personally held beliefs and values. But these theoretical perspectives do not answer the second question: Why do prejudice and discrimination arise in the first place? It is indeed clear that prejudice and discrimination can become part of the historical consciousness of a group or a society once they have emerged. But this does not provide an understanding of the genesis of these phenomena. It is this second question that must now be addressed.

It has already been shown that such general factors as dislike of the unlike, group ethnocentrism, social change, socialization, and even the theory of aggression-displacement do not provide the kind of theoretical specificity to explain either the genesis of prejudice and discrimination or the empirical variations in these phenomena from one group relationship to the next. Similarly, diverse research findings describe a large number of intervening variables such as age, socioeconomic status, place of residence, religious differences between groups, and education, all of which may modify an individual's prejudice or his willingness to discriminate. But, again, these complexly interrelated variables, as significant as they may be, do not provide an answer to the question of the genesis of collective group stereotypes and patterns of discrimination. In essence, these are variables that intervene and create variations from an assumed set of norms. But why do these norms, prejudicial stereotypes, and patterns of discrimination emerge in the first place?

The answer to this question provided in the following discussion, is that prejudice and discrimination emerge from historical instances of intergroup conflict. There are, in effect, three basic propositions that stem from this contention. First, prejudice and discrimination are weapons employed by groups in social conflict. They are conflict techniques that may be used as measures or indices of intergroup conflict. Second, just as social conflict varies from one kind of situation to the next and from one kind of majority-minority relationship to the next, so the emergence and relative strength of prejudice and discrimination will exhibit important variations. Not all instances of social conflict or all kinds of majority-minority relationships will produce the same patterns of prejudice and discrimination. Finally, since it has already been shown that conflict evidences important variations depending upon the social-structural arrangements in which different groups interact, so it may be shown that prejudice and discrimination vary according to these same social-structural arrangements. It was shown in the preceding chapter that there are four typical social locations in which minority groups are situated. They are reward parity with integration, reward parity with segregation, reward deprivation with integration, and reward deprivation with segregation. The task here is to show how and why prejudice and discrimination differ according to these four situations. Before this can be done, the basic contention that prejudice and discrimination emerge from group conflict situations must first be examined in greater detail.

The idea that prejudice, discrimination, and intergroup conflicts are interrelated phenomena is not a new theme in the social sciences. Even during the second half of the nineteenth and early twentieth centuries, such prominent European scholars as Ludwig Gumplowitz and Max Weber argued that racism could best be understood in terms of social and economic group conflicts.[8] While this theme was certainly not

[8]See further the discussion on pp. 259–261.

absent from the formative periods of American sociology, it was not until the early 1950s that sociologists challenged the then widely held view that prejudice causes social conflict. Jesse Bernard observed that, at that time, there was much more psychological than sociological research on this subject. The view that prejudice causes group conflict no doubt resulted from the fact that psychologists tend to view most, if not all, cognitive or subjective variables as independent, rather than dependent, variables. In simple terms, the larger body of social scientific research conceptualized the relationship between prejudice and social conflict in this manner. In contrast, Bernard argued that, from a sociological perspective, it seemed more probable that prejudice and discrimination were the results of historical instances of conflicts between groups (Bernard 1951).

This theme was further emphasized by Simpson and Yinger in the first edition of their text *Racial and Cultural Minorities* 1953:97–127/1965:9–16, 80–108). They contend that both prejudice and discrimination are weapons employed by groups in social conflict. Specifically, they argue that, in social-psychological terms, prejudice functions to legitimate or justify conflict with, and discrimination against, an out-group. These stereotypical, negative descriptions of the enemy become an important component of the in-group ideology. Discrimination can best be understood as a weapon or conflict technique that is designed to neutralize or injure the enemy. Discrimination essentially restricts and limits the activities, and therefore the impact, of a minority group upon society. It neutralizes a group's efforts to change social arrangements, to acquire social resources, and to influence the norms and values of a society.

As Simpson and Yinger point out, they were not the first writers to propose this theory of the relationship between prejudice, discrimination, and conflict. As early as 1948, Oliver Cox in his book *Caste, Class and Race* argued, from a Marxist perspective, that prejudice and discrimination could only be understood as the results of economic conflict and economic exploitation of one group by another. Cox particularly emphasized the idea that race prejudice is merely one component of the larger capitalist ideology. While Cox's work contains an extremely important argument, it also contains the limitations of any strictly Marxist interpretation of social life. Prejudice is not the unique invention of capitalist societies, and economic competition is merely one source of social conflict. Cox's interpretation provides little understanding of the fact noted in Chapter 4 that group conflict may stem from all kinds of resource competition between groups, as well as from value differences between groups. But Cox must be credited with having realized that prejudice and discrimination are not causes of conflict nor are they the results of some deep-seated group instincts. Rather, they emerge from historical instances of group conflict and play important roles as conflict techniques.

One of the most useful standardized research instruments for demonstrating the direct correlation between conflict and prejudice is the *Bogardus Social Distance Scale*. This widely used research technique was first employed by Emory S. Bogardus in the mid-1920s (Bogardus 1925). Typically, respondents are given a large list of names of different minority groups and are asked to indicate the degree to which they would admit members of the different groups to kinship through marriage, into one's social club or church, as a neighbor on the block, as fellow workers on the job, and to citizenship. Each of these categories reflects a different degree of social intimacy; and responses to such questions may be used to compute a measure of social distance, a measure of liking or disliking between members of different groups.

Bogardus himself has compiled the results from college students' responses to his scale in the years 1926, 1946, 1956, and 1966. This information provides a unique longitudinal view of how prejudices toward various groups in the United States have changed over time (Bogardus 1967). Some of these trends suggest quite clearly that the public image of a group is directly related to conflicts between that group and the larger society. For instance, of the thirty different groups listed in the scale in 1926, blacks were ranked twenty-sixth, obviously quite close to the bottom. The data collected in 1946 show that the level of anti-black prejudice in the United States had increased. Blacks were now ranked twenty-ninth on the list of thirty groups. This is hardly surprising, for the early 1940s were marked by a series of tragic race riots in the United States, the most serious of which occurred in the city of Detroit in 1943. Responses to the social distance scale obtained in 1956 show that blacks had moved up to the position of twenty-seven. The early fifties were a period of relative prosperity for both races and, with the exception of consensus-bounded black-white conflicts such as the type that produced the 1954 Supreme Court decision of *Brown v. Board of Education,* this was a period of relative peace between the races. Yet the study conducted in 1966 shows that the social distance between blacks and whites had again become greater. Blacks were again ranked twenty-ninth. This quite clearly is related to the fact that the early sixties witnessed a transition from the Civil Rights Movement to the Black Power Movement, a transition that by the late 1960s would again produce race riots and violence. Moreover, as Bogardus himself points out, an analysis of these several studies in terms of regional variations within the United States reveals that:

> When some members of a racial group become a real competitor in trade or business and win over from natives the larger part of a successful business, antagonistic attitudes toward the whole of the given racial group may find farness expressions of the worst types (Bogardus 1967:32).

Of course, by "farness expressions" Bogardus means expressions of greater social distance between groups. His studies show quite clearly that there is a direct linear relationship between intergroup conflict and prejudice. Some of the trends from these studies illustrate this theory so graphically that it seems almost unnecessary to dwell upon them. For instance, Russians were consistently ranked thirteenth out of thirty groups in both the 1926 and 1946 studies. In 1956, Russians dropped dramatically to the rank of twenty-fourth out of thirty groups and remained at the rank again in 1966. Can one escape the interpretation that the increased level of prejudice toward Russians that appeared between 1946 and 1956 was a function of the period of conflict now referred to as the cold war? These two allies, the United States and the Soviet Union, had become enemies.

Both Bogardus' research as well as studies by the many other researchers who have employed his instrument[9] point to the theory that intergroup prejudice and changes in those prejudices emerge from concrete historical instances of intergroup and even intersocietal conflicts. It must be cautioned that it is not being argued here that there

---

[9]Bogardus' essay (1967) contains an extensive bibliography of additional studies employing the social distance scale.

are never instances in which prejudice itself produces conflict or that there are never strong prejudical views between group members where conflict is absent. It is merely being argued that, in the first instance, social conflict may be viewed as a generative force in the creation of prejudice. As was noted earlier, it is clearly the case that prejudice and discrimination are very likely to become part of the collective historical consciousness of groups and an important feature in the relationship between those groups, even if the original conflict situations that produced prejudice and discrimination lie deep in the historical past. Once patterns of group antagonism are created, they can themselves become contributing factors in renewed instances of intergroup conflict. Prejudice becomes a kind of cognitive resource, a historical residue that may be resurrected in any new potential conflict situation. In this sense, prejudice may contribute to social conflict. But the central argument here is that prejudice and discrimination in the first instance represent weapons of conflict. In the absence of intergroup conflict, it is unlikely that prejudice and discrimination will be found without some prior record of such conflict between groups. Most importantly, ongoing instances of conflict will be measurable in terms of renewed levels of either prejudice, discrimination, or both.

In this context, the four social-structural arrangements in which minority groups become situated may be examined in order to suggest how and why different patterns of conflict produce different patterns of prejudice and discrimination. The four minority group situations, reward parity with integration, reward parity with segregation, reward deprivation with segregation, and reward deprivation with integration, are likely to produce very different central tendencies of prejudice and discrimination when majority-minority conflict occurs. Each of these four situations must be examined in order to explain the tendencies that occur within them.

Reward parity with integration. As was noted in Chapter 4, the kind of majority-minority relationship in which the minority group possesses a significant stock of social resources (reward parity) and shares social space with the majority and other minorities (integration) is most closely approximated in the United States by the major European immigrant religious and ethnic groups. It has also been shown that these minority groups tend to be involved in frequent consensus-bounded conflicts with the majority, and that such conflicts are neither intense nor violent. Given the existence of majority-minority conflict in this type of social arrangement, one is likely to encounter a high degree of prejudice but relatively little discrimination. Why is this the case?

By definition, reward parity with integration is evidence of the fact that the minority group has successfully overcome majority group employed conflict techniques. The minority has attained the very social resources that discrimination, as a conflict technique, is designed to prevent them from obtaining. Large-scale, highly institutionalized practices of discrimination against the minority are, in effect, meaningless. Due to the attainment of reward parity by the minority, discrimination has already proved ineffective. If discrimination is encountered at all, it is likely to be either in the most intimate, private, nonpublic face-to-face situations (choice of marriage partners and friendship networks) or in those institutional sectors that have very little effect upon the lives of minority group members (private social clubs and the like). Even the existence of private social clubs that discriminate may be successfully challenged by the minority. At best, the maintenance of these kinds of institutions is perhaps of symbolic value to the majority but has little real effect upon the quality of life for minority group members. In a sense, when other forms of social discrimination have been overcome by the minority, the "restricted" private club becomes a kind of social anachronism that is out of step with the rest of the social structure.

Moreover, members of minority groups that attain reward parity and choose to integrate are likely to gain positions in major social institutions, especially in political institutions. They are, therefore, in a position to delegitimate both formal and informal types of discrimination. Discrimination against such a minority group no longer constitutes part of the moral order of society. In short, when a minority group occupies the position of reward parity with integration, discrimination is no longer tactically useful or socially sanctioned.

On the other hand, as long as intergroup conflicts persist, there is nothing to prevent the existence or increase of prejudice toward the minority, even if the expression of that prejudice must be handled with care by majority group members in public situations. In psychological terms, prejudice may have an important compensatory function for majority group members. Socially shared negative stereotypes about the minority group, which majority group members may express to one another, may function to release those frustrations and aggressions stemming from conflict that cannot be released in the form of discrimination.[10] Given the fact that discrimination is not a socially sanctioned technique, majority group members may at least console each other with the knowledge that their cause is "just," their side is "right," and that they are not alone in their view that the minority group is an "undesirable lot."

Several trends in the research support the theory that social conflicts between these kinds of minority groups and the majority will be accompanied by high levels of prejudice but not discrimination. Bettelheim and Janowitz (1964), for instance, observe that the strongest expressions of anti-Semitism are found in the upper and middle social strata, precisely those strata in which the larger number of American Jews are located and with which Jews are in frequent situations of conflict and competition. Moreover, institutional discrimination against Jews in the United States has steadily decreased in direct proportion to the ascendency and integration of Jews in the social structure, especially since World War II. College entrance quota systems, which once prevented Jews from entering institutions of higher learning and thus from entering more desirable occupations, have become very much a thing of the past in the United States. Even in the area of intimate social relationships, the intermarriage rates between Jews and non-Jews have steadily increased since the 1957 census data were collected. As was suggested earlier, even though group prejudices remain, intermarriages between white Protestants, Catholics, and Jews resulting from shared social space and life-style have become tolerable though not encouraged.[11]

[10]The use of the terms "frustration" and "aggression" here must be carefully distinguished from the traditional psychological theory of frustration-aggression discussed earlier. The traditional theory maintains that levels of frustration are continually building up in the personality system. The displacement of aggression toward minority group members is viewed as a primary cause of intergroup conflict, prejudice, and discrimination. In contrast, the argument presented here is that the psychological phenomena of frustration and aggression result from concrete instances of intergroup conflict. Given the inability to vent those frustrations through discrimination, prejudice may serve as an alternative channel of release. Again, we are not concerned here with the displacement of "free-floating" aggressions but specifically with the release of those frustrations that are themselves the product of conflict.

[11]See the discussion on pp. 162–164.

Finally, it should be noted that routine patterns of discrimination become exceedingly difficult to employ and enforce when the enemy lives among the in-group. This is especially true when physical distinctiveness is not part of the minority's variation from the social norms. Social integration makes it very difficult to tell the "good guys" from the "bad guys." Even informal types of discrimination become problematic because one can never know whether one of "them" is among "us." An act of discrimination or even the open expression of prejudice may become a *cause célèbre*. In the early days of the Nazi regime when Jews were still rubbing shoulders in the streets with bona fide citizens of the Third Reich, this problem was solved by the requirement that all Jews wear an arm band identifying them as Jews and as different from the other people in the streets. In other words, the Nazi regime had to create some artificial form of physical distinctiveness in order to effectively employ discriminatory practices.

In summary, when a minority group attains both reward parity and social integration with the majority, social conflicts will be manifest in terms of high levels of prejudice but not discrimination. This is because discrimination becomes a meaningless tactic and because discrimination will have been delegitimated by the minority group. The minority possesses a significant share in the social structure and exerts a significant influence upon the reshaping of society's norms.

Reward parity with segregation. The second situation to be examined is that in which the minority group possesses reward parity but has chosen segregated living arrangements in order to preserve its distinctive cultural tradition, values, or life-style. As was noted in Chapter 4, while most third-generation European immigrant groups fit this description, parity with segregation appears to be a more permanent arrangement for Asian-Americans and various social and religious sectarian or communal groups. While minority-group-initiated conflicts tend to be consensus-bounded, most conflicts tend to be initiated by the majority group and are often very intense and violent.

Here, as in the case of parity with integration, reward parity must be viewed as evidence of the fact that the minority has been able to overcome majority group discrimination. Moreover, chosen segregation relegates discrimination to a rather futile and meaningless practice. Discrimination is a pointless endeavor when the group against which one is discriminating has absolutely no desire to integrate or participate in the very social structures and institutions from which they might be excluded. But this does not necessarily mean that absolutely no discrimination will occur.

The critical factor for understanding prejudice and discrimination in this kind of relationship is voluntary social segregation and the infrequent conflicts that accompany it. Over long periods of time, in which little or no conflict is occurring, there is likely to be very little discrimination for the reasons already mentioned. The minority has already attained some level of parity and it is making little or no attempt to integrate. Economic discrimination has already been proven ineffective and social discrimination serves no purpose. For social discrimination is an attempt to neutralize minority group efforts, and, in this case, the minority is not expending efforts to integrate socially. There is nothing to be neutralized. On the other hand, infrequent instances of violence directed toward the minority must be viewed as acts of differential treatment. In other words, violent or intense conflict, attacks of some sort launched by the majority against the minority, are acts of discrimination. Discrimination over time will be at a very low level, if evidenced at all. But those infrequent conflicts between majority and minority are likely to represent the crudest form of social discrimination, violent aggression.

Those periods in which discrimination takes the form of collective aggression will obviously be accompanied by high levels of prejudice. The internment of the Japanese during World War II represents such an instance. While prejudice is likely to become part of the majority group's collective consciousness following and between such periods, there are also some important intervening variables that may produce differing patterns. Given an extremely high degree of segregation between groups, the old adage "out of sight, out of mind" is an apt description of the situation. Religious communal groups such as the Amish, Hasidic Jews, and Quakers are not the objects of extreme prejudice except in areas where they come in contact with members of the larger community. On the other hand, extreme isolation between two groups can serve to sustain group myths and stereotypes. Areas where Jews and Asian-Americans are all but nonexistent may evidence continued prejudice. Group size, the degree of segregation, and the degree to which past instances of conflict affected the larger society are all important variables. In general, though, assuming ongoing contacts and relationships between a majority and a self-segregated minority that has attained reward parity, prejudice—but not discrimination—will be encountered.

A study conducted by Thomas Campbell and Yoshio Fukuyama in the mid-1960s provides an opportunity to test our theory. As part of a large study, Campbell and Fukuyama administered a Bogardus Social Distance Scale to a nationwide sample of 8,500 members of one of the larger white Protestant religious denominations. Their analysis turns to the interesting question of regional variations in group prejudice in different parts of the United States. They observe:

> . . . we also found a slightly higher degree of social distance expressed toward American Indians by parishioners in the Great Plains than by those in metropolitan area churches. While this may give support to the hypothesis that the density of minority groups functions to increase prejudice, our data were not entirely consistent. Respondents in the San Francisco area, for instance, were significantly less prejudiced against Orientals than those in any of the other sample cities where the Oriental population is far less visible (1970:154).

In other words, Campbell and Fukuyama have assumed that prejudice is a function of the two interrelated variables, group visibility and group density (or the relative size of the minority group in a given area). As was noted in our earlier discussion of research findings and theories, these two variables are frequently cited as important determinants of prejudice and discrimination. Yet Campbell and Fukuyama found that, contrary to this interpretation, the one American city included in their study that had the largest relative density of Asian-Americans, San Francisco, was the very city in which people expressed the lowest degree of prejudice toward Asian-Americans. Is their finding, in fact, some sort of unexplainable anomaly, or can an alternative theory account for their research findings?

The theory that has been presented here contends that prejudice and discrimination are the outcomes of social conflict. This does not mean that group density and visibility are entirely irrelevant. Quite to the contrary, both high visibility and minimal density of minority group members may be very important factors in the *initial* emergence of group conflict. But beyond the initial period of contact and conflict between groups, one must give careful attention to the structural arrangements that have evolved between majority and minority, as well as to the conflict tendencies between them. The Asian community in San Francisco represents one of the most outstanding instances of reward parity and chosen segregation of any minority group in the United States. The low frequency of conflict between the two communities, especially the low frequency of majority instigated conflict, is indeed an important factor. It indicates that the majority does not view the minority as a threatening challenge to the social norms and that it is willing to have the Asian community remain separate and autonomous. As has already been suggested, this kind of relationship is likely to exhibit significant residues of prejudice resulting from earlier periods of conflict. This is exactly what Campbell and Fukuyama have found. Yet, the well-established and autonomous Asian community in San Francisco is the object of less prejudice than are Asians in the other American cities studied. The other cities in their study were Louisville, Cincinnati, St. Louis, Detroit, and Hartford. It may be argued that in most of these cities the extremely small size of the Asian population, or the relative absence of Asians altogether, allows for the persistence of old prejudicial stereotypes about the "inscrutable Oriental." It will be recalled that the same explanation has been given for the greater degree of prejudice in rural as opposed to urban areas. Isolation of one group from the next insures the persistence of old, unchallenged myths. It must be remembered that it is not being argued here that social conflict is the only variable affecting prejudice and discrimination. Rather, it is being argued that social conflicts are the initial sources of prejudice and discrimination and that the specific social structures in which groups engage in conflict are important explanatory variables for understanding differences in these phenomena. Unfortunately, Campbell and Fukuyama did not include New York City in their study, for it would have provided an excellent comparative case for theory testing.

Moreover, Campbell and Fukuyama's other finding, that residents of the Great Plains are more prejudiced toward American Indians than residents in metropolitan areas of the country, is entirely consistent with the theory offered here. For, as will be seen, the situation of reward deprivation and segregation is accompanied by intense, often violent conflict as well as by extremely high levels of majority group prejudice and discrimination. Variations in the level of prejudice against American Indians may be understood in terms of social conflict and the structural conditions under which they occur.

Reward deprivation with segregation. There are a large number of groups in the United States whose members suffer the disadvantage of reward deprivation and forced segregation. Among them are blacks, Puerto Ricans, Mexican-Americans, American Indians, the aged poor, migrant workers, and the residents of Appalachia. As was seen in Chapter 4, conflict between these minority groups and the majority (as well as other relatively high status minority groups) tends to be infrequent, though both intense and often violent. Minority-group-initiated conflicts are likely to be consensus-projecting. It has already been seen from Bogardus' study (1967) that majority group prejudice against such a group does decrease, though not immensely, during periods in which conflicts are minimal. Yet social conflicts between a minority that is both deprived of social resources and socially segregated and the majority are likely to be manifested in terms of high levels of both prejudice and discrimination. Moreover, even during those periods between conflicts, prejudice and discrimination are also likely to remain at fairly high levels.

Again, discrimination is a technique designed to neutralize minority group efforts. In the case of deprivation with segregation, the technique of discrimination has served its purpose effectively for the majority. Discrimination is itself a living record of the past conflict encounters between the two groups. It was noted earlier that, in the case of reward parity with integration, prejudice plays a compensatory role for majority group members who are prevented from discriminating. In social-psychological terms, prejudice serves as an alternative form of release for frustrations and aggressions stemming from conflict that cannot be released in the form of discrimination. But where reward deprivation and segregation are encountered, the relationship between prejudice and discrimination is quite different. In this case, the two phenomena reinforce each other. Prejudice becomes an ideological justification for rigid patterns of discrimination. Prejudice both sustains in-group solidarity and justifies in-group discrimination against the minority. But discrimination, in turn, places the minority in an undesirable social position and forces it into a life-style that itself becomes the source of even more prejudicial myth building.

Perhaps the most classic example of this syndrome was the practice of occupational discrimination against Jews in Europe during the late Middle Ages. Because of religious sanctions, most Christians would not enter the profession of money lending. It became one of the few significant occupations open to Jews, and they were encouraged to enter it precisely because it was too "dirty" a business for Christians. This pattern of discrimination soon produced the stereotype of the Jew as a "money-grubbing" individual, a role into which he had, in fact, been forced by collective patterns of discrimination. As Glock and Stark have found (1966), this stereotype of the Jew survives in modern-day American culture.

One need not turn to the Middle Ages to find examples of this kind of syndrome of reinforcement between prejudice and discrimination. The larger number of blacks in the United States are deprived of educational and job opportunities. They are, in effect, made poor and illiterate by collective patterns of discrimination. Once poverty and illiteracy become collective group traits, they may be explained by the majority, not in terms of the effects of systematic discrimination, but in terms of other alleged group traits. Thus, the stereotype alleges that blacks are poor because they are "shiftless" and that they are illiterate because they are stupid. Much the same may be said of the entrapment of people in the welfare system. People accept welfare because they have no other viable means of support, because discrimination prevents them from earning a living. But once the members of a group are forced to become welfare clients, it is argued that they are on welfare because they are lazy or lack pride, not because they are poor. Again, prejudice justifies discrimination, which, in turn, creates collective patterns of living that provide additional fuel for more prejudice and stereotypes.

The case of the *Eta* in Japan provides yet another illustration of this point. The *Eta* are in no way physically, religiously, or culturally distinct from the majority of the Japanese population. They are mostly urban slum dwellers. They are descendents of those social "outcasts" who, in the sixteenth century, were forced into occupations viewed as unclean or undesirable according to the values of Shintoism and Buddhism, both of which have prohibitions against the killing of animals. Thus, the jobs of dog catcher, sandal maker, executioner, prison warden, and a number of other occupations have become the sole means of livelihood for members of the *Eta* (Dore and Aoyagi 1965, in Rose and Rose 1965:88–92). It is, of course, argued that the *Eta* do these jobs because they are unclean as a "people." But the *Eta* are not a "people." They are just like the rest of the population in terms of race, religion, and culture. They just happen to be descendents of people who were forced into these occupations and are themselves the continuing objects of discrimination. There is a striking similarity between the treatment of the *Eta* due to the religious prescriptions of Shintoism and Buddhism and the treatment of the Jews by Christians during the Middle Ages. In both cases, some group had to be found that could be forced to perform social roles that were functional to society but undesirable because of religious sanctions.

In summary, there is a tendency for minority groups that are both deprived of resources and socially segregated to be the objects of mutually reinforcing, high levels of both prejudice and discrimination. This is true both during periods of intense conflict as well as between those periods. The minority group has very little influence in shaping the social norms and lacks the social resources to successfully counteract or prevent discrimination. Prejudicial stereotypes are likely to emphasize both the nature of the minority group's alleged variation from the social norms as well as the way in which the minority group's life-style and position in society (created, of course, by discrimination) are self-created consequences of the group's collective traits.

Reward deprivation with integration. This type of arrangement is one in which the relative frequency of majority-minority conflict is exceedingly low. It will be recalled from Chapter 4 that there are two different kinds of minority groups that occupy this position: groups, such as Women's Liberation, that represent infrequent value threats to the larger society; and groups, such as the handicapped, that are physically distinct but do not exhibit the kind of physical distinctiveness involved in racial distinctions.

Turning first to those groups that emerge from within the social structure in order to fight for some form of contracultural social change, it seems that both prejudice and discrimination are high during periods of conflict but will most probably be relatively low in those periods in which no conflict occurs. This is because such groups only become the object of prejudice and discrimination in periods when they undertake organized, collective action against the social order. In other periods, members of these social movements are indistinguishable from other members of society. This, of course, assumes that this form of contracul-turalism rarely involves physical distinctiveness. Both Women's Libera-tion and various types of ardent pacifist groups have been the objects of extreme discrimination and prejudice in periods of overt conflict. But in the absence of conflict, members of such contracultural groups merge back into the social fabric; and the larger society has relatively little consciousness of their social distinctiveness.

The second category of groups that experience reward deprivation with social integration is the physically handicapped. Clearly, there are prejudicial views about the handicapped. But, as was noted earlier, this form of prejudice emphasizes neither the competitive nature of the out-group nor the "morally reprehensible" character of the group's variance from the social norms. Rather, prejudice here denies the ability of the group to compete at all and is likely to be characterized by an element of paternalistic sympathy rather than hate or antagonism. For this reason, it may be appropriate to say that prejudice in the traditional sense is minimal. But discrimination remains a constant ele-ment in the social relationship between the handicapped and the larger society. It may indeed be the case that conflict between the handicapped and the larger society, if and when it occurs, will evidence the unique pattern of increasing prejudice but decreasing discrimination. This is because, on the one hand, the reduction of discrimination against the handicapped would be consistent with a humanistic social philosophy. To refuse to provide better job opportunities for the handicapped would be—to use an all too trite but apt metaphor—tantamount to stealing from the blind. But the reduction of discrimination against the handicap-ped might well produce increased prejudice. For the larger public might come to see the handicapped as a social competitor and might resent being morally coerced into reducing discrimination. Prejudice is likely to take the form, "I'm all in favor of giving them a chance, but they've really begun to take advantage of us," and "I don't like having them around anyway.'' It must again be stressed that the situation of reward deprivation with integration characterizes a great diversity of groups and is therefore the one type of minority group social location about which it is difficult to generalize.

The central tendencies between prejudice, discrimination, and intergroup conflict are depicted in Table 13. First, when the minority group occupies a position of reward parity with integration, it is most probable that majority-minority conflicts will be manifest in terms of high levels of prejudice, but little if any discrimination. The more the minority group attains parity of resources, the less likely it is that social discrimination will accompany intergroup conflict. Where the minority group occupies the position of reward parity with segregation, the likelihood

TABLE 13. Prejudice, Discrimination, and Social Conflicts: Four Cases of Minority Group Social Location

Minority group social location	Majority group practices	
	Prejudice	*Discrimination*
During periods of social conflict		
Reward parity with social integration	+	−
Reward parity with social segregation	+	+
Reward deprivation with social integration	+	− (physical minorities)
	+	+ (other minorities)
Reward deprivation with social segregation	+	+
Between periods of social conflict		
Reward parity with social integration	+	−
Reward parity with social segregation	+	−
Reward deprivation with social integration	−	+ (physical minorities)
	−	− (other minorities)
Reward deprivation with social segregation	+	+

of conflict producing prejudice is equally great. Here discrimination between periods of conflict will be very unlikely. In this instance, discrimination has no object because the minority does not desire shared social space. Yet, to the degree that overt aggression may be viewed as discrimination, it is accurate to say that parity with segregation will produce discrimination, but only as an immediate manifestation of conflict. This is not the kind of institutionalized discrimination that endures beyond the period of actual conflict.

Reward deprivation with segregation is the one instance in which majority-minority conflict will produce prejudice and discrimination both during the actual period of conflict as well as between those periods. Prejudice and discrimination will reinforce each other and the minority will have little means of overcoming discrimination. Finally, the situation of deprivation with integration must be analyzed in terms of two different kinds of minority groups. Where the minority group is not viewed as a social competitor, for instance, the physically handicapped, discrimination is the more outstanding feature of majority-minority interaction over time. Yet, paradoxically, social conflict is most likely to result in reduced discrimination but increased prejudice. On the other hand, where majority-minority conflict involves the type of minority group that represents a contracultural threat and that emerges from within the existing social structures, neither prejudice nor discrimination will characterize periods of little conflict. But both prejudice and discrimination will emerge with conflict.

In summary, the analysis presented here does not claim to explain all aspects of prejudice and discrimination. If and when a comprehensive theory of prejudice and discrimination is constructed, it must be a theory capable of integrating various research findings about personality systems, social structures, and total societies. The foregoing analysis contributes only one component of such a larger theory. Specifically, it has been argued that prejudice and discrimination are weapons employed by groups in social conflict. Moreover, the patterns of prejudice and discrimination between groups will vary with the very structural arrangements in which those conflicts occur. Clearly, the large assortment of social variables stemming from previous research must be viewed as intervening variables that may account for further variations within the patterns that have been discussed. But the task of fully integrating these various trends lies well beyond the limits of this book. For the moment, it must suffice to have shown that social conflict theory provides a significant degree of explanatory power concerning not only the emergence of prejudice and discrimination but also variations in patterns of prejudice and discrimination from one group relationship to the next.

Knowledge and Power: "A Sociology of Majorities"

The traditional approach of sociologists to the study of majority-minority relationships places great emphasis upon the role of social power. As was noted in Chapter 2, minority groups are, by definition, subordinate groups in society.[12] From this perspective the study of minority groups becomes an important part of the larger field of the study of stratification, the process of ranking, and the distribution of rewards between groups in societies. Yet, as Schermerhorn observes, this trend of analysis often results in a kind of "victimology" (1970:8–9). The study of social power in dominant-subordinate relationships revolves around the themes of how minority groups are kept in lower status positions and how these relationships affect the quality of life for oppressed and disadvantaged minority group members. Although these themes are both scientifically appropriate and socially relevant, they produce a rather incomplete view of majority-minority relationships. While it is essential that the social sciences provide an understanding of the consequences of prejudice and discrimination for minority group members, it is equally important to understand how these patterns of prejudice and discrimination are sustained. As Robert Bierstedt suggests, "a sociology of majorities" (1948) is an essential component of the study of majority-minority relationships.

It has already been noted that socialization is an important factor in the maintenance of patterns of prejudice and discrimination. In the framework of the sociology of knowledge, socialization is a process through which new members of a social collectivity are taught to accept the existing definitions of social reality. It is a continual process through which individuals learn what to expect, what to value, what to know,

[12]See discussion pp. 13–24.

and how to act in society. Jacques Ellul makes this point by suggesting that societies and the groups within them are their own best propaganda. Socialization consists of:

> . . . a progressive adaptation to a certain order of things, a certain concept of human relations, which unconsciously molds individuals and makes them conform . . . (Ellul 1962/1965:64).

In other words, socialization imparts "socially approved knowledge" to the individual, a taken-for-granted perception of society, its power relationships, and the place of one's group and others within it. Unless some form of discrepancy or contradiction should disrupt the order of things, there is little reason for individuals in society, especially members of dominant groups, to ask why things are the way they are. One simply knows that some people are rich and others are poor, that some live in slums, others in shiny new suburbs. The social world becomes a kind of second nature to us. Its injustices, inequalities, and paradoxes achieve an aura of inevitability. Man forgets that he created the social world. The power that the taken-for-granted world holds over us is empirically demonstrated by the fact that even minority groups tend to endorse majority-defined stereotypes about other minority groups in society.[13] This is the very meaning of Gordon's term "cultural assimilation" (1964).[14] The minimal stock of knowledge that members of groups acquire as they assimilate into society includes not only such practical information as what to wear, how to speak the language, how to find a job, and where to get a bus but also knowledge of society's power structures and the "place" of different groups within it. Membership in society requires a knowledge of society's norms. Dominant groups play the largest role in defining normative social reality. In this sense, the old adage "knowledge is power" has an added meaning. The power of dominant groups to define social reality for all other groups reinforces the ability of dominant groups to maintain power over society and the groups within it. The ability to define the rules of the game and the very name of the game is an immense advantage in winning.

---

[13]See the discussion on p. 214.
[14]See the discussion on pp. 82–85.

But the important question that must be addressed here is what happens in the case of a discrepancy? What happens when the taken-for-granted world, the existing social definitions of groups, and their place within the social structure are challenged? In contemporary American society, large numbers of government programs and agencies, as well as private agencies, have openly challenged practices of discrimination and prejudice against the most severely disadvantaged minority groups in the country. Similarly, these groups have played an increasingly greater role in becoming spokesmen in their own behalf. When Gunnar Myrdal and his associates (1944) studied black-white relationships in the United States during the early 1940s, they observed that there was a tragic contradiction between the ideology of democracy embodied in the Constitution and the disgraceful treatment of minority group members, especially blacks. Since the 1940s this contradiction has become an even stronger element in American culture. In spite of the many governmental and privately organized programs designed to overcome these patterns of prejudice and discrimination, they persist. In spite of the efforts of social scientists and educators generally to dispel these myths, they survive. The race riots of the 1960s seem so very similar to those of the 1940s. As the well-known French proverb contends, "While things are always changing, nothing seems to change."

The question that arises is how and why are patterns of prejudice and discrimination maintained in the face of increasing organized efforts to overcome them, and in the face of increasing attempts by the media, especially television, to portray the minority group member as part of the larger family of man, no different from the rest of us? In effect, there exists an immense discrepancy in American culture. The following discussion is but one attempt, from the perspective of the sociology of knowledge, to understand how these old patterns are maintained in the face of such discrepancies. This requires a more detailed examination of the majority side of majority-minority relationships.

The answer to this question is found in Berger and Luckmann's suggestion that the *known* tends to circumscribe the *knowable* (1966). The social world as we know it tends to shape our view of new, and especially discrepant, information. This, of course, assumes that discrepancies created by new knowledge are relevant to the day-to-day concerns of the group being studied (Schutz 1971). It should not be presumed that human knowledge is a closed, internally consistent phenomenon. Rather, individuals live with sundry paradoxes and inconsistencies. The individual's knowledge of the world around him is a fragmentary and incomplete stock of information, most of which is acquired secondhand from other people. Similarly, the *structure of relevance* is ever changing. At a given point in time, it was learned that the atom is not the basic unit of all physical matter. Rather, atoms consist of neutrons, protons, and electrons. This new piece of knowledge sparked some public interest but in no way created a relevant discrepancy for the man in the street's perception of his world. On the other hand, when Galileo during the seventeenth century proclaimed that the sun, not the earth, is the center of the universe, he created a relevant discrepancy for an important segment of the population. The Catholic Church, which was still the official guardian of reality definitions, eventually forced the mad scientist to recant his heretical and "obviously false" views. The theology of the Church was the paramount reality in Galileo's day, and that theology exerted a major influence upon what was knowable in Galileo's world. The history of science is replete with examples of ideas that were born before their time, born before an appropriate intellectual climate and a sufficient social base would support them (Kuhn 1962).

In situations where new knowledge creates a relevant discrepancy, there are at least three frequently encountered cognitive techniques employed by people that allow the known to circumscribe the knowable. These three forms of rationalization each play important roles in sustaining existing prejudices. The first technique may be called *contextual twisting*. In this situation, new knowledge that contradicts the taken-for-granted world is somehow twisted to fit the known facts of reality. Contextual twisting amounts to a reinterpretation of the new information in the context of what is already known. For instance, a prejudiced individual who believes certain stereotypes about blacks, Puerto Ricans, or Jews may suddenly find that a member of one of these groups has moved into his neighborhood or will be working alongside him at the office. Over time, the prejudiced individual may find that his stereotypes do not fit the conduct or personality of the new neighbor or fellow worker. The newly acquired information must be assessed very carefully in terms of what is already known about "them." Typically, contextual twisting results in the claim that "He's not like the rest of them," or "He's an exception to the rule." Contextual twisting can occur whether the new information is acquired firsthand or secondhand. The prejudiced individual may learn that a group of social scientists has found that blacks and whites with similar educational backgrounds and experience perform equally on IQ tests. What does the new information mean? "Well, that's only one small piece of research," or "It must have been an exceptional group of blacks, what about all the rest?" In other words, even the data of science require interpretation. Contextual twisting is a frequently encountered way of making new, potentially discrepant, knowledge conform with known reality.

A second technique for keeping the known world intact is *denial by discrediting the source*. For instance, if the NAACP makes a major press release on discrimination or institutional racism in the United States, the prejudiced response may be "What do you expect them to say?" In spite of the Kerner Commission's (1968) finding that prejudice and discrimination by whites was a major cause of the civil disorders and riots during the mid-1960s, many Americans still contend that the commission's report was slanted and that the riots resulted from "a Communist conspiracy to overthrow the United States government." Impuning the motives and credibility of the source is an important way of rationalizing unpleasant facts that disrupt the existing picture of social reality. Moreover, it should not be assumed that people are equally inclined to act upon both good news and bad news. It is indeed probable that people will fail to act upon unpleasant news, especially if such new knowledge can be defined as simply not relevant to the individual's day-to-day concerns.

A third technique is simply that of *denying the relevance* of new information. An anti-Semite may learn that not all Jews are rich or that some other alleged group stereotype is false. The typical response is "So what?" Obviously, it is always easy for an individual to deny the relevance of new information if that information does not directly interfere with his own daily activities. Few Northerners were troubled by the 1954 Supreme Court decision to desegregate Southern school systems. But Court decisions in the early 1970s demanding busing and desegregation in Northern school systems have been less easily passed off by Northern residents as simply an unfortunate turn of events.

Finally, it should be noted that extreme prejudice does not have to exist in order for members of one social group to reject discrepant information about another group. The initial public response in the United States to the *Keyserling Report* (1964) and Michael Harrington's *The Other America* (1962) was simply disbelief. The life of America's poverty-stricken groups is so different from that of most of the population that many people found these reports literally incredible. Many white middle-class students react the same way to books like Claude Brown's *Manchild in the Promised Land* (1965) or Jonathan Kozol's *Death at an Early Age* (1967). So different are the life experiences of different groups in the same society that the view from "the other side" is often too different to fit the taken-for-granted plausibility structure. Reports of the Nazi extermination camps during World War II were dismissed in this country as "inaccurate exaggerations" even up to the point when the Allies finally entered the death camps and brought out firsthand descriptions of the nightmare. Thus, while the various forms of cognitive rationalization help to sustain prejudice and discrimination in the face of discrepant information, some facts are so discrepant that one need not be strongly prejudiced to disbelieve them. The known tends to circumscribe the knowable. What is knowable in one segment of a society may be entirely implausible in another. The same principle applies to the social distribution of knowledge between different societies.

In summary, dominant groups possess not only the power to define social reality but also the cognitive mechanisms for warding off discrepant challenges to those definitions. If prejudice and discrimination are to be understood and combated, the sociology of majority-minority relationships must pay greater attention to the majority side of the coin. For while it is useful to know the consequences of prejudice and discrimination for minority groups, changing the situation requires an equally clear understanding of how majority groups maintain their taken-for-granted view of the social structure. The foregoing discussion has offered at least one avenue of analysis for developing a sociology of majority groups.

FOR FURTHER READING

ADORNO, T. W., ET AL.

    1950   *The Authoritarian Personality*. New York: Harper & Row. This is the best-known study from a series entitled *Studies in Prejudice*. The authors depict a wide range of personality factors that contribute to the six types of prejudiced personalities described in the book. A comprehensive discussion of the methodological and substantive issues stemming from this work will be found in Christie and Jahoda (1954).

ALLPORT, GORDON

    1954   *The Nature of Prejudice*. Reading, Mass.: Addison-Wesley. This is a comprehensive attempt to enumerate both the social and psychological factors contributing to prejudice.

BECKER, ERNEST

    1962   *The Birth and Death of Meaning*. New York: Free Press. Becker draws widely from the different sciences of man in order to present an integrated view of human nature. His study strongly emphasizes the importance of self-esteem as a motivational force in social conduct.

BERGER, PETER L., AND THOMAS LUCKMANN

    1966   *The Social Construction of Reality*. Paperback ed., 1967. Garden City, N.Y.: Doubleday. A treatise outlining the major components of a sociology of knowledge.

BERNARD, JESSIE

    1951   "The conceptualization of intergroup relations with special reference to conflict," in *Social Forces*, Volume 29 (March), pp. 243–251. Bernard challenged the notion that prejudice causes conflict.

BETTELHEIM, BRUNO, AND MORRIS JANOWITZ

    1950   *Dynamics of Prejudice*. New York: Harper & Row. This well-known study of prejudice among American war veterans stresses the importance of social mobility in conditioning prejudice. Unlike most studies, this one makes an attempt at combining sociological and psychological approaches.

    1964   *Social Change and Prejudice*. New York: Free Press. This work contains the text of their earlier study (1950) as well as an assessment of the value of its findings in the light of more recent research.

BIERSTEDT, ROBERT

    1948   "The sociology of majorities," in *American Sociological Review*, Volume 13, pp. 700–710. Bierstedt's essay is a plea for studies of the majority side of the majority-minority relationship.

BLALOCK, JR., HUBERT M.

1967   *Toward a Theory of Minority-Group Relationships*. New York: Wiley. (Paperback ed., 1970. New York: Capricorn Books.) Blalock's work is one of the few exclusively theoretical treatments of the subject. He proposes some ninety-seven general propositions that may be tested by further research on dominant-subordinate group relationships.

BLUMER, HERBERT

1958   "Race prejudice as a sense of group position," in *Pacific Sociological Review*, Volume 1, pp. 3–7. Blumer's essay is an attempt to examine some of the more constant features of race prejudice. He especially points to the element of social position in this kind of ideology and presents a convincing argument for the collective nature of prejudice.

BOGARDUS, EMORY S.

1925   "Measuring social distances," in *Journal of Applied Sociology*, Volume 9, pp. 299–308. This essay marked the introduction of the Bogardus Social Distance Scale into the sociological literature. It is now a well-known and widely used research technique for measuring prejudice.

1967   *A Forty-Year Racial Distance Study* (booklet). Los Angeles: The University of Southern California. This is a comparative analysis of the responses to the social distance scale of large samples of college students in the years 1926, 1946, 1956, and 1966.

BROWN, CLAUDE

1965   *Manchild in the Promised Land*. New York: Macmillan. (Paperback ed., 1966. New York: Signet Books.) An autobiography of life in an American black ghetto.

CAMPBELL, ERNEST Q., AND THOMAS F. PETTIGREW

1959   *Christianity in Racial Crisis: A Study of Little Rock's Ministry*. Washington, D.C.: Public Affairs. Campbell and Pettigrew focus upon the role and problems of clergymen in the desegregation controversy in Little Rock, Arkansas. A shorter report on their findings appeared in the *American Journal of Sociology*, Volume 64, 1959, pp. 509–516.

CAMPBELL, THOMAS, AND YOSHIO FUKUYAMA

1970   *The Fragmented Laymen*. Philadelphia: United Church Press. This is a major study of the attitudes of laymen in one Protestant denomination, the United Church of Christ. It includes an analysis of intergroup prejudice based upon responses to social distance scales.

CHRISTIE, RICHARD, AND MARIE JOHODA (EDS.)

1954   *Studies in the Scope and Method of the Authoritarian Personality*.

New York: Free Press. As the title implies, this volume contains a collection of essays that explore the many issues raised by Adorno et al.'s landmark study (1950).

CLEAVER, ELDRIDGE

1968   *Soul On Ice*. New York: Dell Publishing Company. Cleaver has played a major role in the Black Panther Party. This volume, which was written while the author was in prison, is a scathing indictment of white America.

COSER, LEWIS

1956   *The Functions of Social Conflict*. Paperback ed., 1965. New York: Free Press. Coser's important study depicts the ways in which social conflict may be viewed as functional for groups and societies.

COX, OLIVER C.

1948   *Caste, Class and Race: A Study in Social Dynamics*. Garden City, N.Y.: Doubleday. Cox argues, from a strictly Marxist perspective, that prejudice and discrimination are the fruits of social conflict, especially economic competition and capitalist exploitation.

DORE, R. P., AND KIYOTAKA AOYAGI

1965   "The buraku minority in urban Japan," in *Minority Problems*. Edited by Arnold M. Rose and Caroline B. Rose. New York: Harper & Row. This brief essay tells the story of the *Eta* minority. It is one of many diverse studies published in this anthology.

DURKHEIM, EMILE

1895   *The Rules of Sociological Method*. Translated by Sarah A. Solvoy and John H. Muller, and edited by George E. G. Catlin, 1953. New York: Free Press. This is Durkheim's methodological treatise in which he stresses the "historicity" of "social facts."

ELLUL, JACQUES

1962   *Propaganda: The Formation of Men's Attitudes*. Translated by Konrad Kellen and Jean Lerner, 1965. New York: Knopf. An essay on consciousness and public opinion in modern society.

GLOCK, CHARLES, AND RODNEY STARK

1966   *Christian Beliefs and Anti-Semitism*. Paperback ed., 1969. New York: Harper & Row. The authors depict the role of the teachings of the Christian churches in conditioning anti-Semitism.

GOFFMAN, ERVING

1963   *Stigma*. Englewood Cliffs, N.J.: Prentice-Hall. Subtitled *Notes on the Management of Spoiled Identity*, this study examines the problems that society creates for individuals with distinctive physical traits.

GRIFFIN, JOHN HOWARD

1961   *Black Like Me*. Boston: Houghton Mifflin. (Paperback ed. New York:

Signet Books.) This is the story of a white author who darkened his skin in order to experience firsthand the life of black Americans.

HARRINGTON, MICHAEL

1962 *The Other America: Poverty in the United States.* Baltimore, Md.: Penguin. This book, along with the Keyserling Report (1964), began the avalanche of literature on poverty in the United States in the 1960s.

KEYSERLING, LEON

1964 *Progress or Poverty.* Washington, D.C.: Conference on Economic Progress. This volume and Harrington's book (1962) began the thrust that resulted in the "Great Society" poverty programs of the Johnson Administration.

KOZOL, JONATHAN

1967 *Death at an Early Age.* Boston: Houghton Mifflin. (Paperback ed., 1968. New York: Bantam.) The story of life in an all-black Boston grammar school is all but unbelievable to those who have not experienced it.

KRIEGEL, LEONARD

1969 "Uncle Tom and Tiny Tim: Some reflections on the cripple as Negro," in *The American Scholar,* Volume 38, pp. 412–430. Kriegel explores the similarities of the social experiences of those with physical deformities and members of racial minorities, in this case blacks. The essay is reprinted in Sagarin's collection (1971).

KUHN, THOMAS

1962 "The structure of scientific revolutions," in *International Encyclopedia of Unified Sciences,* Volume II, Rev. ed., 1970. Chicago: University of Chicago Press. Kuhn has shown through an analysis of the history of the natural sciences that the principle of the known circumscribing the knowable works the same way in science as it does in the everyday world.

LENSKI, GERHARD

1961 *The Religious Factor.* Paperback ed., 1963. Garden City, N. Y.: Doubleday. Lenski's study focuses upon the effects of religion in the social, economic, and political lives of people. The work also contains some data on the relative views that the four racial-religious groups have of each other.

MALCOM X WITH ALEX HALEY

1964 *The Autobiography of Malcolm X.* New York: Grove. This now well-known volume was completed shortly before Malcolm X's murder.

MANNHEIM, KARL

1929 *Ideology and Utopia*. Translated by Louis Wirth and Edward Shils, 1936. London: Routledge & Kegan Paul. (Paperback ed., 1936. New York: Harcourt Brace Jovanovich.) This important work attempts to deal with the problem of values in science and especially in political sociology.

MERTON, ROBERT

1949 "Discrimination and the American creed," in *Discrimination and National Welfare*. Edited by Robert MacIver. New York: Harper & Row. Merton's essay contains the fourfold typology depicting the possible relationships between prejudice and discrimination.

MYRDAL, GUNNAR, ET AL.

1944 *An American Dilemma*. New York: Harper & Row. This was the first major study of racism in the United States.

ROSE, PETER I.

1964 *We and They*. New York: Random House. This is a paperback "short text" on minority groups in American society. Rose's discussion of prejudice and discrimination basically follows the approach of Merton (1949).

SAGARIN, EDWARD (ED.)

1971 *The Other Minorities*. Waltham, Mass.: Ginn. Sagarin's collection is an excellent example of the extended range of groups that may be analyzed through the conceptual approach argued for in the present work. Among the groups considered in this collection are homosexuals, hippies, ex-convicts, dwarfs, and others.

SCHERMERHORN, RICHARD A.

1970 *Comparative Ethnic Relations*. New York: Random House. Schermerhorn's discussion of the role of legitimacy in majority-minority relationships is but one of many stimulating research avenues suggested in this fine book.

SCHUTZ, ALFRED

1944 "The stranger," in *American Sociological Review,* Volume 69 (May), pp. 499–507. Schutz's essay extends the theme originally developed by Simmel (1908b). It was reprinted in Arvid Brodersen (ed.), *Alfred Schutz, Collected Papers, Volume 2* (The Hague: Martinus Nijhoff, 1964), pp. 91–105.

1953 "Common-sense and scientific interpretation of human action," in *Philosophy and Phenomenological Research,* Volume 14 (September), pp. 1-37. This essay includes Schutz's discussion of the concept of "typification." It was reprinted in Maurice Natanson (ed.),

Alfred Schutz, Collected Papers, Volume 1 (The Hague: Martinus Nijhoff, 1962), pp. 3–47.

1971   *Reflections on the Problem of Relevance*. Edited and annotated by Richard M. Zaner. New Haven: Yale University Press. This posthumously published essay is perhaps Schutz's most important examination of human consciousness in the everyday world.

SHIBUTANI, TAMOTSU

1962   "Reference groups and social control," in *Human Behavior and Social Processes*. Edited by Arnold M. Rose. Boston: Houghton Mifflin. This essay is a revision of an article published in the *American Journal of Sociology*, Volume 60, 1955, pp. 562–569. It is an excellent exposition of the problem of social pluralism from the standpoint of reference group theory.

SIMMEL, GEORG

1908a   "Conflict," in *Conflict and the Web of Group-Affiliations*. Translated and edited by Kurt H. Wolff and Reinhard Bendix, 1955. New York: Free Press. Simmel's essay on conflict first appeared as Chapter 4 of his *Soziologie*.

1908b   "The stranger," in *The Sociology of Georg Simmel*. Translated and edited by Kurt H. Wolff, 1950. New York: Free Press. This "essay" actually appeared as an excursus, or footnote, in Simmel's work *Soziologie*. Simmel's theme is expanded upon by Alfred Schutz in his *Collected Papers, Volume 2* (1964). An earlier translation of Simmel's essay will be found in Park and Burgess' *Introduction to the Science of Sociology* (1921).

SIMPSON, GEORGE, AND J. MILTON YINGER

1953   *Racial and Cultural Minorities*. Rev. eds., 1958, 1965, 1972. New York: Harper & Row. This volume is still the only major text on prejudice and discrimination. It contains an excellent bibliography.

STEMBER, CHARLES H.

1961   *Education and Attitude Change: The Effects of Schooling on Prejudice Against Minority Groups*. New York: Institute of Human Relations Press. In addition to this study of prejudice and education, Stember has edited a volume entitled *The Jews in the Mind of America* (New York: Basic Books, 1966).

STRAUSS, ANSELM (ED.)

1934   *The Social Psychology of George Herbert Mead*. Edited by Anselm Strauss. Chicago: University of Chicago Press. The paperback edition of this work appears under the title, *George Herbert Mead on Social Psychology* (Chicago: University of Chicago Press, 1956, rev. ed.,

1964). It is a useful compendium of Mead's writings on the genesis of the social self.

TUMIN, MELVIN M.

1961 *An Inventory and Appraisal of Research on American Anti-Semitism.* New York: Anti-Defamation League of B'nai Brith. This is a useful review of the literature on this subject based upon sources published between 1930 and the late 1950s. Tumin has edited a yearly set of volumes, also sponsored by B'nai Brith, entitled *Research Annual on Intergroup Relations.*

WEBER, MAX

1904 "'Objectivity' in social science and social policy," in *The Methodology of the Social Sciences.* Translated and edited by Edward A. Shils and Henry A. Finch, 1949. New York: Free Press. This is Weber's important essay on the problem of values in science and social policy.

CHAPTER 6
The Concept of Race:
The Social Uses of Science

Old Questions and New Data

In spite of the many similarities between racial and other types of minority groups, the subject of race warrants special attention. Confusion over the very meaning of the word "race" is sufficient to justify its consideration here. One hears of the white race, the human race, the Jewish race, and the German race. While in everyday usage the word "race" is most often employed to mean people of different skin colors, even this use of the term is not necessarily consistent with the scientific meaning of the word. Many researchers in both the natural and social sciences have argued that the term "race" should be discarded entirely. Alleged racial differences are the source of the most extreme instances of prejudice and discrimination in this and many other societies. Gerald Berreman, for instance, contends that in spite of America's otherwise open, class system of stratification, blacks resemble a rigidly segregated caste (1960). Numerous writers have argued that racial minorities in the United States, especially blacks, American Indians, Puerto Ricans, and Mexican-Americans, represent *colonized* peoples, captive victims within an unjust social and economic system. Finally, the subject of race is a critical one for scientific investigation because of the unique and ambiguous role that the sciences have played in creating race ideologies and mythologies.

Anthropologist Ashley Montagu is at least historically correct in asserting that the idea of race is, in essence, a mythological notion. In Montagu's view, race is "man's most dangerous myth" (1942). Yet, it is important to note that race myths are frequently couched in scientific terms. This is not to suggest that the idea of race is exclusively the product of modern scientific thought. Various writers have shown that concepts roughly equivalent to the modern idea of race may be found in such diverse premodern sources as the works of the Greek philosopher Aristotle and the fourteenth century Muslim scholar Ibn Khaldûn (Gossett 1963, Montagu 1965). Yet most students of the subject also agree with Gossett that the contemporary idea of race is a product of the seventeenth century Enlightenment in scientific thought and that the social phenomenon of racism is the invention of nineteenth century Western culture.

There are several basic questions about the concept of race that must be addressed here. First, is there such a thing as race? Second, how are alleged racial differences measured and defined scientifically? Third, and most importantly, what are the social implications of the science of race itself? The customary sociological approach to the subject of race has been to reject the biological concept of race and to focus upon its social aspects. Accordingly, there now exists a large and valuable sociological literature on racial prejudice, discrimination, and racism. The following discussion does not attempt to summarize or supplement that literature in any major way. Rather, the focus here is upon the history of race as a scientific idea and upon the science of race per se. In short, the purpose is to examine the scientific utility and the social consequences of the science of race. Why has this path of investigation been chosen?

The recurrence of racial conflict in the United States has quite predictably resulted in an explosion of literature in American sociology about racism. This literature, following the now-established tradition, ignores the question of race as a biological concept and its implications, if any, for the social sciences. Yet at the same time there has been a resurgence of interest and debate over the biological notion of race in the disciplines of physical anthropology, biology, educational psychology, in newly formed departments of bio-behavioral science, and, of course, in American society. The position that is argued in the following discussion is that race is a social and not a biological phenomenon. Yet the failure of sociologists to examine the other side of this question has begun to appear as an argument *ad hominem*. The implicit argument seems to be that all those who would even seriously examine the biological research on race are racists. This undoubtedly is not the case. In view of the renewed interest in research on blood groups by other social scientists and, most importantly, in view of the controversy stimulated by Arthur Jensen's essay on race and intelligence published in the *Harvard Educational Review* (1969), the failure of most of the sociological literature to reexamine these questions has begun to look like an unwillingness to do so. In short, a failure to recognize the social climate in which one studies and teaches about race can have serious and unintended consequences. As will be seen, some social scientists, in pursuing the avenue of so-called bio-behavioral research have failed to recognize this fact. In contrast, sociologists, by ignoring these new researches, have been equally guilty of ignoring the social context of their work. There is, then, a renewed need for sociologists to consider the biological aspect of the subject of race and to answer once again the argument being made on the other side.

It is important at the outset that the argument presented here be made clear. In turning first to the history of the scientific idea of race, it is argued that the emergence of this concept represents an instance of what Max Weber has called "unintended consequences." Weber observed that the ideas of intellectuals (be they theologians or scientists) often acquire very different meanings in society from those intended by their authors. The transition from the science of race to the ideology of race provides a case study in the growth of an unintended meaning. Those scientists most responsible for the emergence of the idea of race were the least convinced that the new idea was socially or scientifically useful. Moreover, the different kinds of research that have lent the greatest support to the ideology of race have successively proved to be more social folly than scientific fact. In turning secondly to the biological and psychological studies of race, it is contended that these studies must be examined not because they are convincing but precisely because they are not. What is intended, then, is an examination of biological research both on its own grounds as well as a case study in the sociology of scientific knowledge. Our investigation begins with an analysis of the historical emergence of the idea of race.

From Science to Ideology

The Enlightenment in Western thought during the seventeenth century ushered in a new age of scientific and human understanding. The accomplishments of Copernicus (1473–1543), Galileo (1564–1642), and Newton (1642–1727) created what historian Crane Brinton has called a "new cosmology," a new way of viewing the social and natural world (1950/1963:289–318). Foremost among the ideas of the Enlightenment was a firm belief in the unity of man and nature and in the perfectability of man in society. These ideas were the guiding precepts of the young Swiss naturalist Carl Linnaeus (1707–1778), whose famous work *Systema Naturae* was first published in 1735. Linnaeus' scheme of the "great chain of being" was intended to demonstrate not only the unity of all mankind but of all living things. His classification of living things into the categories kingdom, phylum, class, order, family, genus, and species remains the cornerstone around which modern biological science is built. Yet Linnaeus' system also contains a classification of the species "man" according to four color groups. It is important to see that Linnaeus argued that there are fixed biological subgroups of the species man in order to demonstrate the essential order and interrelationships between them. While Linnaeus himself viewed these distinctions between color groups as merely a matter of arbitrary convenience, later students were to place greater emphasis upon the differences rather than the similarities between human populations. Thus, Linnaeus, in his attempt to demonstrate the ordered relationships and unity between all living things, stimulated the quest for human differences.

The list of those who attempted to modify the "Linnaean Web" (Handlin 1957) is endless. For the following discussion, several key figures must serve as historical signposts in the development of the concept of race. One of the most important early challenges to Linnaeus' work was that of George Louis Leclerc, Comte de Buffon (1707–1788).

Buffon was, in fact, the first writer to use the term "race" to describe the various subspecies of man. In contrast to Linnaeus' fourfold classification, Buffon proposed a schema of six racial groups. More importantly, while Linnaeus visualized man as being divided into relatively fixed subspecies, Buffon, in his monumental forty-four volume *Historie naturelle* (1749–1804), contended that the development of human races is a continual, flexible, and ever-changing process. Contrary to Charles Darwin's later claim that man is descended from the ape, Buffon believed that the ape is a subspecies descended from man. His theory was built upon the idea that environmental factors create physiological differences between different animal species and subspecies. This idea was later developed by Jean Baptiste de Monet Lemarck (1744–1829), who argued that adaptive changes in human physiology could be genetically transmitted ("inherited, acquired characteristics"). For the moment, the important point is that Buffon, like Linnaeus before him, saw his works interpreted in a manner very different from what he had intended. While he strenuously argued for the flexibility of animal species and subspecies, his work was viewed as an argument for the fixed nature of human races.

The German scientist Johann Blumenbach (1752–1840) was the first researcher to move beyond the use of skin color as a criterion for devising racial classifications. Blumenbach, often recognized as the founder of physical anthropology, proposed a typology of five races based upon measurements of the human skull. Even though he, too, maintained that his schema was arbitrary and that human diversity was so great as to defy the creation of a reliable classification system, Blumenbach's work stimulated the rapid growth of the sciences of craniology and, later, phrenology. By the mid-nineteenth century the new science, under the leadership of Paul Broca (1824–1880) of the Anthropological Society of Paris, had produced ingenious, if not fanatical, ways of measuring the human head. These studies reached an exacting climax in the work of A. von Török, who claimed to have taken 5,000 different measurements on one human skull! More important was the work of Anders Retzius (1796–1860) who, in 1842, brought standardization to the field with his measurement, the *cranial index*. The craze for measuring human skulls was not restricted to the European continent. In the United States the proslavery physician Samuel George

Morton (1799–1851) and his students Josiah Clark Nott and George Robin Gliddon dedicated themselves to the collection and measurement of human skulls. Morton concluded that by virtue of skull size, the Negro was not simply a variation of the human species but a separate subspecies, and that because of the adaptive changes which Negroes had undergone they were well-suited to the condition of slavery.

Even by the end of the eighteenth century a raging dispute had developed within the camp of the physical anthropologists. One group followed the position of Buffon and Blumenbach in favor of *monogenesis*. Basically, they argued that the biblical account of the creation was correct, that all species of man came from the same origin, and that different human races had evolved from differences in diet, climate, and other environmental factors. Defenders of the *polygenesis* position, mostly advocates of slavery in the United States, believed that the biblical story of all men being created from Adam and Eve was incorrect. The idea that blacks are a different race and not descended from the biblical progenitors was used as a justification for slavery (Harris 1968:80–107). In other words, even by the early nineteenth century the new science of race had become embroiled in social and political ideologies. Science, somewhat at its own invitation, had been put to the service of society.

Undoubtedly, the most important book on the subject of race published during the nineteenth century was Count Arthur de Gobineau's four-volume *Essai sur l'inégalité des races humaines* (1853–1855). Gobineau's ideas are important, not because they are true, but because they were widely read and believed on several continents. Prior to Gobineau, the question of human differences and race had occupied the attention of natural scientists and social philosophers alike. In Gobineau's essay, these two forms of inquiry were blended into a scientific, historical, race mythology. The author of this remarkable treatise was a French nobleman vehemently opposed to the egalitarian philosophy of the French Revolution. Further, Gobineau made no attempt to hide the fact that his essay was intended to justify, on racial grounds, the political rule of the French nobility and the suppression of the masses. He drew upon the most respected scientific sources of his day. The studies of Buffon, Blumenbach, Prichard, Retzius, and Morton were marshalled to demonstrate the existence of racial differences. In order to explain the meaning of these alleged differences, Gobineau resurrected the myth of the "Nordic" or "Aryan" race. The myth stems from an essay by the Roman author Tacitus who, during the first century A.D., attributed the cultural achievements of the Teutons (Germans) to their racial superiority and purity. Tacitus was evidently struck by the cultural traditions of these "outsiders" and, having no other explanation for why some of their customs did not exist in his own homeland, he attributed them to biological inheritance. It is Tacitus, then, who contributes to Western thought the erroneous idea that there is an organic relationship between biology (race) and culture. While Tacitus is the source of this myth, it was Gobineau who brought the idea to prominence in nineteenth century Western scientific and social thought. Gobineau reconstructed the history of man through a blend of biology and mythology. So convinced was Gobineau that the nineteenth century European nobility was descended from pure Aryan stock that he invented for himself an Aryan family tree in which he was shown to be descended from a (fictional) Nordic champion named Ottar Jarl. Gobineau's theme is indeed simple: Superior races produce superior cultures; mixtures between races cause degeneration of the superior race; the salvation of Western man lies in keeping the superior, governing race pure.

Jacques Barzun contends that Gobineau's *Essai,* like Karl Marx's *Capital,* is one of those books that everyone talks about but no one ever reads (1937/1965:50). But this was far from the case in the nineteenth century. The composer Richard Wagner (1813–1883) later cited Gobineau as justification for his racist views, and Wagner's son-in-law, Houston Stewart Chamberlain (1855–1927), built upon Gobineau's ideas in his widely read racist tract *The Foundations of the Nineteenth Century* (1899). So convinced was Chamberlain of the tie between culture and race that he believed one could determine a person's race by simply observing his actions and habits. The line of thought that begins with Gobineau finds its European culmination in Adolf Hitler's *Mein Kampf.* In America, Gobineau's ideas were later revived in Madison Grant's *The Passing of a Great Race* (1916) and Theodore Lothrop Stoddard's *The Rising Tide of Color* (1920). While Grant's book is more frequently cited, it was, in fact, Stoddard's work that fueled public sentiment in the United States for immigration restrictions to stem the flow of alien races into the United States (Gossett

1963:353–364, 390–398). Even Carleton Putnam's booklet *Race and Reason* (1961) is little more than a restatement of Gobineau's basic theme that racial inheritance accounts for the cultural achievements of different groups.

At the very moment Gobineau was creating his scientific-historical myth of the Aryan race, two other men were about to change drastically the pace and shape of the scientific debate over race. The first of them was a social philosopher and founding father of modern social science. In 1852, Herbert Spencer (1820–1903) announced his new idea of *evolution*. A brief seven years later a natural scientist named Charles Darwin (1809–1882) published his revolutionary work *Origin of the Species by Natural Selection* (1859). Like Buffon and Blumenbach before him, Darwin argued that the process of human physiological change (in this case natural selection) was so complex and diverse as to prevent the establishment of clear lines of demarcation between species and subspecies. Darwin's caution on these issues was so great that he avoided using the loaded Spencerian terms "evolution" and "survival of the fittest" until 1871, when his work *Descent of Man* was published. In spite of Darwin's caution, the terms "evolutionism" and "Darwinism" quickly became interchangeable. Darwin's *Origin of the Species* was viewed as documentation for Spencer's already popular ideas of evolution and survival of the fittest (Singer 1931).

The new philosophy of social Darwinism had two important effects on the race debate. First, the raging monogenesis-polygenesis dispute experienced a rapid and ignoble death. If Darwin's assertion that man is descended from the ape was correct, the question of monogenesis or polygenesis was irrelevant. The polygenesists could at least take some solace in the fact that Darwin's position, like their own, refuted the biblical explanation of the origin of man. More importantly, social Darwinism gave added impetus to the search for racial differences. If natural selection produced anything like survival of the fittest, the new anthropological task was to show why one race is more "fit" than the next. As Handlin observes (1957), the ruler and the calipers came into use as never before. In addition, it was presumed that the task of demonstrating the superiority of certain races would include an historical dimension. Accordingly, archaeology and geology became branches of anthropology.

Charles Darwin's unintended contribution to the study of race and the ideology of racism was soon outdone by his cousin Frances Galton (1822–1911). Galton's "law of ancestral inheritance" stipulated that the physical characteristics of animal populations are passed genetically from one generation to the next. Galton and his co-worker Karl Pearson soon graduated from observing dogs to observing men. Their conclusions affirmed that which Gobineau and others had believed all along, that both physical and cultural traits are biologically transmitted within racial groups. Their findings made even clearer the need for preserving superior racial stocks. The Eugenecist Movement, as Galton named his new science of genetics, had an immense impact upon scientific and social thought in both Europe and the United States. In Germany, the prominent social theorist Ludwig Gumplowitz (1838–1909) employed the popular conception of race in his work *Rasse und Staat* (1875). Even after Gumplowitz abandoned the deterministic biological notion of race in favor of a social definition of race, he was still able to depict the path of human history as a continuing series of race conflicts in his work *Der Rassenkampf* (1883). In the United States the ideas of social Darwinism and eugenecism pervaded the thought of sociology's American founders. Sumner, Ross, Giddings, Cooley, and others all followed the racist line (Gossett 1963, Hofstadter 1944).[1]

Through all of this the work of an obscure Austrian monk named Gregor Mendel (1822–1884) went unnoticed. At the turn of the century, a Dutch botanist named Hugo de Vries (1848–1935) rediscovered Mendel's remarkable essay of 1866. Mendel had, of course, concluded that such physical traits as skin, hair, and eye color are genetically transmitted. But Mendel had also found that these physical traits do *not* coincide with what the eugenecists call "races." Rather, variations in the color of hair and eyes and differences in head shapes cut across supposed racial lines. Mendel further showed that his genetic populations, unlike racial populations, are not fixed but highly flexible and internally diverse. Since gene pools, through the chance selection of recessive and dominant genes, are always changing, the existence of certain physical traits in a specific population at one point in time does not prove a direct or continuous relationship to some previous population. Mendel's theory of *discontinuous variation* knocked the

[1]See the discussion on pp. 74–75.

props out from under the social Darwinist, eugenecist, and racist positions. The notions of continuous favorable selection, survival of the fittest, and progress in human evolution are incorrect. Various chance genetic and environmental factors may determine which genetic strains survive and which disappear. In effect, Mendel's published essay of 1866 had already made obsolete the work of men like Galton and Pearson who followed him! Why was Mendel's important work so completely overlooked by the eugenecists during the last half of the nineteenth century? Charles Singer explains this embarrassing scientific fact as follows:

> The explanation lies perhaps in the mental orientation of the naturalists of the time. They were looking always for *series* of variations which led gradually from one species to another. Their experimentation was always between varieties that differed from each other in a large number of characters. These differences concealed such simple numerical relationships as may have existed (1931/1959:569).

In simple terms, the eugenecists were looking for racial differences. Not surprisingly, they found them. But they failed to take account of both similarities between different racial groups as well as important variations within racial groups. Unlike Mendel, they were unable to see the trees for the woods. As will be seen, the issue of whether differences between racial groups are more significant than differences within them remains a major point of contention in the contemporary debate over the idea of race.

Even prior to the shift in thinking about race among natural scientists, which resulted from the spread of Mendel's ideas, a parallel trend was already at work in the newly founded social sciences. In Germany, Max Weber rejected the biological notion of race and argued that race conflicts are best understood in terms of social and economic factors (Manasse 1947). At the same time in France, Emile Durkheim's *The Rules of Sociological Method* (1895) unleashed a double-barreled attack on biological and psychological explanations of social phenomena. For Durkheim, social and cultural facts could only be understood in terms of social and cultural, not biological, categories.[2] In the United States

[2]See the discussion on p. 102.

the pioneering cultural anthropologist Franz Boas (1858–1942) openly led the attack against the racist views of Grant, Stoddard, and others. Through his own careful research, Boas concluded that physical differences within racial and ethnic groups are greater than those between them. He boldly challenged the racists on their unproven contention that cultural traits are biologically transmitted. Boas' thought gradually gained prominence in his own lifetime, and his ideas were further supported after his death by his outstanding students Ashley Montagu, Margaret Mead, and A. E. Kroeber. A similar movement against racism soon developed in American sociology. The racist presumptions of the founding fathers were replaced by the socialization theories of G. H. Mead and other members of the Chicago school tradition, who demonstrated the ways in which social environments create cultural differences between groups. Eventually the works of Dollard (1937) and Myrdal (1944) stressed the role of majority group prejudice and discrimination as opposed to alleged group instincts and genetics.[3]

But these changes in scientific thinking about race were at best gradual and came much too late to retard the growth of scientific racism during the first quarter of the twentieth century in the United States. The tide of racial bigotry culminated in the National Origins Quota Act of 1924. The "lower races," the yellows, the Slavs, the Poles, and the Jews, were all to be excluded from the promised land. The clear purpose of the act was to preserve the Anglo or Aryan race on America's shores. And at the very moment that the tide of scientific racism was subsiding in America, Hitler launched his infamous attack against the "Semitic race" in Europe. That which had begun in the humanistic efforts of the Enlightenment men (Linnaeus, Buffon, and Blumenbach), and which had been compounded by the scientific errors of Spencer, Darwin, Galton, and Pearson, ended in the human catastrophe of Nazi Germany. Science itself, quite unintentionally, has created the modern myth of race that many scientists are today still attempting to dispell. The growth of modern race consciousness and race mythology provides a sobering case study in the unintended consequences and social uses of science. Those scientists most responsible for the creation of the term were the least convinced of its scientific utility. Even as the scien-

[3]See the discussion on pp. 74–75.

tific errors inherent in social Darwinism were falling into disrepute within the scientific community, the concept of race continued to grow in credibility as an "objective" scientific concept in the larger society. While most scientists today reject the concept of race as it was employed by Morton, Broca, Ritzius, Galton, Pearson, and most importantly, Gobineau, it is precisely this now-discarded scientific meaning of the term that enjoys the status of a taken-for-granted scientific fact in most Western societies. Many scientists now reject the use of the term "race," and even among those who continue to employ the term, relatively few scholars view skin color or head shapes as the criteria for devising racial typologies.

But the contemporary state of the debate is best examined in the light of the various kinds of measurements and data that have been and are employed to document the argument that there are significant racial differences between human populations. Only by examining the evidence can the basic questions about race that have been raised here be honestly and adequately answered. For, while sociologists have generally ignored the matter of biological and physiological differences in favor of a purely social analysis of racism, prejudice, and discrimination, natural scientists and anthropologists have continued to study and debate the question of human racial differences.

Measurements and Their Meanings: The Problem of Scientific Knowledge

There are a vast number of human physical traits that have been measured and employed to document the contention that there are significant racial differences between human populations. These traits range from the apparent characteristics of skin and hair color to more complex factors such as blood types and genetically transmitted diseases. Anthropologists have long known that the popularly employed distinction between Caucasoid (white), Negroid (black), and Mongoloid (yellow) races is empirically inadequate. Among those anthropologists who today argue that the term "race" is meaningful, Carleton S. Coon, Stanley Garn, and J. B. Birdsell (1950) suggest a typology based upon six major "stocks" and some thirty-four races within those stocks. William C. Boyd (1950/1958) has alternatively proposed both a fivefold and a twelvefold system. He at least resolves the problem that the American Indians and the Australian aborigine (sometimes called the Australoid race) are not easily placed within the threefold white-black-yellow typology of racial groups.

Even such ostensibly basic human differences as skin color are by no means easy to measure and classify. Through the technique of spectrophotometry, it has been found that there are five, not three, types of skin pigments. Moreover, categorizing individuals according to skin pigment is a difficult and generally unreliable procedure. The degree of overlap between groups, the effects of climatic and other environmental factors upon skin, and the degree of biological mixing between groups are but three factors that complicate the classification of individuals by skin color. Even where such classifications have been made, the extent of color differences within pigment groups is at least as great as those between groups. At best, scientists agree that differences in skin color and pigment have resulted from different degrees of exposure to sunlight. Within all pigment groups, skin colors become darker as populations move closer to tropical climates. This, of course, is entirely consistent with the very early environmentalist theories of Buffon and Blumenbach (Hooton 1931/1946:455–468, Goldsby 1971:90–92).

Hair form is one of the most reliable differences between populations. The three basic types, *ulotrichy* (oval-shaped and tightly curled), *liotrichy* (straight, with a rounded cross section), and *cymotrichy* (wavy, with an intermediate cross-sectional shape) correspond to the three color groups, Negroid, Mongoloid, and Caucasoid. Unlike hair form, both hair and eye color are much more complicated areas of investigation. Here, it is important to distinguish between quantitative and qualitative physiological differences. Both skin color and hair color involve qualitative differences. Much like the difference between apples and oranges, differences in skin and hair color result from qualitatively different kinds of pigment. On the other hand, quantitative differences refer to different quantities of the same substance. As Philip Mason observes, height and weight are probably the simplest examples of quantitative differences between individuals or populations (1970:9–34). Unlike skin and hair color, differences in eye color are quantitative. Different amounts of the same substance in the iris of the eye give the appearance of different eye colors. It is questionable whether both qualitative and quantitative differences should be treated alike for the purpose of making racial classifications. In other words, quantitative differences are differences of degree. Qualitative differences are differences in kind. Both hair and eye color are genetically sex-linked factors, and neither conforms in any simple way with skin color differences between groups. As Simpson and Yinger observe (1953/1965:31), the most reliable generalizations about hair color are that most of the world's population has black hair, and that blonds are a rarity wherever they are found. Turning to eye shape rather than eye color, the only meaningful distinction is between Mongoloid (the eye is slightly recessed with little development of the brow-ridge) and non-Mongoloid (the eye is deeply recessed and overhung by the brow-ridge) (Hooton 1931/1946:480–488, 508–512).

Beginning with the studies of Blumenbach, innumerable ways of measuring the human head have been devised. Most head measurements are, of course, quantitative, not qualitative. For instance, the *cephalic index* is derived by dividing a measurement of the width of the head by another measurement of the length of the head. The three average size ranges tend to correspond to the three color groups of black, white, and yellow. Yet the cephalic index is of little use in determining subspecies within these three groups. As was previously noted, even those anthropologists who do argue that there are significant racial distinctions between human populations according to skin color do not rely upon the black-white-yellow typology. Since the cephalic index is of little use in making distinctions beyond the threefold typology, it would appear to be a relatively weak measure of racial differences. An even less useful measure is the *facial index*, which is also derived from averaging techniques based on measurements and divisions of measurements of the width and length of the head. The three categories, *leptoprosophic* (narrow-faced), *euryprosophic* (broad-faced), and *mesoprosophic* (medium-faced), do not correspond to skin color groups (Hooton 1931/1946:503–507).

Anthropologists are themselves divided on the question of whether these apparent physical differences between groups justify the use of the term "race." As Leonard Lieberman suggests, there are two main camps, "splitters and lumpers" (1968). By "splitters," Lieberman means Stanley Garn (1961), Carleton S. Coon (1962), and others who contend that there are identifiable populations called "races." Within this group, Coon alone seems to believe that cultural inferiority or superiority may be tied to these racial differences (Simpson and Yinger 1953/1965:39). Of course, such pseudoanthropologists as Carleton Putnam (1961) take great stock in this line of anthropological thought. On the other hand, by "lumpers" Lieberman means those writers like Ashley Montagu (1942/1965), Jacques Barzun (1937), and others, who argue that the species *Homo sapiens* is infinitely varied but that these variations do not require or justify the use of the term "race." In their view, the word "race" is an unfortunate misnomer in modern science.

The dispute between the splitters and the lumpers revolves not only around the obvious traits like head shape, hair color, fingerprint patterns, lip shape, eye color, and the like, but extends to more complex differences such as blood types, inheritable diseases, and genetic mutations. For instance, it has been shown that there are different kinds of human earwax. This trait is genetically transmitted, with the more wet type of earwax being predominant in East Asian populations, especially Chinese and Japanese, and the more dry type of earwax occurring more frequently in Caucasoid and Negroid populations. How or why this difference has emerged remains unanswered. It has also been found that members of different groups vary in their ability to taste a slightly bitter chemical compound called PTC. The percentage of individuals who can taste the substance is relatively high in the Mongoloid and Negroid groups and somewhat low in the Australoid group. There are numerous differences of this type between populations, including the fact that the chemical composition of urine differs between groups (Goldsby 1971:55–57).

The most well-known studies of basic constitutional (i.e. internal biological) differences are those of blood groups. The nineteenth century preoccupation of physical anthropologists with measuring human skulls has been replaced in the twentieth century by the search for blood groups. Anyone who has ever donated blood to a blood bank or applied for a marriage license is aware of the blood types A, B, AB, and O. Knowledge of blood types has been an essential factor in saving human lives and in providing various kinds of important medical services and treatments. For instance, researchers have found at least six diseases that appear to be related to these blood types. But the important fact is that the A, B, AB, and O blood groups cut across skin color groups. Blood groups are not racial groups. It is less well known that an entirely different system of blood groups employing the symbols N, M, S, and U has been the subject of intensive biological research. In addition, there are a large number of factors in the blood that must be considered in establishing a classification of blood groups. These include the Rh factor, the Duffy gene Fy[a], the Kelle allele, the allele B, and a number of other blood factors that require much more technical description than is possible here. On the basis of these differences, there may be four, ten, twelve, or any larger number of basic blood groups (Dunn 1960, Goldsby 1971).

Yet another type of blood-related factor that has received a great deal of attention in the United States is the sickle-cell trait. The trait, which is frequently found in American blacks, causes the often-fatal disease sickle-cell anemia. It is also found among blacks in West Africa as well as nonblack populations in southern Asia, Greece, New Guinea, and several other parts of the world. The emergence of the sickle-cell trait appears to be an adaptive response to malaria, a disease that either did or still does flourish in all parts of the world where those populations with the sickle-cell trait live or once lived. In other words, the sickle-cell trait is best understood in terms of demography, not race. There are nonblack populations that exhibit the trait. A similar trait involving the hemoglobin in the blood, which appears only in Southeast Asia and Indonesia, is also related to the presence of malaria (Goldsby 1971:97–101). Knowledge of these factors is of immense value in medical science and clearly demonstrates the diverse biological effects of environment on human populations. They may even be useful in reconstructing historical trends in group migration. But it is highly questionable whether they suggest anything about race. One can only hope that the contemporary anthropological penchant for studying blood types and genetically related diseases will not produce the same kinds of unintended consequences that resulted from earlier scientific excursions into the differences in skin colors and head shapes.

It is indeed possible that physical anthropologists may gain significant information about the migration of human populations through studying human physiological and biological characteristics. On the other hand, it is extremely important that the purposes of such studies and the kinds of scientific inferences to be drawn from them be stated in very clear terms. Thus far, biologists and geneticists have been able to identify a wide variety of biological differences among human populations. In some instances, such as that of the sickle-cell trait, these differences are known to affect the occurrence of a specific disease and are known to have been caused by environmental factors. This kind of research clearly does not lead to the inference of the existence of racial groups. Moreover, biologists have not yet shown that such phenomena as the sickle-cell trait have any other biological significance for the human organism than the specific trait-disease relationship. There is yet another category of findings, such as those concerning the ability or lack of ability of people in different populations to taste the chemical compound PTC, that is nothing more than an observed difference. In other words, it has not even been shown that this difference is of any biological or organic significance. It seems, then, terribly premature to argue that such differences have social or racial implications, when biologists have not yet been able to demonstrate that these kinds of differences have clear biological implications for human organisms. Moreover, it must be emphasized that the older and popularized notion of race as a skin color phenomenon does not correspond to the kinds of blood groups and genetic groups now being studied.

Yet the most controversial research about race has not been the studies of physical anthropologists and biologists but those of educational psychologists. If one grants for the moment that various observed physiological and genetic differences may justify the use of the term "race," and that intelligence tests have shown wide differences in the performance of different racial groups, how are these IQ differences to be explained? The debate over heredity versus environment is far from settled. One group, represented most recently by Arthur Jensen in his controversial essay published in the *Harvard Educational Review* (1969), contends that while both environment and heredity affect intelligence, the ultimate determinant of intelligence differences is heredity. Jensen's work has been criticized on a number of substantive and methodological grounds (Deutsch 1969). But Jensen's respected position in his field has lent renewed force to an argument that has been quite out of vogue among scientists for many years (Baughman 1971). The opposing position, which is still more widely held within the social sciences, is represented in the works of Otto Klineberg (1935, 1944), Thomas Pettigrew (1964), and numerous other anthropologists, sociologists, and educational psychologists.[4] There is little need here to refute in detail the specific and rather technical arguments of Arthur Jensen's essay. This has already been done elsewhere, most notably in Martin Deutsch's reply to Jensen, which also appeared in the *Harvard Educational Review* (1969). Jensen's essay, of course, contains no new data but is, rather, a selective rereading of existing research. As Deutsch has shown, Jensen badly misinterprets the data he uses, consistently ignores methodological complexities and problems inherent in those studies, and completely ignores the larger body of research that contradicts his position. But the important question is not simply whether Jensen is right or wrong but whether the broader assumptions made by Jensen and all others pursuing this kind of research are valid scientific assumptions. There are a number of important issues that predate and encompass Jensen's essay. It is this kind of issue that must be examined here.

One of the most compelling questions raised by the environmentalists is whether there actually is such a thing as "intelligence" and, if so, whether it can really be measured. Philip Mason underscores these issues in his book *Race Relations* (1970). Mason argues that there are at least three different phenomena encompassed by the term "intelligence." First is the genetically endowed potential of the individual. Second is the way in which that potential responds to and is shaped by specific cultural and other environmental factors. Third is the performance of that response on an intelligence test. Only the last phenomenon, the individual's performance, is directly measurable. The second entity, the response of the genetic potential to the environment, is inferred by observing performance. Finally, the first quantity, the genetic endowment, is simply not measurable by any direct means. If the term "intel-

---

[4]An extensive bibliography of research that documents this position will be found in Deutsch's essay (1969).

ligence'' is employed to mean the genetic endowment, clearly there is no way of either directly proving or disproving the argument that heredity determines intelligence.

Since an individual's performance is the only directly measurable source of documentation for the environment-versus-heredity question, there has been extensive scrutiny of the kinds of research instruments that are commonly used to elicit these performances. Many researchers argue that all intelligence, IQ, and aptitude tests are culturally or class biased in some way (Eells et al. 1952). For instance, should a lower-class American Indian child be expected to recognize and manipulate the same kinds of cultural symbols and meanings as his white, middle-class counterpart? Should a lower-class black child living in the South be expected to perform on one of these tests in the same manner as a middle-class black child living in the North? The answer must be no. For the life experiences, the socially taught values, and the familiarity of these children with various kinds of cultural objects, including language, have been very different. For this same reason, adult populations from different kinds of societies, East and West, have been shown to perform differently on intelligence and aptitude tests. In short, the attempts of some researchers to demonstrate racial differences through IQ tests have led many people to overlook the fact that similar differences have been found between various national, ethnic, and class groups both within and between societies. These differences are largely explainable on the basis of the cultural biases of the various tests and the cultural differences between the various groups. Dregger and Miller (1960, 1968) have argued that existing social class differences between blacks and whites in the United States, which have resulted from racial discrimination, make it difficult indeed to find comparable populations where class differences can be held constant for the purposes of research. On the basis of their examination of a large number of studies, Dregger and Miller conclude that the research is so inconclusive that it is impossible to defend either the environmentalist or the hereditary position (1960). Perhaps a more important impediment to this kind of research is the fact that even if one controlled for class differences between the races, this would not justify the assumption that all cultural factors had been controlled. Just because blacks enter the middle class does not mean that they also acquire white middle-class culture. Rather, just as middle-class Jews remain culturally different from middle-class Protestants and Catholics, so middle-class blacks remain culturally distinct from middle-class whites. In other words, present-day social scientists are no more justified in viewing class assimilation as total assimilation than earlier researchers were in viewing ethnic assimilation as total assimilation. Glazer and Moynihan's (1963) observation that ethnic groups assimilate but still remain distinct applies to racial groups as well. Said differently, blacks are an ethnic group possessing distinct cultural traits. This, of course, is the importance of understanding race as a social phenomenon. Just because a so-called racial group changes its social position does not mean that all of its cultural distinctiveness as a group will disappear. Asian-Americans provide a clear illustration of this point. In this context, it becomes difficult to imagine how researchers can actually minimize or eliminate cultural differences for the purpose of examining biological (alleged racial) differences.

Finally, those who place great emphasis upon psychological testing for the purpose of demonstrating racial differences often forget that even those biologists and anthropologists who employ the term "race" readily admit that it is impossible to empirically identify "pure" racial groups. The degree of biological mixing between American blacks and whites has been so great that it would be impossible to find any "pure" Negroids in the United States, even if some agreement could be reached concerning what the composite physiological and genetic characteristics of a "pure" Negroid are. Obviously, any attempt to solve this problem by comparing African blacks and American whites introduces so many additional cultural variables as to make such a comparison meaningless.

In summary, the same methodological problems that prevent disproving the contention that race and heredity determine intelligence also prevent the accumulation of conclusive research findings to prove the argument. In this context, the choice on the part of some scientists to opt for the assumptions that the biological concept of race is scientifically valid, and that there is a connection between race and intelligence, more closely resembles a *deductive,* rather than an *inductive,* philosophy of science. An inductive scientific method requires that the scientist examine carefully the data at hand, making as few assumptions as possible, and then make those claims that are clearly and unequivocally supported by the data. A deductive approach allows the scientist to ask leading questions of his data, so to speak, and then to gather those shreds of evidence that support his original hunches and hypotheses. Clearly, no science is ever purely inductive or deductive. But those opting for the heredity position in the race debate appear to be deductively selecting shreds of evidence in the face of inconclusive data and immense methodological problems. Admittedly, the environmentalists also reveal an element of deductive choice. Again, the very problems that prevent proving one position also prevent disproving it. Yet, the environmentalist position, at the very least, represents the scientific guess that has the least damaging social consequences. Moreover, while all of the research in this area is plagued with methodological complexities, the larger body of that research demonstrates the varying effects of environment quite convincingly (Klineberg 1935, Lee 1951, Bloom, Davis, and Hess 1965, Feuerstein 1968). In this framework, the sociology of knowledge raises an important question: Why have scientists been attempting for so long to demonstrate the effects of race and heredity in the face of successive research failures to do so? Would this scientific question, and the deductive choices that lead to a "yes" answer to the question, be such a recurrent theme in Western science if it were not for the fact that racism has been a social fact in these societies for so long a time? In other words, would scientists be attempting to prove the connection between race and intelligence if racism were not the dominant ideology of the societies in which those scientists live? It is not being argued here that all those who ask the race-heredity-intelligence question are racists. But, rather, it does seem that society itself plays an important role in determining which scientific questions will be asked and, given inconclusive research findings, which deductive answers to these questions will become fashionable in science. There are two important questions here. First, to what extent does society influence the kinds of research questions and answers one finds in science? The frequent response to this question, that science is an "objective" enterprise and that scientists are at least consciously attempting to be objective, provides only half an answer to the question. No science can be completely objective because science is a social institution and is thereby, to some degree, understandable only in the context of the society in which it exists. The second question is, To what extent do the ideas of scientists influence society? Here the response that science is to some degree an objective enterprise is irrelevant and provides no answer at all. As was seen in the foregoing discussion of the history of the idea of race, scientific thought, regardless of its validity, has played an immense role in fueling race ideology in Western societies. Is not the scientist obligated to consider this important fact? This is a crucial issue and will be examined more fully momentarily. First, the question Is there such a thing as race? must be answered.

. In the summer of 1951, a renowned and diverse group of physical anthropologists and geneticists met at UNESCO House in Paris to answer this very question. The official statement that they drafted was subsequently adopted at the Fourth International Congress of Anthropological and Ethnological Sciences in 1952 and has been reprinted in numerous scientific journals around the world. The "Statement on Race" that appeared in the English-language journal *Current Anthropology* in 1961 contends that all men belong to the same single species, *Homo sapiens*, and that the term "race" is a valid classificatory device for both zoological and evolutionary studies of the development of the various different kinds of *Homo sapiens*. Specifically, race is defined as:

. . . groups of mankind possessing well-developed and primarily heritable physical differences from other groups. . . . There are also many populations which cannot easily be fitted into a racial classification . . . [and] the extent of the classificatory subdivisions adopted may legitimately differ according to the scientific purpose in view (UNESCO 1961).

Most importantly, the "Statement on Race" clearly disavows four unproven and untrue racial myths. The "Statement" contends that (1) there is no such thing as a "pure" race, (2) that inherited genetic differences do not produce cultural differences between groups, (3) that there are no innate intellectual or emotional differences between human groups, and (4) that there is no reason to believe that there are any disadvantageous biological consequences resulting from racial mixture.

While the 1951 "Statement on Race" is a useful clarification of some of the most important issues surrounding the concept of race, it has had relatively little impact upon the nonscientific public. Even within the scientific community, the "Statement" has provided more of a framework for the continuing debate rather than an end to that debate. Even the definition of race that is offered in the "Statement" leaves many questions unanswered. Most importantly, what is a "well-developed," "heritable"[5] physical trait? The ostensible traits of black skin, red hair, baldness, and left-handedness all fit this definition. Is the trait for sickle-cell anemia any more "well-developed" or "heritable" than those for congenital heart disease or diabetes? Again, the elements of value and choice enter the social and natural sciences alike. While one researcher may choose to disregard skin color and focus upon blood for the purpose of making racial distinctions, another researcher may make just the opposite decision. It will be recalled that Galton and Pearson overlooked the very kinds of differences that Mendel found to be most significant. Racists have generally found human differences to be more significant than similarities common to the entire species. In science, as in society, men continually choose between alternatives. Different men value the same things differently.

In scientific terms, physical anthropologists and geneticists argue that the concept of race has a valid place in the study of human evolution and zoology. In a sense, they have "agreed to disagree," for the "Statement" maintains that there is no fixed racial classification system and that disagreements between scholars in this area are legitimate. If it is granted that race is a legitimate concept, it is not clear what the scientific implications are of the existence of races. While in 1951 it was at least agreed that there are no intellectual, moral, cultural or emotional differences stemming from race differences, more recent trends in the bio-behavioral sciences, such as Jensenism, seem to be calling these age-old myths back from the past. Ironically, there is not even any agreement concerning the evolutionary or zoological implications of the existence of races, except perhaps the recognition that certain differences exist. We are not all exactly alike, and our differences most probably evolved over some great period of time.

In this context, it will be recalled from our earlier discussion of typologies in the sciences that few typologies are universal in any sense.[6] Rather, every typology emerges in the context of a particular scientific question. It is for this reason that there can legitimately be several

[5]The words "heritable" and "inheritable" mean the same thing—that something can be biologically transmitted from one generation to the next.
[6]See the discussion on p. 33.

different kinds of typologies of minority groups. Similarly, the "Statement on Race" recognizes any number of legitimate racial typologies. The physical anthropologist Sherwood L. Washburn raises the important question regarding the concept of race, "typology for what purpose?" Considering the great diversity of human differences, the inability of scientists to arrive at an agreement about the number of races, and the extremely flexible biological nature of human groups, Washburn argues that the term "race" is far from a useful scientific concept. Since it serves so little scientific purpose, and since its social consequences (racism, prejudice, and discrimination) are so undesirable, the term should be dropped. Washburn succinctly argues:

> I think we should require people who propose a classification of races to state in the first place why they wish to divide the human species and to give in detail the important reasons for subdividing our whole species (1963).

Washburn's argument provides the best answer to the first question that has been raised here. Yes, there are innumerable differences between human populations; there are equally innumerable ways of measuring those differences. But the biological concept of race provides little, if any, understanding of these differences. Why, then, use the concept? The most important thing modern science has learned about race is that science itself has helped to create and sustain race mythologies and racial discrimination. Following W. I. Thomas' often-cited dictum, if men define something as real, it will be real in its social consequences. Modern racism has been fueled by scientific definitions, and it is this fact that ultimately must be recognized by scientists.

Martin Deutsch raises this issue in his reply to Jensen's essay:

> Unfortunately Jensen's article, through its use by attorneys in some desegregation cases and by some legislators with respect to appropriation bills (aside from its overinterpretation in public media) has had a negative effect on social progress; less money for education cannot lead to better education; casting aside court desegregation cannot lead to greater social equality (1969:30).

Deutsch clearly is not calling for a halt to bio-behavioral research, nor is he calling for any infringement upon the academic freedom of scholars to investigate any scientific questions that happen to interest them. But he is reminding scientists that they cannot hide behind the cloak of scientific objectivity in ignoring the social uses and misuses of scientific research findings. The position being argued here demands that first, given the social context of present-day research, scientists have an obligation to specifically disavow misuses of their findings, misinterpretations of their findings, and unwarranted inferences based on their findings that have dire social consequences. Secondly, bio-behavioral scientists have an obligation to make clear the purposes of their research as well as the limits of their rather tentative findings, be they arrived at either inductively or deductively. If someday it is reliably demonstrated that heredity affects social conduct, it is also likely to be found that hereditary factors are as numerous and as complexly interrelated as social scientists now know social influences on behavior to be. Simply because bio-behavioral scientists are now attempting to test the as-yet-unproven hypothesis that there are connections between biology and human conduct does not justify elevating that hypothesis to the status of a proven fact.

Having examined these issues, one returns to the fact that racism, as both a social doctrine and as a pattern of social conduct, is a social reality in contemporary American society. The remaining part of this chapter examines several related dimensions of racism as a social fact.

Some Dimensions of Racism

The ambiguous concept of race in modern science is paralleled by the confusing and controversial term "racism" in modern society. Accusations of institutional racism and racist thought, as well as the claim that the United States is a racist society, appear daily in the press and other media. Countercharges of reverse racism are heard just as frequently. At least one minority group has transformed the connotation of the term "race" by employing the words *La Raza* as a symbol of its group pride and solidarity.[7] What is racism? Is the

[7]The term *La Raza* (the race) has emerged as an important self-reference term for Mexican-Americans. It is their way of saying "black is beautiful" (i.e. that the minority group's distinctiveness is something of which one should be proud, not ashamed).

United States a racist society? Are the terms "racist" and "institutional racism" meaningful concepts for understanding the contemporary American dilemma?

In the specific sense that Gossett (1963) and others have used the term, it is indeed accurate to describe the United States as a racist society. *It is meaningful to speak of racism wherever alleged racial differences between human populations become a major aspect of the social stratification system.* While the idea of race is not of recent origin, it is only in modern times that one finds both a widely accepted social ideology and institutionalized conduct based upon the idea of race. To this extent, minority group spokesmen are correct in asserting that the United States is a racist society. This claim was amply documented in the Kerner Commission's report on civil disorders. The report argued in part that:

> . . . the most fundamental [cause of riots] is the racial attitudes and behavior of white Americans toward black Americans.
>
> Race prejudice has shaped our history decisively; it now threatens to affect our future.
>
> White racism is essentially responsible for the explosive mixture which has been accumulating in our cities since the end of World War II (Kerner et al. 1968:10).

Unfortunately, the Commission's report did not receive wide popular support, nor has American society yet solved the problem of racism.

The fact that the term racism refers to a number of different social phenomena, and that distinctions between them are not frequently made, has undoubtedly contributed to the communications gap between blacks and whites in the United States. Like anti-Semitism, racism is a specific form of prejudice and/or discrimination. Just as prejudice and discrimination may or may not occur together, so racial prejudice and discrimination on the part of individuals may appear together or independently of each other. Similarly, the term "racist" is no more useful a scientific concept than the term "bigot." Obviously, there are individuals who are racially prejudiced and who discriminate. But the same kinds of situational factors that affect prejudice and discrimination generally, also affect racial prejudice and discrimination. It is, therefore, ultimately misleading to employ the terms "bigot" and "racist" as though they were personality types.[8]

While the concept of racism is a useful one for understanding the conflict and controversy in the United States today, it must be admitted that there is no social phenomenon that fits the literal meaning of the term. Racism, like prejudice and discrimination, takes specific forms involving different social groups and situations. If there was any period in American history when racism was empirically manifested in a generally recognizable form, it was during the late nineteenth and early twentieth centuries. During this period, such diverse groups as blacks, Jews, yellows, and numerous other ethnic groups were all viewed as racial groups. Today, the term "racism" refers specifically to antiblack prejudice and discrimination as well as to beliefs and action by whites toward Spanish-speaking Americans and American Indians. Even black-white relationships involve subtle cultural nuances that transcend the popular notion of racism, meaning color prejudice. For instance, African blacks who speak with a "broken handwriting" are often treated differently than native American blacks. Even though he is black, the African may enjoy some of the benefits of being a foreigner, a stranger (Simmel 1908, Schutz 1944). In other words, even racial prejudice and discrimination must be examined carefully in terms of additional situational variables, in this case that of ethnic differences. Even where the concept of race is involved, patterns of prejudice and discrimination change with different groups and situations. In spite of these difficulties, it is still useful to define racism as *any instance in which social beliefs and conduct based upon alleged racial differences are a major part of the stratification system in society.*

Within this framework, it is additionally useful to distinguish between several different forms of racism. Racism may be either collective or individual. Just as individuals may express prejudice or discriminate, so institutions, in their norms and practices, may embody racism. Moreover, prejudice and discrimination may be either intended or unintended. The term *subjective racism* may be used to refer to instances where prejudice and discrimination are conscious and intended. *Objective racism* refers to situations in which racial prejudice and discrimina-

---

[8]See the discussion on pp. 201–206.

tion result as unintended or nonconscious outcomes of human action. The failure to distinguish between these different dimensions of racism, individual, institutional, intended, and unintended, has contributed to social misunderstandings about racism.

Minority group spokesmen have made great rhetorical use of the term "institutional racism." The term "institutional racism" has been employed to make two kinds of claims. First, it is argued that the prevailing patterns of conduct in American institutions are discriminatory. Second, it is contended that the ethos and norms of American institutions reveal underlying racist ideas, prejudice. There can be little quarrel with either of these two claims. But minority group spokesmen often fail to distinguish between objective (unintended) and subjective (intended) racism. Their error lies in the assumption that collective patterns of prejudice and discrimination are always accompanied by individual intent. This is not always the case. To recall an example discussed earlier,[9] a black real estate salesman who refuses to sell homes to blacks in white sections of town participates in an institution that contains an ethos of racial prejudice, and he commits a discriminatory act. But he is not prejudiced against blacks, nor is his discrimination intentional. There are, in fact, situations in which individuals are largely unaware of the discriminatory effects or consequences of their actions. There is, then, a great need for minority group representatives to distinguish between racism, be it individual or collective, that is intended and racism that is objective—an unintended consequence of individual or collective conduct.

Moreover, even when it is recognized that racism is frequently unintended or unconscious on the part of the individual, the overall thrust of many minority group leaders has been to place blame and guilt upon members of the white community for the suffering of minority groups. This is not to suggest that prior absence of intent or a prior state of unconsciousness about the consequences of one's actions absolves one of guilt or responsibility for those consequences. On the contrary, regardless of the original intent, white Americans must recognize their responsibility for the effects of their actions once those effects become known. In the same way, it has already been argued here

9See the discussion on p. 203.

that scientists are obligated to recognize the social context of their research and especially to disavow misuses of their findings. The disclaimers, ''I didn't mean it that way,'' or ''It's none of my business,'' are morally indefensible once the individual is actually aware of the effect of his actions upon other people. But the more important point for the moment is that the fixation of minority group leaders on the question of guilt and the admission of guilt by white Americans has been counterproductive. To understand why this is the case, one must consider white America's reactions to the accusation of racism.

White Americans have either denied the existence of racism in any form or have refused to accept the blame for patterns of discrimination that are objective. The typical argument is that individuals cannot be blamed or expected to acknowledge guilt for institutional arrangements that they did not create or intend to create. In essence, there are two important errors that create the communications gap. Minority group leaders and many younger group members have fixated on the task of getting individuals to admit *guilt* for patterns of objective racial discrimination. The desire to assign guilt is related to the failure to distinguish between subjective and objective racism. On the other hand, white society has failed to accept *responsibility* for either subjective or objective racial discrimination. Denying guilt for institutional racism has clouded the more important task of accepting both individual and collective responsibility for solving the problem. The debate over racism would be greatly simplified if spokesmen for both sides would distinguish the types of racism involved. Such a clarification of the issues would allow the debate to move to the more important question of how racism in any form may be eliminated. In terms of the life experiences of individuals who are victims of racism, it matters little whether discrimination is intended or unintended. The important question is not guilt but responsibility for rectifying the situation. As long as both groups operate with tacit and erroneous assumptions about the nature of racism, it is unlikely that the debate will be moved to the level of problem solving.

In summary, this chapter has focused upon the unique history and consequences of a rather questionable scientific idea, the concept of race. There can be little doubt that the scientific debate over the concept will continue. At best, it can be hoped that scientists and laymen alike will develop a greater awareness of the social context and consequences of the science of race, as well as an appreciation of the complexities and limitations of scientific research on the subject. As was suggested earlier, the very existence of the race question in modern science cannot be fully understood without considering the role of racism, as a social phenomenon, in those societies in which scientists investigate the subject of race. In the face of a scientific stalemate over the utility of the idea of race as a biological concept, the fact remains that racial differences are socially defined and acted upon in a way that has dire consequences not only for minority group members but for society as a whole.

FOR FURTHER READING

BARZUN, JACQUES
　1937　*Race: A Study in Superstition.* Rev. ed., 1965. New York: Harper & Row. Barzun's historical survey of what he calls "race-thinking" begins with the Nordic myth and covers the period ending with World War II.

BAUGHMAN, EARL E.
　1971　*Black Americans.* New York: Academic. This volume reviews a large part of the research concerning intelligence, biology, social psychology, and sociological aspects of the situation of American blacks.

BERREMAN, GERALD D.
　1960　"Caste in India and the United States," in *American Journal of Sociology,* Volume 64, pp. 120–127. This comparison of the social situation of the "untouchables" in India with that of blacks in the United States makes a strong case for viewing the lower stratum of the American stratification system as a caste rather than a class.

BLOOM, B., A. DAVIS, AND R. HESS (EDS.)
　1965　*Compensatory Education for Cultural Deprivation.* New York: Holt, Rinehart & Winston. This volume contains research reports given at a conference in 1964. It contains a variety of studies done in different national settings that point to the importance of environmental-social factors in producing changes in children's achievement levels on IQ tests.

BOYD, WILLIAM C.
　1950　*Genetics and the Races of Men.* Rev. ed., 1958. Boston: Boston University Press. The revised edition of Boyd's work suggests a typology of twelve racial groups based upon blood types.

BRINTON, CRANE
  1950 *Ideas and Men*. Rev. ed., 1963. Englewood Cliffs, N.J.: Prentice-Hall.
         A standard intellectual history of Western man.
COON, CARLETON S., STANLEY M. GARN, AND J. B. BIRDSELL
  1950 *Races*. Springfield, Ill.: C. C. Thomas. In this unique joint venture,
         these three authors acknowledge that races are in essence Mendelian,
         ever-changing populations. Nonetheless, they propose a typology of
         thirty-two races.
COON, CARLETON S.
  1962 *The Origin of Races*. New York: Knopf. Coon argues for a system
         of five basic racial groups. He also contends that racial differences
         should be attributed to polygenesis (parallel origins and development)
         rather than to the more popular notion of successive differentiation.
         He is one of the few anthropologists to suggest that racial differences
         are related to cultural superiority and inferiority.
DEUTSCH, MARTIN
  1969 "Happenings on the way back to the forum: Social science, IQ,
         and race differences revisited," in *Harvard Educational Review*,
         Volume 39, pp. 1–35. Deutsch's reply to Jensen is one of the best
         summaries of the problems with Jensen's analysis.
DOBZHANSKY, THEODOSIUS
  1962 *Mankind Evolving*. New Haven: Yale University Press. This book
         offers a wide survey of the subject and its history. Zoologist Dobzhan-
         sky, who has written numerous volumes, is highly respected by social
         and natural scientists alike.
DOLLARD, JOHN
  1937 *Caste and Class in a Southern Town*. New Haven: Yale University
         Press. Dollard's work was one of the first in the sociological approach
         to race. The emphasis is entirely upon prejudice and discrimination
         as explanatory variables, not physiology or biology.
DREGGER, R. M., AND K. S. MILLER
  1960 "Comparative psychological studies of Negroes and whites in the
         United States," in *Psychological Bulletin*, Volume 57, pp. 361–402.
         A useful review of the research. The authors contend that the
         methodological problems involved, as well as the noncomparability
         of different samples, make any resolution of the race and intelligence
         question impossible.
  1968 "Comparative psychological studies of Negroes and whites in the
         United States: 1959–1965," in *Psychological Bulletin Monograph
         Supplement*, Volume 70 (Number 3, Part 2). A supplement to Dregger
         and Miller's earlier (1960) review of the research.

DUNN, L. C.
  1960 *Heredity and Evolution in Human Populations*. Cambridge, Mass.: Harvard University Press. Dunn is one of the leading students of genetic and blood factors related to racial differences.

DURKHEIM, EMILE
  1895 *The Rules of Sociological Method*. Translated by Sarah A. Solvoy and John H. Muller, and edited by George E. G. Catlin, 1953. New York: Free Press. Durkheim's emphasis upon the collective nature of "social facts" was intended to refute biological and psychological explanations of social phenomena.

EELLS, KENNETH, ET AL.
  1952 *Intelligence and Cultural Differences*. Chicago: University of Chicago Press. A collection of essays that examine different aspects of cultural bias in intelligence tests.

FEUERSTEIN, R.
  1968 "The role of social institutions and subsystems in the causation, prevention, and alleviation of retarded performance: A contribution to a dynamic approach" (paper presented at the Peabody-NIMH Conference on Social-Cultural Aspects of Mental Retardation). Nashville, Tenn.: June, 1968. Feuerstein's research, which was conducted in Israel, shows dramatic changes in the test performances of retarded children when they are given the benefit of more stimulating social environments. This type of research points to quite the reverse of the position taken by Jensen (1969).

GARN, STANLEY M.
  1961 *Human Races*. Springfield, Ill.: C. C. Thomas. Garn's approach to racial classification stresses nine major geographical areas with thirty-two local races or breeding populations.

GOBINEAU, COUNT ARTHUR DE
  1853–
  1855 *Essai sur l'inégalité des races humaines*. Translated by Adrian Collins. 1915. London: Heinemann. This translation contains only the first volume of Gobineau's four-volume tract, which argues that superior races produce superior cultures.

GOLDSBY, RICHARD A.
  1971 *Race and Races*. New York: Macmillan. This paperback text is written by a biologist. The book contains an up-to-date summary of much of the research on racial differences.

GOSSETT, THOMAS
  1963 *Race: The History of an Idea in America*. Dallas, Tex.: Southern Methodist University Press. This excellent book is generally viewed

as the basic source on its subject. Gossett traces the idea of race in the United States from the colonial period to the present. His chapters on race, science, and religion are particularly good (Chapters 6 and 7).

GRANT, MADISON

1916 *The Passing of a Great Race*. New York: Scribner. This was one of the most widely read racist books of the first quarter of the twentieth century. The "great race" was, of course, white Anglo-Saxon Protestantism.

HANDLIN, OSCAR

1957 *Race and Nationality in American Life*. Boston: Little Brown. (Paperback ed., 1957. Garden City, N.Y.: Doubleday.) This is a brief and highly readable collection of essays on the rise of racial and ethnic prejudice in the United States.

HARRIS, MARVIN

1968 *The Rise of Anthropological Theory*. New York: T. Y. Crowell. This work contains a useful discussion of the rise of racial thinking in anthropology.

HOFSTADTER, RICHARD

1944 *Social Darwinism in American Thought 1860–1915*. Philadelphia: University of Pennsylvania Press. Like so many of the late Richard Hofstadter's studies of American thought and life, this one is most comprehensive and most readable.

HOOTON, ERNEST A.

1931 *Up from the Ape*. Rev. ed., 1946. New York: Macmillan. While there has been a great deal of new research since the last edition of this book, it still contains a most comprehensive discussion of heredity and race (pp. 423–771). It is particularly useful for information on observable traits such as head shape, eye color, and the like.

JENSEN, ARTHUR

1969 "How much can we boost IQ and scholastic achievement?" in *Harvard Educational Review*, Volume 39, pp. 1–123. Jensen argues that heredity is the most important influence upon intelligence, and that for this reason such catch-up programs as Head Start are bound to produce only limited results. This essay has had such an impact in opening up the old issue of heredity versus environment that some have renamed the heredity position "Jensenism."

KERNER, OTTO, ET AL.

1968 *Report of the National Advisory Commission of Civil Disorders*. New York: Bantam. The commission's report clearly places the blame for racial strife and riots at the door of white Americans.

KLINEBERG, OTTO

1935   *Negro Intelligence and Selective Migration.* New York: Columbia
University Press. This is the first major study demonstrating the effect
of social environment on the performance of American blacks on
IQ tests.

KLINEBERG, OTTO (ED.)

1944   *Characteristics of the American Negro.* New York: Harper & Row.
Klineberg has been one of the leading challengers of the notion that
race and intelligence are genetically linked.

LEE, E. S.

1951   ''Negro intelligence and selective migration: A test of the Klineberg
hypothesis,'' in *American Sociological Review,* Volume 16, pp.
227–233. Lee presents a retest of Klineberg's early findings (1935)
that IQ scores of southern blacks increase after they move to the
North. The research supports the contention that environment has
an effect upon intellectual development.

LIEBERMAN, LEONARD

1968   ''The debate over race: A study in the sociology of knowledge,''
in *Phylon,* Volume 29, pp. 127–141. Lieberman argues that the scientific view of race has changed along with the social view of race
as changes in the social structure have occurred.

MANASSE, ERNST MORITZ

1947   ''Max Weber on race,'' in *Social Research,* Volume 14, pp. 191–221.
The author reviews Weber's various pronouncements on the subject
of race and stresses Weber's rejection of the biological notion of
race as a factor in group conflict.

MASON, PHILIP

1970   *Race Relations.* New York: Oxford University Press. This short paperback text contains a fine review of the issues in the field. Topics
include both physical and social aspects of race.

MONTAGU, ASHLEY

1942   *Man's Most Dangerous Myth: The Fallacy of Race.* Rev. ed.,
1964. New York: Harcourt Brace Jovanovich. Montagu argues that the
concept of race should be discarded.

1965   *The Idea of Race.* Lincoln, Neb.: University of Nebraska Press. A
brief set of lectures containing Montagu's basic position against the
use of the term. This work and the one listed above (1942) only
begin the long list of Montagu's writings on the subject.

MYRDAL, GUNNAR, ET AL.

1944   *An American Dilemma: The Negro Problem and Modern Democracy.*
New York: Harper & Row. This work has become a classic and

is still a relevant treatment of the extent of prejudice and discrimination in the United States.

PETTIGREW, THOMAS F.

1964   *A Profile of the Negro American*. New York: Van Nostrand Reinhold. Pettigrew's work has become a standard reference volume for those seeking social facts rather than mythological fictions.

PUTNAM, CARLETON

1961   *Race and Reason* (booklet). Washington, D.C.: Public Affairs. This modern example of racist thought became required reading in the Louisiana school system in the year of its publication. It is a prime example of the social uses of anthropology.

SCHUTZ, ALFRED

1944   "The stranger," in *American Journal of Sociology*, Volume 69 (May), pp. 499–507. Schutz amplifies Simmel's theme of the special and somewhat privileged treatment given to those who take the social role of the stranger. This essay was reprinted in Arvid Brodersen (ed.), *Alfred Schutz, Collected Papers, Volume 2* (The Hague: Martinus Nijhoff, 1964), pp. 91–105.

SIMMEL, GEORG

1908   "The stranger," in *The Sociology of Georg Simmel*. Translated and edited by Kurt H. Wolff, 1950. New York: Free Press. While numerous sociologists have commented upon the role of the stranger, Simmel's essay is the best known, and for good reasons.

SIMPSON, GEORGE, AND J. MILTON YINGER

1953   *Racial and Cultural Minorities* (Rev. eds., 1958, 1965, 1972). New York: Harper & Row. A major text on prejudice and discrimination.

SINGER, CHARLES

1931   *A History of Biology*. Rev. ed., 1959. New York: Abelard-Schuman. A very readable history that goes as far as the turn of the century. It is an excellent source for the basic ideas of biologists from Hippocrates to Mendel.

STODDARD, THEODORE L.

1920   *The Rising Tide of Color Against White World-Supremacy*. New York: Scribner. This book contains the same theme as Grant's (1916) and was in fact even more widely read and more influential than the latter.

UNESCO

1951   "Statement on the nature of race and race differences," reprinted in various places, including *Current Anthropology,* 1961, Volume 2, pp. 304–306. This document is part of UNESCO's program to combat racism and represents the ''official'' position of an international group of anthropologists and geneticists. It was officially adopted at the Fourth International Congress of Anthropological and Ethnological Sciences in 1952.

WASHBURN, SHERWOOD L.

1963 ''The study of race,'' in *American Anthropologist,* Volume 65, Part 1, pp. 521–531. This essay was a presidential address to the American Anthropological Association. Washburn argues that the term ''race'' should be eliminated unless those proposing to use the term can justify the utility and purpose of dividing the human species for scientific investigation.

CHAPTER 7
Epilogue: The Problem of "Multiple Realities"

One of the unique features of the social sciences is that social life may be examined in terms of a number of different units of analysis. The individual, the group, and the total society may each fruitfully be employed as yardsticks against which social reality may be measured and understood. As C. Wright Mills observes, biography, society, and history are but three different aspects of the same events (1956). The constant challenge is to connect these different levels of analysis and meaning. This study has primarily focused upon total social structures and the group relationships within them. Yet a humanistic perspective in the social sciences demands that the foregoing analysis be assessed in terms of its meaning for individuals. What does the pluralistic structure of American society and other societies like it mean for the people who live day-to-day within them?

The concept of social differentiation, which was discussed earlier,[1] provides an appropriate starting point for answering this question. Life in a simple, undifferentiated society differs in many ways from daily experience in a highly differentiated, pluralistic society. In less diverse societies the various social roles played by individuals typically overlap and reinforce one another. Even in Europe during the late Middle Ages,

[1]See the discussion on p. 24.

the roles and values involved in social, religious, and economic activities were greatly interrelated. Religion provided the overarching values for family life, and the family was an economic institution.[2] These kinds of interrelationships break down as societies become more internally complex. The separation between major institutions and the roles and values acted out within them requires what Peter Berger has called *alternation* on the part of the individual (1963:51–52). The skills and values of the work role are often unrelated to, or even in conflict with, those of family, civic, religious, and political life. Each performance in the individual's *role set* is situated in a different social context, a different set of social meanings. The ability of the individual to alternate between these different settings is a prerequisite for living in a highly differentiated society.

Erving Goffman suggests the term *identity kit* for describing the assortment of role identities that each individual carries with him (1959). The various role identities—I am a father, a business executive, an elder in the church, a graduate of my state university—are labels that tell us who we are in society. Moreover, the different identities in one's identity kit are of various shapes and sizes. Some of them are very specific and are important only during certain times of the week or day. Being a good salesman is very important during work hours, but one alternates to being a good husband and father once the work day has ended. In contrast to these more specific role identities, some self-concepts are relevant most, if not all of the time. Such identities as I am a man, an American, and an Irish Catholic are less easily changed or altered. Even though the individual may not be fully conscious of these parts of his identity kit at all times, they provide a taken-for-granted identity backdrop against which more specific roles are acted out. While social psychologists have not yet devised an easily employed typology of social roles, there are certainly qualitative differences between alternating and changeable roles, such as occupation and membership in various kinds of voluntary associations, and those larger role categories that are less easily changed and that are transported from one institutional setting to the next. The latter are often called *integrative* or *master roles*. The integrative role identities that provide

[2]See, for instance, Daniel Bell's essay on the demise of "family capitalism" (1960).

overarching meanings for daily life cluster around the very social variables that create minority status in society. Race, physical handicaps, and ethnicity, as well as strongly held religious or social beliefs, create minority status for groups and become integrative role identities for the individuals in those groups.

One of the most important aspects of living in a pluralistic society is that minority group members are always, to some degree, caught between their identities as members of the larger society and their identities as members of their particular groups. Being black, Irish, Puerto Rican, Jewish, or Mexican has different meanings depending upon the audience to which that role is being played. Minority group members must continually cope with *multiple realities*,[3] different majority and minority group interpretations of what it means to be a member of a given physical, cognitive, or behavioral minority. Moreover, the different majority and minority definitions of what a "hyphenated" identity means may conflict with each other. The individual may not value these different meanings and role prescriptions equally. As depicted in Table 14, there are four possible ways in which both minority groups and individuals within them may value these multiple identities.

The first situation is one in which the meanings and role requirements of being a minority group member may differ between the two communities, but the individual may generally either enjoy or accept both definitions of his identity. An American Jew may have a strong and proud self-concept of being Jewish and may derive a great deal of enjoyment and self-esteem from his Jewish religious, cultural, and organizational activities. He may also be content with what it means to be Jewish in the larger society. There is no conflict between being an American *Jew* and a Jewish *American*. The two role definitions are compatible and the individual complies appropriately with the social roles expected of him in the different settings. In terms of group relationships, this is essentially the situation of peaceful coexistence that earlier students of American society envisioned in their notion of cultural pluralism.

The second situation depicted in Table 14 is one of role conflict.

---

[3]The concept of "multiple realities" is used here in a slightly different sense from that of Alfred Schutz, who coined the term (1945).

TABLE 14. Multiple Realities: Role Choices and Pluralistic Identities[a]

Individual's response to majority role definition	Individual's response to minority role definition	Role situation	Role technique(s)
1. +	+	Multiple role compatibility	Multiple role compliance
2. −	+	Role conflict	Role distance or role change
3. +	−	Role conflict	Role distance or role change
4. −	−	Multiple role conflict	Multiple role rejection and role change

[a]Plus and minus signs indicate the individual's preference or dislike for majority and minority groups' definitions of his social role as a minority group member.

An American black or Puerto Rican may reject the role of being black or Puerto Rican in the larger society but may be comfortably at home within the minority subculture. Two choices are open to such an individual. First, he may employ *role distance* while still acting out those roles in the majority institutions that are not consistent with his own self-image. The term "role distance" refers to the perceptual distance between an individual's view of himself and the social roles he plays that he knows are not the "real" him (Goffman 1961). All people employ some degree of role distance in everyday life. We are all called upon to give convincing performances that we would rather not give. But the task of continually employing role distance in terms of one's master social role is a difficult and frustrating business. Depending upon how severely stigmatized[4] one's minority identity is in the larger society, individuals may tire of this kind of role playing. "Playing up to Whitey" has its limits. Many American blacks have overcome

[4]For a discussion of this term see pp. 216–217.

the continual strain of "playing up to Whitey" by "putting on Whitey." Similarly, many American Jews resent having to deal, in degrading situations, with *goyim*[5] but tolerate such role playing because "after all, they are *goyim*." Both of these examples demonstrate that a sense of in-group solidarity, a sense of gamesmanship, and a sense of humor can all go a long way in allowing individuals to tolerate roles that they dislike.

In some instances, employing role distance is not a tolerable alternative for the individual, and role change becomes the only way of resolving the conflict. It is difficult to effect complete role change without physically leaving the host society. Yet separatism, militancy, and a high degree of participation in minority-group-controlled social institutions may all be viewed as ways in which individuals (and groups) resolve such role conflicts. The Afro-American Culture Movement as well as the Black Panthers represent attempts to redefine the meaning of blackness and the roles of blacks in American society. The situation of Chinese-Americans represents a highly successful instance of role change through the maintenance of parallel social and economic institutions.

The third situation depicted in Table 14 is one in which the individual rejects the minority group's self-definition of its distinctiveness and may attempt to effect either role change or role distance within the minority community. The experience of the second-generation European immigrants was of this type. Rejecting the Old World meanings of being Italian, Irish, or Polish, individuals barely tolerated the traditions of their parents while moving out of the ethnic ghettos and often anglicizing their names. In psychological terms, the most distressing instance of this kind of situation is when individuals attempt to deny entirely any identification as a minority group member, in the face of a society that simply refuses to let people forget "who" they are.

Finally, it is often possible for an individual to reject both the minority and majority group definitions of his master social role. There are at least three common responses to multiple role conflict. The first is complete physical withdrawal. If one rejects being a *Mexican*-American and being an *American*-Mexican, one may seek a new place of

[5]This is a derogatory term used by Jews to refer to non-Jews.

residence, another society in which Mexican identity is something different from that which both the majority and minority in the United States say it is. A second possibility is social deviance. Having no reference group with which one identifies in a positive sense, one may attempt to seek some third alternative reference group that violates the norms and social definitions of both the majority and minority. Finally, one may attempt to effect role change within both communities at the same time. Groups and individuals who adopt this technique of resolving multiple role conflict run the risk of being viewed as a "plague on both houses," but they do occasionally succeed. When the NAACP first began, it was viewed disdainfully by both the white and black communities in the United States. It was calling for new role definitions of blackness in both communities, and its leaders were viewed as revolutionaries. In the early 1960s, the Black Panthers and Afro-American Culture advocates were in a somewhat similar position.

The problems of role choices between multiple role realities may be even more complex than the twofold choice situations depicted in Table 14. One of the best literary examples of such a situation is found in Piri Thomas' autobiography *Down These Mean Streets* (1967). Thomas is faced with at least three role choices: white, black, and Puerto Rican identity. His autobiography provides episodic views of how he vacillates between these three different worlds, finally coming to grips with the meaning of yet a fourth self-concept, that of being a Puerto Rican of mixed parentage in a pluralistic society.

The stress created by pluralistic identities becomes particularly acute with certain "rites of passage" in society. The members of a mixed marriage are suddenly thrust into a situation of multiple realities. The Protestant girl married to the Jewish boy may opt for yet a third identity group, the Unitarian Church. The Italian-American adolescent first entering a large university and leaving the protective enclave of his ethnic community may suddenly become aware of the multiple realities and identity choices that are open to him. The middle-class black college graduate, finding that he is suddenly the token representative of his race at the office, faces a new situation of multiple realities that demands role choices. The blind student who, for the first time on a college campus, finds that there are options for defining his handicap is faced with multiple realities. In short, pluralistic societies require of all minority group members a continual set of reality conflicts that may be resolved in a number of ways. The essential meaning of social pluralism is choice both for the society and for the groups and individuals in the society. The challenge is to create a social environment in which groups and individuals may choose voluntarily the identities they wish to play out. Far from being a schizophrenic handicap, the challenge of multiple realities becomes a playing field for the expression of the diversity and freedom of the human condition.

FOR FURTHER READING

BELL, DANIEL
    1960   *The End of Ideology.* New York: Free Press. This collection of essays contains Bell's essay, "The breakup of family capitalism."
BERGER, PETER L.
    1963   *Invitation to Sociology.* Garden City, N.Y.: Doubleday. This widely read introduction to sociological thought contains Berger's interesting idea of alternation.
GOFFMAN, ERVING
    1959   *The Presentation of Self in Everyday Life.* Garden City, N.Y.: Doubleday. This book has become a standard reference work in the area of role theory.
    1961   *Encounters: Two Studies in the Sociology of Interaction.* Indianapolis, Ind.: Bobbs-Merrill. This volume contains Goffman's essay on role distance.
    1963   *Stigma: Notes on the Management of Spoiled Identity.* Englewood Cliffs, N.J.: Prentice-Hall. Here Goffman employs the theoretical framework developed in his earlier work (1959) to analyze the social roles of the "stigmatized."
MILLS, C. WRIGHT
    1956   *The Sociological Imagination.* New York: Oxford University Press. This is Mills' well-known work on the nature of sociological thinking and the problems of contemporary sociological analysis.
SCHUTZ, ALFRED
    1945   "On multiple realities," in *Philosophy and Phenomenological Research,* Volume 5 (June), pp. 533–576. This brief essay is the source of the term "multiple realities." It was reprinted in Maurice

Natanson (ed.), *Alfred Schutz, Collected Papers, Volume 2* (The Hague: Martinus Nijhoff, 1962), pp. 207–259.

THOMAS, PIRI
1967   *Down These Mean Streets*. New York: Knopf. (Paperback ed., 1968. New York: Signet Books.) This is one of the best recent autobiographical treatments of the meaning of minority status.

Index of Names

Abramson, Harold J., 19, 41–42
Adamic, Louis, 69, 87–88
Adams, Romanzo, 71, 88
Addams, Jane, 68, 88
Adorno, T. W., 196, 243
Allport, Gordon, 196–197, 215–216, 243
Aoyagi, Kiyotaka, 232–233, 245
Aristotle, 251
Aron, Raymond, 98, 183–184

Barzun, Jacques, 256, 264, 279
Baughman, Earl E., 267, 279
Becker, Ernest, 204–205, 243
Beecher, Lyman, 59, 88
Bell, Daniel, 282, 287
Bellah, Robert, 169, 184
Berger, Bennett, 77, 84, 88
Berger, Peter L., 6, 11, 17, 34, 42, 197, 239, 243, 287, 292
Bernard, Jessie, 221, 243
Berreman, Gerald D., 250, 279
Berry, Brewton, 33, 42
Bettelheim, Bruno, 210–213, 226, 243
Bierstedt, Robert, 217, 237, 243
Birdsell, J. B., 261, 280
Blalock, Hubert M., Jr., 6, 11, 42, 200, 218, 244

Bloom, B., 270, 279
Blumenbach, Johann, 254–255, 257, 260, 262–263
Blumer, Herbert, 6, 8, 11, 197, 207, 244
Boas, Franz, 260
Bogardus, Emory S., 222–223, 231, 244
Bonaparte, Napoleon, 64–65
Boyd, William C., 261–262, 279
Bressler, Marvin, 77, 88
Brinton, Crane, 253, 280
Broca, Paul, 254, 261
Brown, Claude, 217, 242, 244
Buffon, George Louis Leclerc, Comte de, 253–254, 257, 260, 262
Burgess, E. W., 112, 188
Burke, Kenneth, 101, 184

Campbell, Ernest Q., 205, 244
Campbell, Thomas, 229–231, 244
Campisi, P. J., 75, 88
Carr, Edward Hallet, 50, 89
Chalmers, David M., 61, 68, 89
Chamberlain, Houston Stewart, 256
Chavez, Cesar, 146–147
Child, Irvin L., 40, 42, 75, 89
Christie, Richard, 196, 244–245
Cleaver, Eldridge, 217, 245

Index of Subjects

Aborigine, Australian. *See* Race, typologies of
Africa, blacks in, as different from American blacks, 269, 277
   intergroup relations in, 28, 30. *See also* South Africa
Age, effects on prejudice, 209–213, 219
Aged poor, as a minority group in the United States, 14, 35, 181
   position in the social structure, 136
Amalgamation, as an aspect of assimilation, 84
   defined, 63
   doctrine of, 63–67, 70
   research on, 70–73
   theory of, 67, 70–73, 180
   criticism of, 104–109, 139, 152
Amana Community, as a minority group, 37
American Indians, colonization of, 153–155, 250
   conflict techniques of, 123, 143, 147
   economic deprivation of, 133
   position of, in the social structure, 136, 231
   prejudice and discrimination against, 35–36, 84, 202, 217, 229, 230–233

American Jewish Committee, conditions leading to formation of, 127–128
   as a self-defense organization, 120
American Protectionist Association (APA), 60–61
Amish, as objects of prejudice and discrimination, 228
   self-segregation of, 171
Anarchists, deportation of, 62
"Anglo-conformity," doctrine of, 53, 70. *See also* Assimilation, doctrine of
Anomie, prejudice and discrimination, 215–216
Anthropological Society of Paris, 254
Anthropology, disputes over race within, 261–262, 263–264, 273–274
   early studies of race, 254–255, 257
Anti-Defamation League of B'nai Brith, conditions leading to formation of, 127–128
Anti-Semitism, on the part of blacks, 32
   factors producing, 226
   in Middle Ages, 232–233
   research about, 214–216
   results of, 127–128
   resurgence of, in United States, 4
   as a specific form of prejudice and/or discrimination, 275